Born in Chatham, Kent, **HENRY STEDMAN** has been writing guidebooks for over fifteen years now and is the author or co-author of half a dozen titles, including Trailblazer's *Kilimanjaro*, *Coast to Coast Path* and all three books in the *South-West Coast Path series* as well as *The Bradt Guide to Palestine* and the *Rough Guides* to *Indonesia* and *Southeast Asia*. When not travelling or writing, Henry lives in Hastings editing other people's guidebooks, maintaining his Kilimanjaro website and arranging climbs on the mountain through his company, Climb Mount Kilimanjaro.

DAISY is Henry's dog, though any assumption that ownership equates with control is entirely wrong in this instance. Two parts trouble to one part Parson's Jack Russell, Daisy has also walked all 630 miles of the South-West Coast Path.

Author

Hadrian's Wall Path First edition: 2006; this fourth edition: June 2014

Publisher Trailblazer Publications
The Old Manse, Tower Rd, Hindhead, Surrey, GU26 6SU, UK
info@trailblazer-guides.com, www.trailblazer-guides.com

British Library Cataloguing in Publication Data
A catalogue record for this book is available from the British Library

ISBN 978-1-905864-58-4

© **Trailblazer** 2006, 2008, 2011, 2014: Text and maps

Series Editor: Anna Jacomb-Hood **Editor**: Nicky Slade
Cartography: Nick Hill **Illustrations**: © Nick Hill (pp76-7), Rev CA Johns (pp78-9)
Proof-reading: Jane Thomas **Layout**: Bryn Thomas **Index**: Jane Thomas
Photographs (flora): © Bryn Thomas **All other photographs**: © Henry Stedman

All rights reserved. Other than brief extracts for the purposes of review no part of
this publication may be reproduced in any form without the written consent of the
publisher and copyright owner.

The maps in this guide were prepared from out-of-Crown-
copyright Ordnance Survey maps amended and updated by Trailblazer.

Acknowledgements

I'd like to thank Nick Hodgson of Arbeia for his explanation of the archeological dig near
Albermarle Barracks; David McGlade, National Trail Officer for Hadrian's Wall, for his
usual advice and help; and Les at The Old Repeater Station for his hospitality. Thanks are
also due to those I met on the trail (and the readers who wrote in) all kindly offering thoughts
and suggestions. In no particular order: Norman Craik, Linda, Richard and Thomas Sherbon
(Australia); Murray Turner and David Twine (Tavistock); Andy O'Sullivan (Appleby);
Simon Thornton, James Fuller and James Murray (London/Sussex); Ruth Seymour and
Rachel Morgan (Somerset); Keith Frayn; Sheila Patterson; Fred Leverentz; Darcy R. Fryer;
Keith Dunbar; Don Jewell; Michael Scarlatos; Rachel Howell; Leonie M Wilding; Ken, Rich
& Sophie Eames; John Nichols; Kornelie Oostlander-Vos; Cathy Rooke and Ingrid Strobl.

  Away from the trail I'd like to thank, firstly, Charlie Loram, the first series editor, for
all the work he did before I even put pen to paper or foot to path. Also thanks to everyone
at Trailblazer: Nicky Slade for editing; Jane Thomas for proofreading and the index; Nick
Hill for the maps and illustrations; and, as ever, to Bryn, for keeping me in work.

A request

The author and publisher have tried to ensure that this guide is as accurate and up to date
as possible. Nevertheless, things change. If you notice any changes or omissions, please
write to Trailblazer (address above) or email us at ✉ info@trailblazer-guides.com. A free
copy of the next edition will be sent to persons making a significant contribution.

Warning: long-distance walking can be dangerous

Please read the notes on when to go (pp14-16) and outdoor safety (pp68-70). Every effort
has been made by the author and publisher to ensure that the information contained herein
is as accurate and up to date as possible. However, they are unable to accept responsibility
for any inconvenience, loss or injury sustained by anyone as a result of the advice and information given in this guide.

Photos – Front cover and this page: Looking back towards Housesteads and beyond.
Previous page: The undulating terrain east of Walltown Crags.
Overleaf: Passing fields of dazzling oilseed rape near Halton Shields.

Updated information will be available on: ✉ www.trailblazer-guides.com

Printed on chlorine-free paper by D'Print (☎ +65-6581 3832), Singapore

★ trailblazer

Hadrian's Wall
PATH

59 large-scale maps & guides to 29 towns and villages
PLANNING – PLACES TO STAY – PLACES TO EAT
WALLSEND TO BOWNESS-ON-SOLWAY

HENRY STEDMAN

TRAILBLAZER PUBLICATIONS

Contents

Contents

ABOUT THIS BOOK

This guidebook contains all the information you need. The hard work has been done for you so you can plan your trip from home without the usual pile of books, maps and guides.

When you're all packed and ready to go, there's comprehensive public transport information to get you to and from the trail and detailed maps and town plans to help you find your way along it. The guide includes:

● All standards of accommodation with reviews of campsites, bunk-houses, hostels, B&Bs, guesthouses and hotels
● Walking companies if you want an organised tour and baggage-carrying services if you just want your luggage carried
● Itineraries for all levels of walkers
● Answers to all your questions: when to go, degree of difficulty, what to pack, and how much the whole walking holiday will cost
● Walking times and GPS waypoints
● Cafés, pubs, tearooms, takeaways, restaurants and shops for buying supplies
● Rail, bus and taxi information for all villages and towns along the path
● Street plans of the main towns both on and off the Wall: Newcastle, Wylam, Corbridge, Hexham, Haltwhistle, Brampton and Carlisle
● Historical, cultural and geographical background information

MINIMUM IMPACT FOR MAXIMUM INSIGHT

Man has suffered in his separation from the soil and from other living creatures ... and as yet he must still, for security, look long at some portion of the earth as it was before he tampered with it. **Gavin Maxwell**, *Ring of Bright Water*, 1960

Why is walking in wild and solitary places so satisfying? Partly it is the sheer physical pleasure: sometimes pitting one's strength against the elements and the lie of the land. The beauty and wonder of the natural world and the fresh air restore our sense of proportion and the stresses and strains of everyday life slip away. Whatever the character of the countryside, walking in it benefits us mentally and physically, inducing a sense of well-being, an enrichment of life and an enhanced awareness of what lies around us.

All this the countryside gives us and the least we can do is to safeguard it by supporting rural economies, local businesses, and low-impact methods of farming and land-management, and by using environmentally sensitive forms of transport – walking being pre-eminent.

In this book there is a detailed and illustrated chapter on the wildlife and conservation of the region and a chapter on minimum-impact walking, with ideas on how to tread lightly in this fragile environment; by following its principles we can help to preserve our natural heritage for future generations.

INTRODUCTION

Just when you think you are at the world's end, you see a smoke from East to West as far as the eye can turn, and then under it as far as the eye can stretch, houses and temples, shops and theatres, barracks and granaries, trickling along like dice behind – always behind – one long, low, rising and falling, and hiding and showing line of towers. And that is the Wall!

Rudyard Kipling, *Puck of Pook's Hill*

On 23 May 2003, Britain's 13th National Trail, Hadrian's Wall Path, was opened in the border country between England and Scotland. The trail (84 miles/135km from end to end) follows the course of northern Europe's largest surviving Roman monument, a 2nd-century fortification built on the orders of the Emperor Hadrian in AD122. The Wall marked the northern limits

> **The trail follows the course of northern Europe's largest surviving Roman monument**

of Hadrian's empire – an empire that stretched for 3000 miles across Europe and the Mediterranean all the way to the Euphrates.

To say that creating such a path had been problematic would be something of an understatement. This was the first National Trail to follow the course of a UNESCO World Heritage Site. As such, every time a fencepost, signpost or waymark was driven into the ground,

Walking east towards Crag Lough (see p157) along a fine section of the Wall.

The walk begins at Segedunum, the most easterly fort on the Wall, and follows the River Tyne through Newcastle (**above**) and past the city's seven bridges.

an archaeologist had to be present to ensure that the integrity of the Wall was not in any way compromised. To give you an indication of just how careful they had to be, it took *ten years* before the Hadrian's Wall Path was finally opened to the public. By comparison, it had taken the 2nd and 6th legions of the Roman army only six years to build the actual Wall!

Since its opening many have walked the trail and all seem to agree that the difficulties involved in its creation were well worth it, allowing the walker to follow in the sandal-steps of those who built it with the trail itself rarely diverting from the course of the Romans' barrier by more than a few hundred metres. And, though there's only about ten miles of the Wall left and it hardly ever rises to more than half its original height, it – or at least the route it would have taken – makes for a fascinating trekking companion. Punctuated by forts, milecastles and turrets spaced evenly along its length, the Wall snaked over moor and down dale through Northumberland and Cumbria, between the Roman fort of Segedunum (at the appropriately named Newcastle suburb of Wallsend) in the east and the mouth of the Solway River in the west. It's an incredible feat of engineering, best appreciated in the section from Housesteads to Cawfield Quarry where the landscape is so bleak and wild that human habitation and farming never really took a hold. It is here that the Wall stands most intact, following the bumps and hollows of the undulating countryside – as integral a part of the scenery now as the whinstone cliffs on which it is built. Here, too, are

some of the best-preserved fortresses, from the vast archaeological trove at Vindolanda, set just off the Wall to the south, to the subtle charms at Birdoswald and the beautifully situated Housesteads itself.

After the Romans withdrew the Wall fell into disrepair. What we see as a unique and awe-inspiring work of military architecture was to the local landowners a

Above: A small shelter and a little garden mark the end of the walk on the banks at Bowness-on-Solway.

Right: A decent stretch of Roman Wall at Willowford Farm, just outside Gilsland (51 miles down, 33 to go!)

convenient source of ready-worked stones for their own building purposes. The Wall is part of the fabric of many of the major constructions built after the Romans left: the churches, priories and abbeys that lie just off the Wall, such as those at Hexham and Lanercost; the Norman castles at Carlisle and Newcastle; the Military Road which we follow for part of the walk; the stronghouses at Thirlwall and Drumburgh – all beautiful, historically important buildings. And all of them incorporate stones from the Wall. Yet even where its destruction was total, the Wall's legacy continues to echo through the ages in the names of the villages that lie along the route: Wallsend, Wallend, Wallhouses, Walton, Wall village and Oldwall are just some of the place names that celebrate the Wall. The past is inseparable from the present.

Quite apart from the architectural and historical interest, all around the Wall is scenery of breathtaking beauty

Quite apart from the architectural and historical interest, all around the Wall is scenery of breathtaking beauty, from the sophisticated cityscape of Newcastle to the wild, wind-blasted moors of Northumberland, the pastoral delights of Cumbria and the serenity of Bowness-on-Solway, an Area of Outstanding Natural Beauty and a haven for birdwatchers and those seeking peaceful solitude. After all, what other national trail passes through Paradise (a

suburb of Newcastle), Heavenfield (before Chollerford) and even Eden (the river flowing through Carlisle)!

Yet perhaps the best feature of the Wall is that all its treasures are accessible to anyone with enough get-up-and-go to leave their armchair. The path itself is regarded as one of the easiest National Trails, a week-long romp on a grassy path through rolling countryside with the highest point, Green Slack, just 345m above sea level. (That said, there are still a couple of tiring stages and one brief perusal of the book at the Kings Arms in Bowness, in which hikers who've just finished their trek give their thoughts, will give you an idea of just how tough many people find the walk – and few in number indeed are those who consider it easy.) The waymarking is clear and, with the Wall on one side and a road a little distance away on the other, it's very difficult to lose one's way. There are good facilities, from lively pubs to cosy B&Bs, friendly, well-equipped bunkhouses and idyllic little tearooms. And for those for whom completing the entire trail is over-ambitious, there are good transport connections,

The waymarking is clear and it's very difficult to lose one's way

There's a great variety of scenery on this walk: it's not just about the Wall. On some stretches, such as between Carlisle and Bowness-on-Solway (**below**), almost all evidence of the Wall has disappeared (see p200).

including a special Hadrian's Wall Country bus (the AD122). With a little planning, you can arrange a simple stroll along a short section of the trail, maybe take in a fort or museum on the way, then catch the bus back to 'civilisation'. While for those who prefer not to follow any officially recognised National Trail, the path also connects to 43 other walks, details of which are readily available from one of the half-dozen or so tourist offices serving the trail.

So, while the Wall no longer defines the border between Scotland and England (90% of Northumberland, an English county, actually lies to the north of the Wall, and at no point does the wall actually coincide with the modern Anglo-Scottish border), it nevertheless remains an inspiring place and a monument to the breathtaking ambition of both Hadrian, the youthful dynamic emperor, and of Roman civilisation itself. And this trail is a great way to appreciate it.

HOW DIFFICULT IS THE HADRIAN'S WALL PATH?

The Hadrian's Wall Path is just a long walk. Indeed, many rate this as the easiest of the national trails in the UK. At only four to seven days long, it's one of the shortest too. (Indeed, there's a guy called Elvis from Haltwhistle who completed it in one 30-hour stretch for charity.)

Below: The trig point at Green Slack (see p159), at 345m, is the highest point on the path.

❑ HADRIAN'S WALL HIGHLIGHTS

Trying to pick one particular section that is representative of the entire trail is impossible because each is very different. Undoubtedly if I had to recommend one highlight it would be from **Chollerford to Steel Rigg** (see pp144-58), with its excellently preserved Wall, its milecastles and Wall forts. The landscape is the most dramatic here, too, as you ride the crests and bumps of the various crags. David McGlade, the National Trail Officer for Hadrian's Wall, prefers the **Walltown section** of the Wall (see pp162-80), **Birdoswald and Segedunum forts** (the former for the views, the latter for its presentation), and the **Solway Estuary** (see pp199-212) because of its birdlife.

But just because these sections are my favourites does not mean that the others should be dismissed. The cityscape and suburbs of Newcastle, the absorbing roadside tramp from Heddon-on-the-Wall to Chollerford, the gentle rolling countryside of Cumbria, and 'The Land that Time Forgot' near Bowness are all worth experiencing.

Age seems to be no barrier to completing the walk either. While updating the third edition I walked with a friend, Peter Fenner, who (and I am sure he won't mind my revealing this) was just a month shy of his 78th birthday. So there's no need for crampons, ropes, ice axes, oxygen bottles or any other climbing paraphernalia, because there's no climbing involved. All you need to complete the walk is some suitable clothing, a bit of money, a rucksack full of determination and a half-decent pair of calf muscles.

That said, it is a fairly wild walk in places. Regarding safety, there are few places on the regular trail where it would be possible to fall from a great height, unless you stray from the path near the crags; and with the Wall on one side and a road on the other, it's difficult to get lost too. Nevertheless, you may find a compass or GPS unit (see p17) useful.

Your greatest danger on the walk is from the weather. Thus it is vital that you dress for inclement conditions and always carry a set of dry clothes with you. Not pushing yourself too hard is important too, as over-exertion leads to exhaustion and all its inherent dangers; see pp68-70.

But really, while it is no mean achievement to complete the walk, this is nevertheless a straightforward but fairly exhausting stroll by the standards of northern Britain and should be enjoyed and appreciated as such.

The route is well marked with the familiar National Trail 'acorn' signposts, arrows and other waymarks, so keeping to the trail shouldn't really be a problem.

HOW LONG DO YOU NEED?

Most people take around six days to complete the walk

Most people take around six days to complete the walk, making it one of the shorter national trails. Of course, if you're fit there's no reason why you can't go a little faster, if that's what you want to do, and finish the walk in five days (or even less), though you will end up having a different sort of trek to most of the other people on the trail. For where theirs is a fairly relaxing holiday, yours will be more of a sport. What's more, you won't have much time to enjoy the forts and other attractions, one of

See p31 for some suggested itineraries covering different walking speeds

the main reasons for visiting the Wall in the first place. There's nothing wrong with this approach – *chacun à son goût*, as the French probably say. However, what you mustn't do is try to push yourself too far. That road leads only to exhaustion, injury or, at the absolute least, an unpleasant time.

When deciding how long to allow for the trek, those intending to camp and carry their own luggage shouldn't underestimate just how much a heavy pack can slow them down. On p31 there are some suggested itineraries covering different walking speeds. If you have only a few days, don't try to walk it all; concentrate instead on one area such as the popular central section, or the quieter Cumbrian section from Carlisle to Bowness.

When to go

SEASONS

Britain is a notoriously wet country and the north of England is an infamously damp part of it. '*Hadrain*' as one witty souvenir T-shirt puts it and it's fair to say that few trekkers manage to complete the walk without suffering at least one downpour; two or three per trek are more likely, even in summer. That said, it's equally unlikely that you'll spend a week in the area and not see any sun at all, and even the most cynical of trekkers will have to admit that, during the trekking season at least, there are more sunny days than showery ones. The **trekking season**, by the way, starts at Easter and builds to a crescendo in August, before steadily tailing off in September. By September's end, few indeed are the trekkers who attempt the whole trail, although there are plenty of people on day walks, and by the end of October many places close down for the winter.

Unusually, the authorities in charge of maintaining the path request that walkers do **not attempt the trail in winter** (which they define as October to April), when the path is at its most fragile; they do not, however, rule out walking in Wall country altogether; see the box on pp64-5 for more details.

There are two further points to consider when booking your trip. Firstly, remember that most people set off on the trail at a weekend. This means that you'll find the trail quieter **during the week** and as a consequence you may find it easier to book accommodation. Secondly, towards the western end of the walk, the trail through the Solway Marshes is prone to flooding. While this won't affect when you set off (at least, not if you are starting at the eastern end of it), you do need to be aware of the time of the high tides and plan your walk through

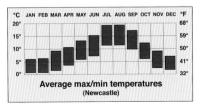

Average max/min temperatures
(Newcastle)

the marshes so that you are not there during high tide; the box on p199 gives advice on how to do this.

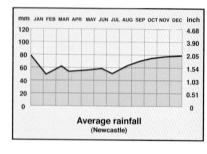

Average rainfall
(Newcastle)

Spring
Find a dry week in springtime (around the end of March to mid-June) and you're in for a treat. The wild flowers are coming into bloom, lambs are skipping in the meadows, the grass is green and lush, and the path is not yet badly eroded. Of course, finding a dry week in spring is not easy but occasionally there's a mini-heatwave. Another advantage with walking at this time is that there will be fewer trekkers and finding accommodation is relatively easy, though do check that the hostels/B&Bs have opened. Easter is the exception; the first major holiday in the year when people flock to the Wall.

Summer
Summer, on the other hand, can be a bit *too* busy but even over the most hectic weekend in August I find it's never insufferable. Still, the chances of a prolonged period of sunshine are of course higher at this time of year than any other, the days are much longer, all the facilities and public transport are operating and the heather is in bloom, turning some of the hills around the crags a fragrant purple. My advice is this: if you're flexible and want to avoid seeing too many people on the trail, avoid the school holidays, which basically means ruling out the tail end of July, all of August and the first few days of September. Alternatively, if you crave the company of other trekkers, summer will provide you with the opportunity of meeting plenty of them, though do remember that you **must book your accommodation in advance**, especially if staying in B&Bs or similar accommodation. Despite the higher than average chance of sunshine, take clothes for any eventuality – it will probably still rain at some point.

Autumn
September is a wonderful time to trek, when many of the tourists have returned home, the path is clear and blackberries provide sustenance for the weary walker along the trail. I think that the weather is usually fairly good too, at least at the beginning of September, though I'll admit I don't have any figures to back this claim. The B&Bs and hostels will still be open at least until the end of the month. By then the weather will begin to get a little wilder and the nights will start to draw in. The trekking season is almost at an end.

Winter
The National Trail authorities ask that you do not walk the trail during winter, to give the path a rest and prevent damage. It is also a little more dangerous to

trek at this time, with few people around, a cold climate and a slippery trail. But while I advise against walking the actual trail, there is nothing to stop you trying one of the circular winter trails near the Wall. For leaflets with suggestions for walks you can take in Wall country that don't actually encroach on the main trail and any unexcavated archaeological treasures see 🖳 www.nationaltrail.co .uk/hadrians-wall-path/leaflets.

RAINFALL

At some point on your walk it will rain; if it doesn't, it's fair to say that you haven't really lived the full Hadrian's Wall experience properly. The question, therefore, is not whether you will be rained on but how often. As long as you dress accordingly and take note of the safety advice given on pp68-70, this shouldn't be a problem.

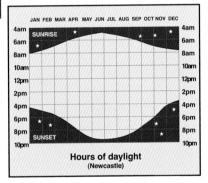

Hours of daylight
(Newcastle)

DAYLIGHT HOURS

If walking in autumn or early spring (I'm assuming you're not going to walk in winter), you must take account of how far you can walk in the available light. It won't be possible to cover as many miles as you would in summer. Remember, too, that you will get a further 30-45 minutes of usable light before sunrise and after sunset depending on the weather.

In June, because the path is in the far north of England, those coming from the south may be surprised that there's enough available light for trekking until at least 10pm. Conversely, in winter you will be equally amazed how quickly the nights draw in. Bear this in mind if walking outside the summer season.

❑ FESTIVALS AND ANNUAL EVENTS

As one of the emptiest parts of England, it is perhaps not surprising that there is a dearth of traditional annual festivals, at least when compared to other parts of the country. That's not to say that events don't happen, it's just that the many fairs, festivals and other happenings do not have the weight of tradition or history behind them. Though many of the activities do take place annually, it's not necessarily at the same time each year. Nevertheless, a look at the official Hadrian's Wall website does give a reasonable list of things going on, from lectures to Easter-egg hunts, guided tours to Roman re-enactments, bat walks to falconry displays, and it's very possible that your trip will coincide with at least one event.

For more details and a complete list of what's on throughout the year, see 🖳 www.visithadrianswall.co.uk.

PLANNING YOUR WALK 1

Practical information for the walker

ROUTE FINDING

With the Wall to follow, it's difficult to get lost on this walk. The route is well marked with the familiar National Trail 'acorn' signposts, arrows and other waymarks, so keeping to the trail shouldn't really be a problem. Nevertheless, you may find a GPS unit (see below) useful.

ACCOMMODATION

The trail guide (Part 6) lists a fairly comprehensive selection of places to stay along the length of the trail. You have three main options: camping, staying in hostels/bunkhouses/camping barns, or using B&Bs/guesthouses/hotels. Few people stick to just one of these options the whole way, preferring, for example, to camp most of the

---

❑ **Using GPS with this book**

I never carried a compass, preferring to rely on a good sense of direction ... I never bothered to understand how a compass works or what it is supposed to do ... To me a compass is a gadget, and I don't get on well with gadgets of any sort.　　　　　　　　　　　**Alfred Wainwright**

While Wainwright's acolytes may scoff, other walkers will accept GPS technology as an inexpensive, well-established if non-essential, navigational aid. To cut a long story short, within a minute of being turned on and with a clear view of the sky, **GPS receivers** will establish your position as well as elevation in a variety of formats, including the British OS grid system, anywhere on earth to an accuracy of within a few metres. These days most **smartphones** have a GPS receiver built in and mapping software available to run on it (see box p40).

　　　The maps in the route guide include numbered waypoints; these correlate to the list on pp216-8, which gives the grid reference as well as a description. You can download the complete list of these waypoints for free as a GPS-readable file (that doesn't include the text descriptions) from the Trailblazer website: 🖳 www.trailblazer-guides.com.

　　　Bear in mind that the vast majority of people who tackle the Hadrian's Wall Path do so perfectly successfully without a GPS unit. Instead of rushing out to invest in one, consider putting the money towards good-quality waterproofs or footwear instead.

time but spend every third night in a hostel, or perhaps use hostels where possible but splash out on a B&B every once in a while.

When booking accommodation, remember to ask if a pick-up and drop-off service is available (usually only B&Bs provide this service). Few of the B&Bs actually lie on the Wall, and at the end of a tiring day it's nice to know a lift is available to take you to your accommodation rather than having to traipse another two or three miles off the path to get to your bed for the night.

The facilities' table on pp32-3 provides a quick snapshot of what type of accommodation is available in each of the towns and villages along the way, while the tables on p31 provide some suggested itineraries. The following is a brief introduction to what to expect from each type of accommodation.

Camping

There are campsites all the way along the Hadrian's Wall Path except in Newcastle and Carlisle. That said, few people choose to camp every night on the trail. You're almost bound to get at least one night where the rain falls relentlessly, soaking equipment and sapping morale, and it is then that most campers opt to spend the next night drying out in a hostel or B&B. There are, however, many advantages with camping. It's more economical, for a start, with most campsites charging from £6. There's rarely any need to book either, except possibly in the very high season, and even then you'd be very unlucky not to find somewhere.

Campsites vary; some are just the back gardens of B&Bs or pubs; others are full-blown caravan sites with a few spaces put aside for tents. Showers are usually available, occasionally for a fee though more often than not for free. Note that **wild camping** (ie not in a regular campsite) is not allowed.

Camping is not an easy option; the route is wearying enough without carrying your accommodation around with you. Should you decide to camp, therefore, I advise you to look into employing one of the baggage-carrying companies mentioned on p26. Of course this does mean that it will cost more and that you will lose a certain amount of freedom as you have to inform the company, at least a day before, of your next destination – and stick to it – so that you and your bag can be reunited every evening. What's more, make sure that the baggage companies deliver to campsites – not all of them do.

❏ Joining the YHA

The YHA still has its fans and, despite the name, anybody of any age can join them. This can be done at any hostel or by contacting the **Youth Hostels Association of England and Wales** (☎ 0800-019 1700, 🖳 www.yha.org.uk). The cost of a year's membership is £15 per year or £20 if paying by credit card (£5/10 for anyone under 26 when paying by debit/credit card) but you do get discounts at various trekking outlets and on certain railcards. Having secured your membership, YHA hostels are easy to book, either online or by ringing the YHA, or each individual hostel separately. You don't need to be a member to book/stay at a YHA hostel but will be charged an additional sum (usually around £3) per night.

Bunkhouses/camping barns and hostels

The term '**bunkhouse**' can mean many different things, though usually it's nothing more than a converted barn in a farmer's field with a couple of wooden benches to sleep on. Sleeping bags are usually necessary in these places. While not exactly the lap of luxury, a night in a bunkhouse is probably the nearest non-campers will get to sleeping outside, while at the same time providing campers with shelter from the elements should the weather look like taking a turn for the worse. Some of the better bunkhouses provide a shower and simple kitchen with running water and perhaps a kettle, and occasionally pots, pans, cutlery and crockery.

Since the first edition of this guide, the number of **youth hostels** on the trail has dropped alarmingly. The closure of the hostel in Jesmond, Newcastle, can be added to the closures at Acomb and Greenhead (the latter is now a private hostel) over the past decade, while the hostel at Birdoswald has since 2013 taken only groups and the one at Carlisle is, by necessity, open only during the summer holidays (as it is actually accommodation for students for the rest of the year). In other words, there are now only two YHA hostels left on the trail, the one at Carlisle I've just mentioned and the one at Once Brewed (which, incidentally, is open only for pre-booked groups between December and February). On top of this, if you are travelling in April/May or September, ie at the beginning or end of the trekking season, you may find them shut for two or three days per week, or that they are entirely taken over by school groups, leaving trekkers shut out; contact the YHA (see box opposite) or the relevant hostel to find out the exact opening dates. Even in high season neither of the YHAs on the route is staffed during the day and trekkers have to wait until 4 or 5pm before checking in. Finally, the cost of staying in a hostel, once breakfast has been added on, is in most instances not that much cheaper (starting at £15 for members, though more usually around £20) than staying in a B&B.

Bed and breakfast

Bed and Breakfasts (B&Bs) are a great British institution and many of those along the Hadrian's Wall Path are absolutely charming, with buildings often three or four hundred years old and some even made with Wall stones! There's nothing mysterious about a B&B; as the name suggests, they provide you with a bed in a private room and a cooked breakfast (see below) – unless you specify otherwise beforehand – though they range in style enormously.

Rooms usually contain either a double bed (known as a double room), or two single beds (known as a twin room) though sometimes twin beds can be pushed together to make a double bed. Family rooms are for three or more people; sometimes this means there is a double bed with (a) separate single bed(s) or bunk beds. Rooms are often en suite but in some cases the facilities are shared or private, though even with the latter the bathroom is never more than a few feet away. Most rooms have a TV and tea/coffee-making facilities.

An evening meal (usually around £12-20) is often provided at the more remote or bigger places, at least if you book in advance. If not, there's nearly

PLANNING YOUR WALK

always a pub or restaurant nearby or, if it's far, the B&B owner may give you a lift to and from the nearest place with food.

B&B rates B&Bs in this guide start at around £30 per person (pp) for two people for the most basic accommodation. Most charge around £35-40pp. Solo trekkers should take note: single rooms are not so easy to find so if you are on your own you will often end up occupying a double/twin room, for which you'll usually have to pay a single occupancy supplement (upwards of £10). Rates are sometimes discounted for stays of two or more nights.

PLANNING YOUR WALK

❏ **Should you book your accommodation in advance?**

When walking the Hadrian's Wall Path, it's essential that you have your night's accommodation booked by the time you set off in the morning, whether you're planning to stay in a hostel or a B&B. Nothing is more deflating than to arrive at your destination at day's end only to find that you've then got to walk a further five miles or so, or even take a detour off the route, because everywhere in town is booked.

That said, there's a certain amount of hysteria regarding the booking of accommodation, with many websites, B&Bs and other organisations suggesting you book at least six months in advance. Whilst it's true that the earlier you book the more chance you have of getting precisely the accommodation you require, booking so far in advance does leave you vulnerable to changing circumstances. Booking a full six months before setting foot on the trail is all very well if everything is to go to plan but if you break your leg just before you're due to set off or, God forbid, there's another outbreak of foot and mouth, all you'll end up with is a lot of lost deposits. By not booking so far in advance, you give yourself the chance to shift your holiday plans to a later date should the unforeseen arise.

In my experience, the lack of accommodation is not as bad as some suggest, at least not outside the high season (ie the summer period coinciding with the long school holidays in the UK). Outside this period, and particularly in April/May or September, as long as you're flexible and willing to take what's offered, with maybe even a night or two in a hostel if that's all there is, you should get away with booking just a few nights in advance, or indeed just the night before. The exceptions to this rule are at weekends, when everywhere is busy, and where accommodation is very limited. Campers, however, have more flexibility and can often just turn up and find a space.

In summary, therefore, my advice is this: it's always worth phoning ahead to book your accommodation. If you are staying in **B&Bs** and walking in high season this should be done months in advance if you have a preference for specific B&Bs. If, on the other hand, you're not too bothered which B&B you stay in, are trekking in April/May or September and don't mind the possibility of having to walk a mile or two off the route to get a room, you can probably get away with booking your accommodation a night or two before. If you can book at least a few nights in advance, however, so much the better, and at weekends it's essential you book as soon as you can.

If staying in **hostels or bunkhouses**, the same applies though do be careful when travelling out of high season as many hostels close for a couple of days each week and shut altogether from around November to Easter. Once again, it's well worth phoning at least one night before and well before that if it's a weekend, to make sure the hostel isn't fully booked or shut.

Campers, whatever time of the year, should always be able to find somewhere to pitch their tent at a campsite, though ringing in advance can't hurt and is often appreciated; it will at least mean you can confirm that the campsite is still open.

Guesthouses, hotels, pubs and inns

The difference between a B&B and a guesthouse is minimal, though some of the better guesthouses are more like hotels, offering evening meals and a lounge for guests. Pubs and inns also offer bed and breakfast accommodation and prices are no more than in a regular B&B.

Hotels usually do cost more, however, and some might be a little irritated with a bunch of smelly trekkers turning up and treading mud into their carpet. Most on the Hadrian's Wall Path, however, are used to seeing trekkers and welcome them warmly. Prices in hotels start at around £25-30 per person, though occasionally you can get some special deals with the larger hotel chains in Newcastle and Carlisle that can be as low as £19. Hotel and pub rates may not include breakfast.

FOOD AND DRINK

Breakfast and lunch

Stay in a B&B and you'll be filled to the gills with a cooked **English breakfast**. This usually consists of a bowl of cereal followed by a plateful of eggs, bacon, sausages, mushrooms, tomatoes and possibly baked beans or black pudding, with toast and butter, and all washed down with coffee, tea and/or juice. Enormously satisfying the first time you try it, by the fourth or fifth morning you may start to prefer a lighter continental breakfast. If you have had enough of these cooked breakfasts and/or plan an early start, ask if you can have a packed lunch instead of breakfast. Your landlady or hostel can usually provide a **packed lunch** (indicated by the Ⓛ symbol in the text) at an additional cost (unless it's in lieu of breakfast), though of course there's nothing to stop you preparing your own lunch (but do bring a penknife if you plan to do this), or going to a pub (see below) or café.

Remember to plan ahead; certain stretches of the walk are virtually devoid of eating places (the stretch from Chollerford to Housesteads for example – save for a couple of vans that usually set up in summer along the way – and from there to Walltown Quarry) so read ahead about the next day's walk in Part 6 to make sure you never go hungry.

Cream teas

Whatever you do for lunch, don't forget to leave some room for a cream tea or two, a morale, energy and cholesterol booster all rolled into one delicious package: a pot of tea accompanied by scones served with cream and jam, and sometimes a cake or two. The jury is out on whether you should put the jam on first or the cream but either way do not miss the chance of at least one cream tea.

Evening meals

Pubs are as much a feature of the walk as moorland and sheep, and in some cases the pub is as much a tourist attraction as any Roman fort or ruined priory. The **Robin Hood Inn** (see p120) to the west of Whittledene Reservoir, is one example, as are **The Keelman** (see p110) at Newburn and **The Hadrian Hotel** (see p126) at Wall (both just off the trail), the historic **Twice Brewed** (see p160)

near Steel Rigg and the recently renovated *Samson Inn* (see p174) at Gilsland. The *King's Arms* (see p213) at Bowness-on-Solway is also something of an institution, where those who've walked from Newcastle can celebrate their achievement with a certificate (available from the bar) and beer (ditto), jot down their thoughts on the path in the 'trekkers book' they keep there, and worry those who are just about to begin the walk with their tales from the trail. There are also several great pubs in the towns near the path, in particular *The Golden Lion* and *The Wheatsheaf* (see p134) at Corbridge and, my favourite, the cosy *Black Bull* (see p168) at Haltwhistle.

Most pubs have become highly attuned to the desires of trekkers and offer lunch and evening meals (often with a couple of local dishes and usually some vegetarian options), some locally brewed beers, a garden to relax in on hot days and a roaring fire to huddle around on cold ones. The standard of the food varies widely, though, is usually served in big portions, which is often just about all trekkers care about at the end of a long day. In many of the villages the pub is the only place to eat out. Note that pubs may close in the afternoon, especially in the winter months, so check in advance if you are hoping to visit a particular one, and also if you are planning lunch there as food serving hours can change.

That other great British culinary institution, the **fish 'n' chip shop**, can be found in Newcastle, Carlisle, and towns off the Wall such as Haltwhistle, Brampton and Hexham; as can Chinese and Indian **takeaways**, which are usually the last places to serve food in the evenings, staying open until at least 11pm.

Self catering on the trail

Except for when the trail passes through the cities of Newcastle and Carlisle, there aren't actually that many shops where you can buy provisions along the path. Heddon-on-the-Wall has a small store that's combined with its petrol station and Chollerford likewise (though even smaller). But with the demise of the shop-cum-post-office at Gilsland the only other places where you can buy anything to eat are the gift shops at the forts of Chesters, Housesteads, Birdoswald and Carvoran, and the informal refreshment stalls established at such places as Haytongate, Bleatarn, Crosby-on-Eden, Grinsdale and Drumburgh (this last one known as *Laal Bite*). These places are, on occasion, absolute lifesavers: the biggest, such as Haytongate, Crosby-on-Eden and Drumburgh, provide a small hut in which hikers can cower from the elements and take advantage of the refrigerated cans, chocolate bars, crisps, even a hot drinks machine. The other

❏ **Local breweries**
When it comes to drinking, there are any number of local breweries competing to slake the thirst of trekkers with real ales, stouts and bitters. Of particular interest to trekkers, maybe, is the **Hadrian and Border** brewery (🖥 www.hadrian-border-brew ery.co.uk), based in Newcastle. A merger of two breweries, Hadrian and Border's beers include Coast to Coast (4.4%), Reiver's IPA (4.4%) and Rampart (4.8%). Also in Northumberland, and only a short hike from the trail, **High House Farm Brewery** (🖥 www.highhousefarmbrewery.co.uk) is based on a farm in the village of Matfen and boasts a visitor's centre, tearoom and, of course, a well-stocked bar from where you can sample one (or more) of their beers, many of which are named after the farm's animals such as Ferocious Fred (4.8%), the farm bull, and the seriously strong Cyril the Magnificent (5.5%), named in honour of the cat. Another brewery that will be of interest to Wall Walkers is **Big Lamp** (🖥 http://biglampbrewers.co.uk), the North-East's oldest micro-brewery, based at the Keelman pub (see p110) just off the trail at Newburn. Brews include the delicious Summerhill Stout and the appropriately named Blackout (11%!). Not too far away, **Wylam Brewery** (🖥 www.wylambrewery.co.uk) is now based at Heddon-on-the-Wall and is perhaps most famous for its Rocket, a 5% strength best bitter. A fourth brewer from this neck of the Wall, **Mordue**, produces the divine Workie Ticket (4.5%), 2013 Champion Best Bitter of Britain and a cracking pint.

Heading into Cumbria, another brewery of interest is Cockermouth's **Jennings of Cumberland** (🖥 www.jenningsbrewery.co.uk), the most ubiquitous brewer in Cumbria. Further boosting Cumbria's reputation for fine brewing, **Geltsdale Brewery** (🖥 www.geltsdalebrewery.com) is based in part of the Old Brampton Brewery (which was originally founded in 1785), from where they produce eight different brews including a lager, AD78, which is named after the year that Governor Agricola finally brought Britain under control.

ones, such as those at Bleatarn and Grinsdale, are little more than small boxes in which the provisions are kept. All of them, however, are unsupervised, and thus rely on an honesty-box system (where you put the correct money into a tin or moneybox to pay for what you've consumed). As some of these 'stalls' are actually run by the children of local families, please don't abuse their trust by walking off without paying. See Part 6 for more details.

Drinking water
There are plenty of ways of perishing on the Hadrian's Wall Path but given how damp the north of England is, thirst probably won't be one of them. Be careful, though, for on a hot day in some of the remoter parts after a steep climb or two you'll quickly dehydrate, which is at best highly unpleasant and at worst might-ily dangerous. Always carry some water with you and in hot weather drink three or four litres a day. Don't be tempted by the water in the streams; if the cow or sheep faeces in the water don't make you ill, the chemicals from the pesticides and fertilisers used on the farms almost certainly will. Using iodine or another purifying treatment will help to combat the former, though there's little you can do about the latter. It's a lot safer to fill up from taps instead.

MONEY

Outside Newcastle and Carlisle, **banks** (and ATMs) are few and far between on the Hadrian's Wall Path – indeed, there is only one place, Heddon-on-the-Wall, which boasts an ATM, though there are plenty in the towns (Hexham, Corbridge, Haltwhistle and Brampton) that lie a mile or two off the trail. See the town and village facilities table on pp32-3 for details. **Post offices**, however, provide a very useful service. You can get cash (by debit card) for free at any post office counter if you bank with most banks or building societies. For a full list see 🖳 www.postoffice.co.uk/branch-banking-services. Another way of getting money in your hand is to use the **cashback** system: find a store that will

---

PLANNING YOUR WALK

❏ Information for foreign visitors

● **Currency/money** The British pound (£) comes in notes of £100, £50, £20, £10 and £5, and coins of £2 and £1. The pound is divided into 100 pence (usually referred to as 'p', pronounced 'pee') which come in silver coins of 50p, 20p, 10p and 5p and copper coins of 2p and 1p. Cash (see p39) is the most welcome form of payment though debit/credit cards are accepted in some places. Up-to-date exchange rates can be found at 🖳 www.xe.com/ucc.

● **Business hours** Most **shops** and main **post offices** are open at least from Monday to Friday 9am-5pm and Saturday 9am-12.30pm. Many choose longer hours and some open on Sundays as well. However, some also close early one day a week, often Wednesday or Thursday. **Banks** are usually open 10am-4pm Monday to Friday. **Pub hours** are less predictable as each pub may have different opening hours. However, most pubs on the Hadrian's Wall Path continue to open daily between 11am and 11pm (some close at 10.30pm on Sunday) and **some still close in the afternoon**.

● **National (Bank) holidays** Most businesses are shut on 1 January, Good Friday (March/April), Easter Monday (March/April), the first and the last Monday in May, the last Monday in August, 25 December and 26 December.

● **School holidays** Generally as follows: a one-week break late October, two weeks around Christmas and the New Year, a week mid-February, two weeks over Easter, a week at the end of May, and from late July to early September. Private-school holidays fall at the same time, but tend to be slightly longer.

● **Documents** If you are a member of a National Trust organisation in your country bring your membership card as you should be entitled to free entry to National Trust properties and sites in the UK.

● **EHIC and travel insurance** The European Health Insurance Card (EHIC) entitles cardholders to any necessary medical treatment under the UK's National Health Service (NHS) while on a temporary visit here; treatment is given only on production of the card so take it with you. However, the EHIC is not a substitute for proper medical cover on your travel insurance for unforeseen bills and for getting you home should that be needed. Also consider cover for loss and theft of personal belongings, especially if you are camping or staying in hostels, as there will be times when you'll have to leave your luggage unattended.

accept a debit card and ask them to advance cash against the card. However, you will almost always need to buy something.

Note that, with few local stores, pubs or B&Bs accepting credit or debit cards, and few places where you can get money out along the way, it is essential to carry plenty of **cash** with you, though do keep it safe and out of sight (preferably in a moneybelt). A chequebook could prove very useful as back-up, so that you don't have to keep on dipping into your cash reserves, especially as most B&Bs don't accept credit cards.

OTHER SERVICES

An increasing number of places offer **internet access** and/or **wi-fi** including most B&Bs and bunk barns. Most villages away from the Wall have a **grocery store**, often with a **post office** in part of it, and nearby you'll usually find a **phone box**.

● **Weights and measures** The European Commission is no longer attempting to ban the pint or the mile: so, in Britain, milk can be sold in pints (1 pint = 568ml), as can beer in pubs, though most other liquid including petrol (gasoline) and diesel is sold in litres. Distances on road and path signs will also continue to be given in miles (1 mile = 1.6km) rather than kilometres, and yards (1yd = 0.9m) rather than metres. The population remains divided between those who still use inches (1 inch = 2.5cm), feet (1ft = 0.3m) and yards (3ft = 1 yard = 0.9m) and those who are happy with millimetres, centimetres and metres; you'll often be told that 'it's only a hundred yards or so' to somewhere, rather than a hundred metres or so.

Most food is sold in metric weights (g and kg) but the imperial weights of pounds (lb: 1lb = 453g) and ounces (oz: 1oz = 28g) are frequently displayed too. The weather – a frequent topic of conversation – is also an issue: while most forecasts predict temperatures in Celsius (C), many people continue to think in terms of Fahrenheit (F; see the temperature chart on p14 for conversions).

● **Smoking** The ban on smoking in public places relates not only to pubs and restaurants, but also to B&Bs, hostels and hotels. The ban is in force in all enclosed areas open to the public – even if they are in a private home such as a B&B. Should you be foolhardy enough to light up in a no-smoking area, which includes pretty well any indoor public place, you could be fined £50, but it's the owners of the premises who carry the can if they fail to stop you, with a potential fine of £2500.

● **Telephone** From outside Britain the international country access code for Britain is ☎ 44 followed by the area code minus the first 0, and then the number you require. Within Britain, to call a landline number with the same code as the landline phone you are calling from, the code can be omitted: dial the number only. If you're using a mobile phone that is registered overseas, consider buying a local SIM card to keep costs down. Mobile phone reception is generally good on and around Hadrian's Wall Path.

● **Time** During the winter, the whole of Britain is on Greenwich Mean Time (GMT). The clocks move one hour forward on the last Sunday in March, remaining on British Summer Time (BST) until the last Sunday in October.

● **Emergency services** For police, ambulance, fire or mountain rescue dial ☎ 999 or the EU standard number ☎ 112.

PLANNING YOUR WALK

There are **outdoor equipment shops** in Carlisle, Newcastle and Hexham; **pharmacies** in those towns as well as Corbridge and Brampton; and **tourist information centres** at Newcastle and Carlisle as well as off the Wall at Corbridge, Hexham, Haltwhistle and Brampton. At Newburn and Once Brewed there are visitor centres for the Riverside Park and Northumberland National Park respectively.

WALKING COMPANIES

It is, of course, possible to turn up with your boots and backpack at Wallsend and just start walking, with little planned save for your accommodation (see box on p20). The following companies, however, are in the business of making your holiday as stress-free and enjoyable as possible.

Baggage carriers and accommodation booking

There are several **baggage-carrying companies** serving the Hadrian's Wall Path, from national organisations such as Sherpa Van Project to companies that consist of little more than one man and his van. With all these services you can book up to the last moment, usually up to around 8pm the previous evening, though it's cheaper if you book in advance. Do shop around as the costs (usually around £8 to take your bag to your next destination) and maximum weight (15-20kg) vary between companies. They have a minimum number of bags that they will transfer from the same address (usually two).

Nearly all these companies offer **accommodation booking** as well. Alternatively you can contact the tourist information centres as most also offer accommodation booking (see box p42).

● **Brigantes Walking Holidays** (☎ 01756-770402, 🖳 www.brigantesenglish walks.com) charges approx £8pp per day; they prefer bags to be less than 17kg.

● **Explore Britain** (☎ 01740-650900, 🖳 www.explorebritain.com) charges £40 per day for up to six bags.

● **Hadrian's Haul** (☎ 07967-564823, 🖳 www.hadrianshaul.com) is one of the cheapest at around £5 per bag with a maximum weight limit of 18kg per bag.

● **Sherpa Van Project** (baggage transfer ☎ 01748-826917, accommodation booking ☎ 01609-883731; 🖳 www.sherpavan.com) charges from £8 per bag; minimum two bags with a maximum weight per bag of 20kg.

● **Walkers' Baggage Transfer Co** (☎ 0871-423 8803; 🖳 www.walkersbags .co.uk) charges from £5 per bag with an 18kg weight limit.

Self-guided holidays

Self-guided basically means that the company will organise accommodation, baggage transfer, transport to and from the walk, and various maps and advice, but leave you on your own to actually walk the path. Most companies offer walks between March/April and the end of October. In addition to the 'standard' itineraries summarised below, just about all the companies can tailor your holiday to suit your requirements.

● **Absolute Escapes** (0131-240 1210, 🖳 www.absoluteescapes.com; Edinburgh) Offer trips of 5-8 days along the whole of the Wall in either direction.

PLANNING YOUR WALK

● **Brigantes Walking Holidays** (☎ 01756-770402, 💻 www.brigantesenglish walks.com; North Yorks) Can put together a walking holiday for you (generally seven walking days but any length/direction is possible). Also operates a baggage carrying service (see p26).

● **Celtic Trails** (☎ 01291-689774, 💻 www.celtic-trails.com; Chepstow) Offer a 4-day 'Best of the Wall' walk from Corbridge to Irthington, and complete Wall walks of 6-11 days. They also offer two standards of accommodation; regular B&Bs as well as their 'Classic plus' grade for anyone who wants to splash out on some days, or even for the whole walk.

● **Contours Walking Holidays** (☎ 01629-821900, 💻 www.contours.co.uk; Derbyshire) Offers various walks along the entire Wall ranging from 5 to 11 days; walks can be done in either direction. They also offer a 'Best of Hadrian's Wall' tour (5-6 days) which omits the less rewarding stages east of Heddon-on-the-Wall and west of Carlisle; a highlights tour (4-5 days) from Corbridge to Brampton; and a 'Hadrian's Wall Short Break' (2-3 days) that takes in the most dramatic section of the Wall between the fascinating fort of Cilurnum at Chollerford and Lanercost.

● **Discovery Travel** (☎ 01904-632226, 💻 www.discoverytravel.co.uk; York) Offer standard self-guided walks of 6-9 nights as well as a 5-night 'Highlights of Hadrian's Wall' package from Chollerford to Lanercost; can organise walks in both directions.

● **Explore Britain** (☎ 01740-650900, 💻 www.explorebritain.com; Co Durham) Offers various walks of about 4-5 days with two covering just the Wall's picturesque centre, and the third a 4-day trip exploring the path while based in Carlisle (two days walking only).

● **Footpath Holidays** (☎ 01985-840049; 💻 www.footpath-holidays.com; Wilts) Run single-centre guesthouse-based self-guided (selected parts) walks for 5-7 days with Hexham as the base.

● **Hadrian's Wall Ltd** (☎ 01434-603499, 💻 www.hadrianswall.ltd.uk; Northumberland) As the name suggests, this company, which is based next to the Wall, specialises in Hadrian's Wall. They offer self-guided, part-guided and tailor-made treks in either direction and with a range of accommodation levels. They are also the only company to offer a camping trek (💻 www.hadrianswall adventure.co.uk); the trek operates west to east and includes 6 nights camping, beginning on a Friday night. The cost includes tent hire, campsite fees and luggage transfer – the tents are set up for you by the time you arrive at the end of the day's walk, and they have a field kitchen to provide a cooked breakfast. They can also provide packed lunches and equipment hire.

● **Let's Go Walking** (☎ 01837-880075; 💻 www.letsgowalking.com; Devon) Offers 8-night/9-day trips (with 7 actually spent on the trail); can make bespoke trips.

● **Macs Adventure** (☎ 0141-530 8886; 💻 www.macsadventure.com; Glasgow) Offers trips of 4-9 days along the whole of the Wall in either direction, as well as 'Best of Hadrian's Wall' itineraries that travel between Corbridge and Gilsland. They will also tailor-make holidays.

PLANNING YOUR WALK

● **Mickledore Travel** (☎ 01768-772335; ☐ www.mickledore.co.uk; Keswick) A number of self-guided tours ranging from a 3-day short break on the most dramatic central section of the wall, between Humshaugh and Gilsland, to a walk of 6-10 days (in either direction) over the entire length of the path. Luggage transfer and packed lunches are optional.

● **Open Book Visitor Guiding** (☎ 01228-670578, ☐ greatguidedtours.co.uk; Cumbria) A company with over 30 years' experience; they can arrange self-guided holidays in either direction and for the whole walk or just part of it.

● **Load Off Your Back** (☎ 01707-331133; ☐ www.loadoffyourback.co.uk; Herts) The 'self-guiding' arm of Ramblers Worldwide Holidays (see below) offers trips of 5-9 days.

● **NorthWestWalks** (☎ 01257 424889; ☐ www.northwestwalks.co.uk; Wigan) Offers itineraries from 5 nights/4 days walking to 10 nights/9 days walking. Can tailor make as required.

● **Shepherds Walks Holidays** (☎ 01669-621044 ; ☐ www.shepherdswalks .co.uk; Northumberland) Offer trips of 6-10 days along the whole of the Wall in either direction as well as highlights tours.

● **Sherpa Expeditions** (☎ 020-8577 2717; ☐ www.sherpa-walking-holidays.co.uk; London) Offers an 8-day 'Inn-to-Inn' walking tour along the whole Wall.

● **The Walking Holiday Company** (☎ 01600-713008; ☐ www.thewalkinghol idaycompany.co.uk; Monmouth) Offers trips of 4-10 days along the whole of the Wall in either direction. Can tailor-make as required.

Group/guided walking tours

If you don't trust your map-reading skills or simply prefer the company of other walkers as well as an experienced guide, the following will be of interest. Packages nearly always include meals, accommodation, transport arrange-ments, minibus back-up and baggage transfer. Have a good look at each of the companies' websites before booking as each has their own speciality. Note that there is nearly always a single supplement for solo travellers.

● **Hadrian's Wall Ltd** (see p27) They offer a range of part-guided walks; the guide will accompany walkers for one or two days and will focus mainly on the central part of the Wall.

● **NorthWestWalks** (see above) Offers one itinerary each year of 7 nights/6 days walking.

● **Open Book Visitor Guiding** (see above) Carol Donnelly has been guiding tours along the Wall for over 35 years and she and her team of guides can arrange walks/tours for any size of group. Also run coach tours along the Wall.

● **Ramblers Worldwide Holidays** (☎ 01707-331133; ☐ www.ramblerscoun trywide.co.uk; Herts)   Offers a 6-day walk from Heddon-on-the-Wall to Bowness; two hotels, one near Hexham, one in Carlisle, provide the accommo-dation during your walk. The walks operate approximately once a month between April and August.

● **Shepherds Walks Holidays** (see above) Offer guided walks for the whole Wall and day walks as well as the hire of a private guide.

Budgeting

England is not a cheap place to go travelling and while the north may be one of the cheaper parts, the towns and villages on the Hadrian's Wall Path are more than used to seeing tourists and charge accordingly. You may think before you set out that you are going to try to keep your budget to a minimum by camping every night where it's possible and cooking your own food but it's a rare trekker who sticks to this rule. Besides, the B&Bs and pubs on the route are amongst the path's major attractions and it would be a pity not to sample the hospitality in at least some of them.

If the only expenses of this walk were accommodation and food, budgeting for the trip would be a piece of cake. Unfortunately, in addition, there are all the little extras that push up the cost of your trip: getting to and from the path, beer, cream teas, stamps and postcards, internet use (though this is increasingly becoming free now), buses here and there, baggage carriers, phone calls, laundry, memory cards for your camera, souvenirs, entrance fees (to minimise these it is worth being a member of English Heritage/National Trust)... it's surprising how much these add up.

CAMPING

You can survive on less than £15 per person per day if you use the cheapest campsites, don't visit a pub, avoid all the museums and tourist attractions in the towns, cook all your own food from staple ingredients and generally have a pretty miserable time of it. Even then, unforeseen expenses will probably nudge your daily budget above this figure. Include the occasional pint, and perhaps a pub meal every now and then, and the figure will be nearer £20 a day.

BUNKHOUSES/CAMPING BARNS AND HOSTELS

The charge for staying in a bunkhouse or YHA hostel varies according to its quality and range of facilities. Bunkhouses on the Hadrian's Wall Path range widely, as shown in the price range of £10-40 per person with most about £12-15. Breakfast is usually extra, at least in the cheaper bunkhouses. YHA hostel rates (for members) start at around £16 at Once Brewed, £24 at Carlisle, while the private hostel in Newcastle starts at £19 and at Greenhead it's £15. Overall, it can cost from around £30 per day, or £40 to live in a little more comfort, enjoy the odd beer and go out for the occasional meal.

B&Bs, GUESTHOUSES AND HOTELS

B&B rates start at £30pp per night but can easily be at least twice this, particularly if you are walking by yourself and are thus liable to pay single supplements. Add on the cost of lunch and dinner and you should reckon on about £50 minimum per day. Staying in a guesthouse or hotel would probably push the minimum up to £60.

Note that B&B rates are often discounted for stays of two or more nights.

Itineraries

Part 6 of this book has been written from east to west, though there is of course nothing to stop you from tackling it in the opposite direction, and there are advantages in doing so – see below. To help you plan your walk there is a **planning map** (opposite the inside back cover) and a **table of village/town facilities** (pp32-3), which gives a run-down on the essential information you will need regarding accommodation possibilities and services.

You could follow one of the suggested itineraries (see opposite) which are based on preferred type of accommodation and walking speeds or, if tackling the entire walk seems a bit ambitious, you can tackle it a day or two at a time. To help you, we discuss the highlights of the Hadrian's Wall Path on p13 and you can use public transport to get to the start and end of the walk. The public transport map and service details are on pp46-8. Once you have an idea of your approach turn to Part 6 for detailed information on accommodation, places to eat and other services in each village and town on the route. Also in Part 6 you will find summaries of the route to accompany the detailed trail maps.

SUGGESTED ITINERARIES

The itineraries in the boxes opposite are based on different accommodation types, camping, hostels and B&Bs, with each one divided into three alternatives depending on your walking speed. They are only suggestions so feel free to adapt them. **Don't forget** to add your travelling time before and after the walk.

WHICH DIRECTION?

It's more common for Wall walkers ('Wallkers'?) attempting the entire trail to start from Newcastle and head west. The main reason seems to be because the official trail guide and the majority of those guidebooks that have followed in its wake were written from east to west. The justification put forward by the author of the official guide is that it seems 'more natural' to walk out of a big city into the open country, and I suppose there's some truth in that. Around 60% of Wall walkers seem to agree. Furthermore, the scenery improves the further west you go – up to a point – and the turrets and milecastles are also numbered from east to west (see box p114) as that is the direction that the Romans built the Wall. What's more, as it's more popular to walk from east to west, those trekkers who prefer a bit of company will find more people heading in their direction.

STAYING IN B&Bs

Relaxed		Medium		Fast	
Place	**Approx Distance**	**Place**	**Approx Distance**	**Place**	**Approx Distance**
Night	miles/km		miles/km		miles/km
0 Newcastle		Newcastle		Newcastle	
1 Newburn	11/18	Heddon	15/24	Chollerford	30/48
2 East Wallhouses	7.5/12	Chollerford	15/24	Gilsland	21/34
3 Chollerford	11.5/18.5	Once Brewed	12/19.5	Carlisle	19/30.5
4 Once Brewed	12/19.5	Walton	16/26	Bowness	14/22.5
5 Gilsland	9/14.5	Carlisle	12/19.5		
6 Newtown	9/14.5	Bowness	14/22.5		
7 Carlisle	10/16				
8 Bowness	14/22.5				

STAYING IN BUNKHOUSES/CAMPING BARNS/HOSTELS

Relaxed		Medium		Fast	
Place	**Approx Distance**	**Place**	**Approx Distance**	**Place**	**Approx Distance**
Night	miles/km		miles/km		miles/km
0 Newcastle		Newcastle		Newcastle	
1 Heddon	15/24	Heddon	15/24	Heddon	15/24
2 Green Carts Farm	16/25.5	Old Repeater Stn	19/30.5	Once Brewed	27/43.5
3 Old Repeater Stn	3/5	Greenhead	15/24	Walton	16/25.5
4 Once Brewed	8/13	Crosby	14/22.5	Carlisle *	12/19.5
5 Greenhead	7/11	Boustead Hill	14/22.5	Bowness	14/22.5
6 Walton	9/14.5	Bowness	7/11		
7 Carlisle *	12/19.5				
8 Bowness	14/22.5	* seasonal			

CAMPING

Relaxed		Medium		Fast	
Place	**Approx Distance**	**Place**	**Approx Distance**	**Place**	**Approx Distance**
Night	miles/km		miles/km		miles/km
0 Newcastle*		Newcastle*		Newcastle*	
1 Heddon *	15/24	Heddon *	15/24	(East) Wallhouses	21/34
2 Wall	14/22.5	Wall	14/22.5	Once Brewed	22/35.5
3 Old Repeater Stn	5/8	Once Brewed	14/22.5	Carlisle *	27/43.5
4 Once Brewed	9/14.5	Walton	15/24	Bowness *	14/22.5
5 Greenhead *	6/9.5	Boustead Hill	19/30.5		
6 Walton	9/14.5	Bowness *	7/11.5		
7 Carlisle *	12/19.5				
8 Boustead Hill	7/11.5				
9 Bowness *	7/11.5				

* Places marked with an asterisk have no campsite but do have a camping barn/bunkhouse/hostel though the hostel in Carlisle is seasonal

PLANNING YOUR WALK

VILLAGE AND

Place name (Places in brackets are a short walk off Hadrian's Wall path)	Distance from previous place § approx miles/km	Bank/ Cash Machine (ATM) £=charge	Post Office	Tourist Information Centre (TIC) National Park Centre (NPC)
Newcastle/Wallsend		✔	✔	TIC
Newburn	**11/18**			
(Wylam)	(1/1.6)	✔£	✔	
Heddon-on-the-Wall	**4/6**	✔£	✔	
East Wallhouses	**6/9.5**			
Port Gate (A68)	**4/6.4**			
Wall	**4/6.4**			
Chollerford	**1/1.6**			
(Humshaugh)	1/1.6			
Corbridge–Hexham–Acomb alternative route				
(Corbridge)	(3/4.8 from Halton)	✔	✔	TIC
(Hexham)	(4.5/7.2)	✔	✔	TIC
(Acomb)	(1.5/2.4)		✔	
(Old Repeater Stn)	(0.5/0.8)			
(Grindon)	(2/3.2)			
Housesteads	**9/14.5**			
Steel Rigg	4/6.4			
(Once Brewed)	0.25/0.4			NPC/TIC
(Haltwhistle)	(2/3.2)	✔	✔	TIC
Carvoran	**5.5/8.8**			
(Greenhead)#	(0.3/0.5)			
Gilsland	**2.5/4**			
Birdoswald	**2/3.2**			
Banks	**2.5/4**			
(Lanercost Priory)	(0.75/1.25)			TIC
Walton	**2.5/4**			
Newtown	**2/3.2**			
(Brampton)	(2/3.2)	✔	✔	TIC
(Laversdale)	(0.6/1)			
Crosby-on-Eden	**5/8**			
Carlisle	**5/8**	✔	✔	TIC
Grinsdale	**3.5/5.6**			
(Monkhill)	1/1.6			
Burgh-by-Sands	**3.5/5.6**			
(Boustead Hill)	(0.3/0.5)			
Drumburgh	**2.5/4**			
Glasson	**1/1.6**			
Port Carlisle	**2.5/4**			
Bowness-on-Solway	**1/1.6**			

TOTAL DISTANCE   84 miles/135.5km

§ Distances in **bold** are between places directly on the trail; distances in brackets are the distances off the path but not necessarily from the previous place mentioned.

PLANNING YOUR WALK

TOWN FACILITIES

Eating Place ✔=1 ✔✔=2 ✔✔✔=3+ (✔)=seasonal	Food Store	Campsite	Hostels YHA/ H (IndHostel)/ B (Barn or Bunkhouse)	B&B-style accommodation ✔=1 ✔✔=2 ✔✔✔=3+	Place name (Places in brackets are a short walk off Hadrian's Wall path)
✔✔	✔		H	✔✔✔	**Newcastle**
✔✔				✔	**Newburn**
✔	✔			✔✔	(Wylam)
✔✔	✔		B	✔✔	**Heddon-on-the-Wall**
✔✔✔		✔		✔✔	**East Wallhouses**
(✔)				✔	**Port Gate (A68)**
✔		✔		✔	**Wall**
✔✔	✔	✔		✔	**Chollerford**
✔	✔			✔	(Humshaugh)
Corbridge–Hexham–Acomb alternative route					
✔✔✔	✔			✔✔✔	(Corbridge)
✔✔✔	✔			✔✔✔	(Hexham)
✔✔✔				✔✔✔	(Acomb)
		✔(u)	H	✔	(Old Repeater Stn)
			B	✔	(Grindon)
✔				✔	**Housesteads**
			B	✔✔	**Steel Rigg**
✔		✔✔	YHA & B	✔✔	(Once Brewed)
✔✔✔	✔	✔✔	B	✔✔✔	(Haltwhistle)
✔✔					**Carvoran**
✔✔		✔	H & B	✔✔	# (Greenhead)
✔✔				✔✔✔	**Gilsland**
✔(✔)			B		**Birdoswald**
		✔		✔	**Banks**
✔				✔	(Lanercost Priory)
✔	✔(r)	✔	B	✔✔	**Walton**
				✔	**Newtown**
✔✔✔	✔			✔✔✔	(Brampton)
		✔			(Laversdale)
✔	✔(r)	✔		✔	**Crosby-on-Eden**
✔✔✔	✔		YHA (seasonal)	✔✔✔	**Carlisle**
	✔(r)				**Grinsdale**
✔	✔		B		(Monkhill)
✔✔	✔				**Burgh-by-Sands**
			B	✔✔	(Boustead Hill)
	✔(r)	✔			**Drumburgh**
✔	✔			✔	**Glasson**
✔		✔	B	✔	**Port Carlisle**
✔(✔)			B	✔✔	**Bowness-on-Solway**

✔(u) = no official campsite though can camp nearby; ask the locals
✔(r) = unmanned refreshments stall with honesty box or vending machine
(Greenhead) this includes Holmhead which is on the Wall

PLANNING YOUR WALK

But, that said, there are arguments that could be made for walking the other way, from Solway to Wallsend; and having trekked both ways now, I'm inclined to think this direction is slightly superior. For one thing, the prevailing winds in the UK tend to blow in from the west, and thus will be at your back if walking from west to east, which is preferable to struggling against a force nine (though, to be fair, the winds aren't too severe in summer). Secondly, just as the official guide says that it's better to walk out of a city into the countryside, it could also be argued that a big city makes a suitably grand place to finish a trail – and Newcastle certainly has any number of bars, clubs and restaurants in which to celebrate the completion of a successful walk. Thirdly, I think you get a better view of the crags (on your way into Thirlwall) and can understand a little more how the Wall was laid out by travelling in this direction (and yes, of course, you can just look back and see the same view if travelling westwards – but it's a rare trekker who actually does). It's also a lot easier getting away from Newcastle at the end of the trail than it is from Bowness – and struggling to find a bus or lift that will take you away from the Solway and back to 'civilisation' is not something you want to be doing after you've walked 84 miles. And finally, isn't there something poetic about finishing a walk along the Wall at a place called Wallsend?

As the majority of trekkers will, I imagine, continue to walk from east to west, that is the way this book has been written. That said, those who prefer to swim against the tide of popular opinion and walk west to east should find it easy to use this book too.

TAKING DOGS ALONG THE HADRIAN'S WALL PATH

The Hadrian's Wall Path is actually not that dog-friendly. Much of the land through which the path passes is grazed by livestock and dogs must be kept on a lead; the number of B&Bs, bunkhouses, guesthouses and even campsites that accept dogs is surprisingly low; and even the odd pub refuses to allow dogs inside, leaving you to sup your shandy in a storm while other walkers crowd around the open fire inside. Furthermore, there are few litterbins on the trail where you can throw away poo bags after you've cleaned up after your dog; many's the time I've walked along the trail with my rucksack festooned with Daisy's little 'hand-warmers' swinging from the straps due to a lack of anywhere suitable to deposit them.

It's fair to say that dog owners must be a resilient breed to put up with the privations they suffer for the sake of their pet. Still,

despite all the moans it *is* possible to walk from one end to the other with your dog and many are the rewards that await those prepared to make the extra effort required to bring their best friend with them. Don't underestimate the extra work involved in bringing your pooch to the path. Just about every decision you make will be influenced by the fact you've got a dog: how you plan to travel to the start of the trail, where you're going to stay, how far you're going to walk each day, where you're going to rest and where you're going to eat in the evening etc etc. The decision-making begins well before you've set foot on the trail. For starters, you have to ask – and be honest with – yourself: can your dog really cope with walking ten-plus miles a day, day after day, for a week or more? And just as importantly, will he or she actually enjoy it? If you think the answer is yes to both, then you need to start preparing accordingly.

For detailed information about taking a dog along the path see p219.

What to take

Deciding how much to take can be difficult. Experienced walkers know that you should take only the bare essentials but at the same time you must ensure you have all the equipment necessary to make the trip safe and comfortable.

KEEP YOUR LUGGAGE LIGHT

Experienced backpackers know that there is some sort of complicated formula governing the success of a trek, in which the enjoyment of the walk is inversely proportional to the amount carried. Carrying a heavy rucksack slows you down, tires you out and gives you aches and pains in parts of the body that you never knew existed. It is imperative, therefore, that you take a good deal of time packing and that you are ruthless when you do; if it's not essential, don't take it.

HOW TO CARRY IT

If you are using one of the baggage-carrier services, you must contact them beforehand to find out what their regulations are regarding the weight and size of the luggage you wish them to carry. Even if you are using one of these services, you will still need to carry a small **daypack**, filled with those items that you will need during the day: water bottle or pouch, this book, map, sun-screen, sun hat, wet-weather gear, some food, camera, money and so on.

If you have decided to forego the services of the baggage carriers you will have to consider your **rucksack** even more carefully. Ultimately its size will depend on where you are planning to stay and how you are planning to eat. If you are camping and cooking for yourself you will probably need a 70- to 95-litre rucksack, which should be large enough to carry a small tent, sleeping bag, cooking equipment, crockery, cutlery and food. Those not carrying their home with them should find a 40- to 60-litre rucksack sufficient.

When choosing a rucksack, make sure it has a stiffened back and can be adjusted to fit your own back comfortably. Don't just try the rucksack out in the shop: take it home, fill it with things and then try it out around the house and take it out for a short walk. Only then can you be certain that it fits. Make sure the hip belt and chest strap (if there is one) are fastened tightly as this helps distribute the weight more comfortably with most of it being carried on the hips. Carry a small daypack inside the rucksack, as this will be useful to carry things in when leaving the main pack at the hostel or B&B.

One reader wrote in with the eminently sensible advice of taking a **waterproof rucksack cover**. Most rucksacks these days have them 'built in' to the sack, but you can also buy them separately for less than a tenner. Lining your bag with a strong **bin liner** is another sensible, cut-price idea. Finally, it's also a good idea to keep everything wrapped in plastic bags inside the rucksack; I usually place all these bags inside a bin-bag which then goes inside the rucksack. That way, even if it does pour with rain, everything should remain dry.

FOOTWEAR

Boots

Only a decent pair of strong, durable trekking boots are good enough to survive the rigours of the Hadrian's Wall Path. Don't be tempted by a spell of hot weather into bringing something flimsier. Make sure, too, that your boots provide good ankle support, for the ground can occasionally be rough and stony and twisted ankles are commonplace. Make sure your boots are waterproof as well: these days most people opt for a synthetic waterproof lining (Gore-Tex or similar), though a good-quality leather boot with dubbin should prove just as reliable in keeping your feet dry. Finally, your boots should be thoroughly 'broken in' so they're comfortable and not likely to cause blisters.

In addition, many people bring an extra pair of shoes or trainers to wear off the trail. This is not essential but if you are using one of the luggage-carrying services and you've got room in your luggage, why not? One reader said he found it more comfortable to wear lighter shoes on the Newcastle section of the walk.

Socks

If you haven't got a pair of the modern hi-tech walking socks the old system of wearing a thin liner sock under a thicker wool sock is just as good. Bring a few pairs of each.

CLOTHES

I have sent you ... pairs of socks from Sattua, two pairs of sandals and two pairs of underpants ...   Tablet 346 of the **Vindolanda Postcards** (see p161)

In a country notorious for its unpredictable climate it is imperative that you pack enough clothes to cover every extreme of weather, from burning hot to bloomin' freezing. Modern hi-tech outdoor clothes come with a range of fancy names and brands but they all still follow the basic two- or three-layer principle, with an inner base layer to transport sweat away from your skin, a mid-layer for warmth and an outer layer to protect you from the wind and rain.

A thin lightweight **thermal top** of a synthetic material is ideal as the base layer as it draws moisture (ie sweat) away from your body. Cool in hot weather and warm when worn under other clothes in the cold, pack at least one thermal top. Over the top in cold weather a mid-weight **polyester fleece** should suffice. Fleeces are light, more water-resistant than the alternatives (such as a woolly jumper), remain warm even when wet and pack down small in rucksacks; they are thus ideal trekking gear.

Over the top of all this a **waterproof jacket** is essential. 'Breathable' jackets cost a small fortune (though prices are falling all the time) but they do prevent the build-up of condensation.

Leg wear

Some hikers find trekking trousers an unnecessary investment and any light, quick-drying trouser should suffice. Jeans are heavy and dry slowly and are thus not recommended. A pair of **waterproof trousers** *is* more than useful, however, while on really hot sunny days you'll be glad you brought your shorts. Thermal **long johns** take up little room in the rucksack and could be vital if the weather starts to close in.

Gaiters are not essential but, again, those who bring them are always glad they did, for they provide extra protection when walking through muddy ground and when the vegetation around the trail is dripping wet after bad weather.

Underwear

Three or four changes of underwear is fine. Any more is excessive, any less unhygienic. Because backpacks can cause bra straps to dig painfully into the skin, women may find a **sports bra** more comfortable.

Other clothes

You may like to consider a woolly **hat** and **gloves** – you'd be surprised how cold it can get up on the moors even in summer – and a **sun hat**.

TOILETRIES

Once again, take the minimum. **Soap**, **towel**, a **toothbrush** and **toothpaste** are pretty much essential (although those staying in B&Bs will find that most provide soap and towels anyway). Some **toilet paper** could also prove vital on the trail, particularly if using public toilets (which occasionally run out).

Other items: **razor**; **deodorant**; **tampons/sanitary towels** and a high factor **sun-screen** should cover just about everything.

FIRST-AID KIT

A small first-aid kit could prove useful for those emergencies that occur along the trail. This kit should include **aspirin** or **paracetamol**; **plasters** for minor cuts; **moleskin**, **Second Skin** or some other treatment for blisters; a **bandage** or elasticated joint support for supporting a sprained ankle or a weak knee; **anti-septic wipes**; **antiseptic cream**; **safety pins**; **tweezers** and **scissors**.

GENERAL ITEMS

Essential
Everybody should have a **map**, **torch**, **water bottle or pouch**, **spare batteries**, **penknife**, **whistle** (see p68 for details of the international distress signal), some **emergency food** and a **watch** (preferably with an alarm to help you make an early start each day). Those with weak knees will find a **walking pole** or **sticks** essential. Those who've also walked in Scotland will recognise the importance of taking **insect repellent** to ward off midges, though they're not so bad here.

If you know how to use it properly you'll also find a **compass** extremely handy. Some people find a **mobile phone** invaluable too, and reception is

---

❑ The Hadrian's Wall Path Passport
A simple piece of folded card, the Passport nevertheless could be an important measure in protecting the Wall – because it is available May to October only and thus encourages walkers to view the trail as a summertime-only activity – as well as providing walkers with a bit of fun and some proof that they actually did walk the entire trail. Open up the passport and you'll find seven blank spaces; the idea is to collect seven stamps from various places along the trail. Get the full set and you qualify for the right to purchase a commemorative badge and certificate from either the Segedunum Roman Fort (or Asda opposite) or the King's Arms in Bowness-on-Solway.

The passport scheme is run by the Hadrian's Wall Trust and thus, with the demise of the Trust, its future is perhaps less certain than it once was. That said, given the popularity of the passport amongst both walkers and local businesses, the National Trail Officer David McGlade thinks that even if the Trust's scheme did have to finish, the local businesses would join together to create their own 'passport' scheme.

The **'stamping stations'** are located at:

● **Segedunum Roman Fort, Wallsend**; also the **TOTAL petrol garage** and **Asda Supermarket customer services desk** There is a stamp inside the main entrance to the museum, available during museum opening hours only, and also one by the rear entrance to the museum which is available outside these hours; alternatively, the garage is just 150 metres east of Segedunum and Asda is across the road.
● **Robin Hood Inn** One mile west of the Whittledene Reservoir in a box outside the front door.
● **Chesters Roman Fort** Inside the entrance to the museum during opening hours; outside these hours a stamping box is provided attached to the wall on the road at the entrance to the car park – though it's not easy to spot.
● **Housesteads** At the Visitors' Centre/reception during opening hours.
● **Birdoswald Roman Fort** Inside the main entrance during opening hours; outside these hours a stamping box is provided by the main entrance.
● **Sands Sports Centre, Carlisle** Inside the café; available only during the centre's opening hours.
● **The Banks Promenade** or **the King's Arms, Bowness-on-Solway** The Promenade stamp is available at any time, while the pub is officially open daily 11am to 11pm from Easter to September, 5.30-11pm the rest of the year.

usually pretty good. For arranging a lift from the Wall to the B&B it can also be invaluable – just don't forget the charger!

Useful items and luxuries

Suggestions here include a **book** for days off or on train and bus journeys, a camera, a pair of **sunglasses**, **binoculars**, a **vacuum flask** for hot drinks and an **iPod/iPad**.

CAMPING GEAR

Both campers and those intending to stay in the various bunkhouses/camping barns en route will find a sleeping bag essential. A two- to three-season bag should suffice for summer. Campers will also need a decent bivvy bag or tent, a sleeping mat, fuel and stove, cutlery, pans, a cup and a scrubber for washing up.

MONEY AND DOCUMENTS

(Also see Money, p24) Cash machines (ATMs) are infrequent along the Hadrian's Wall Path. Not everybody accepts **debit** or **credit cards** as payment either – though some B&Bs and many restaurants now do. As a result, you should always carry a fair amount of **cash** with you, just to be on the safe side. A **chequebook** from a British bank is useful in those places where credit cards are not accepted. Crime on the trail is thankfully rare but you may want to carry your money in a **moneybelt**, just to be safe.

Don't forget your **Hadrian's Wall Path Passport** (see box opposite).

If you are a member of **English Heritage** or the **National Trust**, bring your **membership cards**; membership of English Heritage in particular will save you money at the sights along the path, allowing free entrance to the Roman forts and other attractions.

MAPS

The hand-drawn maps in this book cover the trail at a scale of 1:20,000. This large scale, combined with the notes and tips written on the maps, should be more than enough to stop you losing your way. Nevertheless, some people like to have a separate map of the region; such maps can prove invaluable should you need to abandon the path and find the quickest route off the trail in an emergency. They also help in identifying local features and landmarks and devising possible side trips.

Perhaps the best map for the whole walk is the *Hadrian's Wall Path* (Walker's Route) strip map (1:40,000) published by Harvey Map Services (🖥 www.harveymaps.co.uk). The only criticism that can be levelled against it is that it only covers a narrow strip either side of the path in any detail, thus making it difficult for trekkers to identify far-off peaks and other landmarks.

The Ordnance Survey (🖥 www.ordnancesurvey.co.uk) also produce a waterproof strip map (OL43) that covers the central section of the trail (centred

> **❏ Digital mapping**
> There are a number of software packages available on the market today that provide Ordnance Survey maps for a PC or smartphone. The two most well known are Memory Map and Anquet, but more suppliers join the list every year. Maps are supplied not in traditional paper format, but electronically, on DVD or USB media, or by direct download over the Internet. The maps are then loaded into an application, also available by download, from where you can view them, print them and create routes on them. Additionally, the route can be viewed directly on a smartphone or uploaded to a GPS device. If your smartphone has a GPS chip, you will be able to see your position overlaid onto the digital map on your phone.
>
> Many websites now have free routes you can download for the more popular digital mapping products. Anything from day walks to complete Long Distance Paths. It is important to ensure any digital mapping software on your smartphone uses pre-downloaded maps, stored on your device, and doesn't need to download them on-the-fly, as this may be expensive and will be impossible without a signal.
>
> Smartphones and GPS devices should complement, not replace, the traditional method of navigation (a map and compass) as any electronic device is susceptible to failure and, if nothing else, battery failure. Remember that battery life will be significantly reduced, compared to normal usage, when you are using the built-in GPS and running the screen for long periods.
>
> **Stuart Greig**

on Haltwhistle and Hexham) at a scale of 1:25,000 as part of their Explorer Outdoor Leisure series. In addition, you'll need Explorer Active maps 314, 315 and 316 to cover the rest of the trail. They now also offer a 'Getamap' service, an online map application where you can download their maps, tailor them to your requirements and, for example, plot on routes, add notes and photos and so on. A twelve-month subscription for this service is currently £19.99 – cheaper than buying the required paper maps.

While it may be extravagant to buy all these maps, members of Ramblers' (see box p42) can make use of their library which allows them to borrow up to ten maps for up to six weeks free of charge.

In 2010 English Heritage published *An Archaeological Map of Hadrian's Wall* (£7.99). Beautiful, fascinating and insightful, the map includes sites both along and near the Wall. Probably for those with a specialist interest in the Wall's history and archaeology only, nevertheless this is, in my opinion, the most absorbing map on the Wall and its surroundings.

RECOMMENDED READING

There is a wealth of books on the Wall, as you'd expect, so the following is a mere overview of the better, or at least newer works. Some of these books can be found in the tourist information centres and at the reception desks of the Roman forts en route. As well as stocking many of the titles listed below, these places also have a number of books about the towns and villages en route, usually printed by small, local publishers. Furthermore, each of the visitor centres of the major English Heritage historical attractions such as Housesteads, Chesters and Corbridge publishes their own guidebook to the site.

The journalist and author Hunter Davies, who was born at the western end of the trail, has written the historical travelogue *A Walk Along the Wall* (Frances Lincoln; originally published in 1974), the result of spending a year trekking along and studying the wall. *Hadrian's Wall*, by David Breeze and Brian Dobson, is part of the Penguin History Series and deals with the history of the Wall as well as the day-to-day activities of those who lived in its shadow, both soldiers and locals, during the Roman occupation.

On a similar subject, *Hadrian's Wall in the Days of the Romans*, by Ronald Embleton and Frank Graham (WJ Williams & Son Books Ltd), does exactly what it says on the cover; *Hadrian's Wall AD122-410* by Nic Fields (Osprey Publishing) covers much the same ground. Newer, *The Wall: Rome's Greatest Frontier* (Birlinn Ltd) by Alistair Moffatt, also deals with the building of the Wall and is perhaps the best read of the three and has a good section on the Vindolanda postcards. One of the leading Wall experts, Anthony R Birley, has produced a biography of the enigmatic man behind the Wall: *Hadrian, The Restless Emperor* (Routledge), though it must be said that the text is a little dry.

Locally produced, *The Great Wall of Britain – A Walk Along Hadrian's Wall* (Hayloft) by the illustrator Anton Hodge, is a travelogue-cum-geographical-historical-tour of the Roman Wall. You may find it locally, or on 🖥 www. amazon.co.uk or you can visit the author's website: 🖥 http://anton hodge.co.uk/the-great-wall-of-britain. In a similar 'travelogue' vein is Bob Bibby's *On the Wall with Hadrian* (Eye Books).

English Heritage produce their own historical guide to the Wall, titled simply *Hadrian's Wall*, written by Stephen Johnson and published by BT Batsford.

Finally, for those looking to walk in the region during the winter season, *The Roman Ring* (Shepherd's Walks) by Mark Richards provides details on two trails – called the Moss Troopers' Trail and the Roman Ring – which, whilst still

---

❑ **Fantastic historical websites**
🖥 **www.roman-britain.org** In my opinion the best website on the history and ruins of Hadrian's Wall, this is a non-commercial site seemingly written by enthusiasts whose love and knowledge of all things Roman is astounding. The site includes details of the Wall's construction, a study of the visible remains of the Wall and a whole load of stuff on Roman Britain. Just great.
🖥 **www.hadrians.com** A website dedicated to the man who ordered the construction of the Wall, including studies of his family, as well as the food, clothes, homes and work of those who lived during his reign.
🖥 **www.bbc.co.uk/history/ancient/romans** The BBC's website on the Romans, includes some useful timelines and interesting articles by various boffins.
🖥 **www.britannia.com/history/h30.html** Described as the American gateway to the British Isles, this website is great for an overview of British history, with the address above dealing specifically with Roman Britain.

giving walkers plenty of opportunity to explore the Roman history of the region, visit the Wall only sporadically. With walkers advised against walking the Wall in winter to minimise damage to the path and the archaeology underneath, this book thus provides a decent alternative to the main Hadrian's Wall Path.

❏ SOURCES OF FURTHER INFORMATION

Trail information (online)

🖳 **www.nationaltrail.co.uk/hadrians-wall-path** The essential first stop for those looking to walk the Wall, this is the official site of the Hadrian's Wall Path. Check out the slideshow, maps, sections on accommodation and publications. Best of all, register with them and they'll send you a whole load of relevant pamphlets and brochures, including the Wall Passport (see box p38).

🖳 **www.visithadrianswall.co.uk** The most complete website on the Wall itself, this is the website of Hadrian's Wall Country – and thus, unlike the website above, is not specifically for walkers – with lists of tour agencies, accommodation, events, history and the latest news.

🖳 **www.haltwhistle.org** Website of the Haltwhistle Tourist Office, with a link to 🖳 **www.heartofhadrianswall.com**, giving information about places to stay, eat and services in the central area of the Wall.

🖳 **www.golakes.co.uk** Website that concentrates on the Lake District though does contain pages on Carlisle and the Hadrian's Wall Path.

Tourist information centres (TICs)

Tourist information centres are based in towns throughout Britain and provide all manner of locally specific information and an accommodation-booking service (in many cases a 10% deposit is payable which is deducted from the final bill and sometimes a booking charge (£2-4) as well. The centres listed below are on or close to the Hadrian's Wall Path: **Newcastle** (see p83); **Corbridge** (see p134); **Hexham** (see p140); **Haltwhistle** (p166); **Brampton** (now run by volunteers; see p186) and **Carlisle** (see p196). **Once Brewed** (see p158) is a National Park Visitor Centre but also has a tourist information centre.

Organisations for walkers

● **Backpackers' Club** (🖳 www.backpackersclub.co.uk) A club aimed at people who are involved or interested in lightweight camping through walking, cycling, skiing and canoeing. They produce a quarterly magazine, provide members with a comprehensive advisory and information service on all aspects of backpacking, organise weekend trips and also publish a farm-pitch directory. Membership is £12 a year.

● **The Long Distance Walkers' Association** (🖳 www.ldwa.org.uk) An association of people with the common interest of long-distance walking. Membership includes a journal, *Strider*, three times per year giving details of challenge events and local group walks as well as articles on the subject. Information on over 730 paths is presented in their *UK Trailwalkers' Handbook* (£13.95 to members, £18.95 otherwise). Individual membership is £13 a year whilst family membership for two adults and all children under 18 is £19.50 a year.

● **Ramblers** (formerly Ramblers' Association; 🖳 www.ramblers.org.uk) Looks after the interests of walkers throughout Britain. They publish a large amount of useful information including their quarterly *Walk* magazine (£3.40 to non-members). Membership costs £32/43 individual/joint.

Guidebooks

The Hadrian's Wall Path Trust's *The Essential Companion to Hadrian's Wall Path National Trail* by David McGlade and Janine Howorth is a guide to all those vital services – cash machines, parking, food, accommodation, water taps and so on – as well as providing notes on conservation and other essentials. Written by the Wall's very own National Trail Officer, it was last updated in 2011 and costs £4.95 from ⌨ www.hadrianswallshop.co.uk.

However, the *Companion* is now actually a little dated, and with the winding down of the Hadrian's Wall Trust its future is uncertain, though the National Trail Officer is hopeful it will appear again, updated and possibly in electronic format.

If you are a seasoned long-distance walker, or even new to the game and like what you see, check out the other titles in the Trailblazer series; see p226.

Flora and fauna field guides

Collins Bird Guide, with its beautiful illustrations of British and European birds, continues to be the favourite field guide of both ornithologists and laymen alike. Their *Trees of Britain & Europe* is also OK if you've room in your rucksack and don't know your ash from your alder. Collins also produce guides to the above and *Mushrooms*, *Butterflies*, *Insects*, *Wild Flowers* and *Birds* as part of their *Gem* series – a collection of cracking guides that are only slightly larger than a pack of playing cards and thus ideal for trekking with.

A rather odd book – but charming in its way – is John Miles' *Hadrian's Wildlife* (Whittles Publishing) which looks at the animals, birds and landscape that would have existed in the region when the Wall was being built.

There are also several field guide apps for smart phones and tablets, including those that can aid in identifying birds by their song as well as by their appearance.

DVDs

There's a very pleasant video, *Edge of Empire*, that's produced by Striding Edge and the Ordnance Survey, in which Eric Robson takes us on a journey along the 73 miles and two millennia of the Wall. The *Lost Treasures of the Ancient World* series (Cromwell Productions) has a 48-minute documentary on the Wall; the DVD has features including a 'Test your Knowledge' section.

There is also now a DVD dedicated to the trail itself, *Hadrian's Wall Path National Trail*, narrated by Anthony Burton. Best of all, however, is *Hadrian's Wall from the Air* (£4.99 plus postage), a 45-minute DVD of the Wall filmed from above. A preview can be seen and copies ordered from ⌨ www.hadrian swallshop.co.uk. They have also produced a DVD, *Illuminating Hadrian's Wall* (£4.99 plus postage), that celebrates the night of 13 March 2010 when the entire length of the Wall was lit by over a thousand volunteer torch-bearers and supporters.

Getting to and from the Hadrian's Wall Path

Carlisle and Newcastle are the main transport hubs for the trail and conveniently they all but bookend the path, with Carlisle near the western end and the Newcastle suburb of Wallsend at the eastern end. Both are well connected by public transport to the rest of the country and indeed Europe; see box below. However, it should be noted that some of the other places on the trail are less well connected, both east and west of Carlisle.

PLANNING YOUR WALK

❏ **GETTING TO BRITAIN**

● **By air** Newcastle (🖳 www.newcastleairport.com) and Manchester (🖳 www.manchesterairport.co.uk) are the two major international airports serving the Hadrian's Wall Path but for most foreign visitors it is still one of the London airports that provides them with their first taste of England. Nevertheless, if you've no business in London, do check out flights to Newcastle (from Europe) and Manchester (from Europe and the USA). Of the two, Newcastle Airport is the closest to the Wall. From Manchester Airport to Carlisle it's just over two hours by train.

Other airports that are fairly close include Leeds Bradford (🖳 www.leedsbradfordairport.co.uk) and Durham & Teeside (🖳 www.durhamteesvalleyairport.com; 7 miles/11km outside Darlington).

● **From Europe by train** Eurostar (🖳 www.eurostar.com) operates the high-speed passenger service via the Channel Tunnel between Paris/Brussels and London. Conveniently, the terminal in London is St Pancras International, which is next to King's Cross, the station for departures to Newcastle. Euston, the station for trains to Carlisle, is only a five-minute walk away in the other direction on Euston Rd.

For more information about rail services from Europe, contact your national rail provider or Railteam (🖳 www.railteam.eu).

● **From Europe by coach** Eurolines (🖳 www.eurolines.com) have a huge network of long-distance coach services connecting over 500 cities throughout Europe to London. Check carefully: often, once expenses such as food for the journey are taken into consideration, it doesn't work out much cheaper than flying, particularly when compared to the prices of some of the budget airlines.

● **From Europe by ferry (with or without a car)** There are numerous ferries plying routes between ports around the UK and those in Ireland and continental Europe. However, the most convenient for Hadrian's Wall Path is DFDS Seaways (🖳 www.dfdsseaways.co.uk) with a service connecting Newcastle and Amsterdam daily. Special buses run from Newcastle Central to connect with the ferries. Also worth considering is P&O Stena Line (🖳 www.poferries.com) which operates services daily between Hull and Zeebrugge/Rotterdam.

A useful website for further information is 🖳 www.directferries.com.

● **From Europe by car** Eurotunnel (🖳 www.eurotunnel.com) operates the shuttle train service for vehicles via the Channel Tunnel between Calais and Folkestone taking just 35 minutes.

NATIONAL TRANSPORT

By train

Both Newcastle and Carlisle lie on the main England–Scotland rail links. All timetable and fare information can be obtained from **National Rail Enquiries** (☎ 08457-484950 – operates 24hrs; 💻 www.nationalrail.co.uk) or the relevant train companies. Tickets can be bought through the latter or from websites such as 💻 www.trainline.com.

Newcastle lies on the East Coast (💻 www.eastcoast.co.uk) line. Services connect Newcastle with London King's Cross, York and Edinburgh at least twice an hour and during the rush hour around five times an hour. It takes around three hours from London to Newcastle. In addition, the Trans-Pennine Express (💻 www.tpexpress.co.uk) operates from Manchester to Newcastle via York, Northallerton, Darlington & Middlesbrough (1-2/hr, journey time around 3 hours).

Carlisle is connected to London Euston, Manchester and Glasgow via the West Coast main line, with services operated by Virgin Trains (💻 www.virgin trains.co.uk; 1-2/hr); Euston to Carlisle takes less than four hours. Carlisle also has connections to Leeds (6-7/day) thanks to the scenic Settle to Carlisle line (💻 www.settle-carlisle.co.uk) through the Yorkshire Dales National Park.

Northern Rail (💻 www.northernrail.org) operate several lines in the north of England including links between Carlisle and Leeds. Similarly, and perhaps most usefully of all, **Hadrian's Wall Country Line** connects Newcastle and Carlisle via Haltwhistle and Hexham (see p48).

By coach

The principal coach (long-distance bus) operator in Britain is **National Express** (💻 www.nationalexpress.com). Coach travel is generally cheaper (though with the excellent advance-booking train fares and special deals offered by the train companies, that is not always the case now) but the journey time is longer than if travelling by train (both London to Newcastle and London to Carlisle take at least six hours). There are currently four coaches each to Newcastle (first at 9.30am, last 11.30pm) and Carlisle (first at 9am, last 7.30pm).

In addition, a second coach company, **Megabus** (💻 http://uk.megabus .com) has a similar service to Newcastle though only one service daily (or, rather, overnight) from London to Carlisle.

By car

There are reasonable road connections to Hadrian's Wall. Access from the western side is along the M6 from the south (junctions 42, 43 and 44) and A74 (M) from Glasgow to Carlisle. Access from the eastern side is along the A1(M) to Newcastle; take the city-centre exit and follow signs for Wallsend; or take the A19 and follow the signs for Wallsend from there. The A68 links Edinburgh and Darlington and bisects the trail around Corbridge. Finally, the A69 between Newcastle and Carlisle runs parallel to the Wall, usually around 2-5 miles (3-8km) south of it, and is the main access route.

PLANNING YOUR WALK

GETTING TO THE START AND END OF THE TRAIL

Between Wallsend and Newcastle

There are several ways to get to Wallsend from Newcastle – you can take a bus (Stagecoach No 22, 3/hr) from Central Station, or the Metro train on the Tyne loop via Monument. For further information on public transport in Newcastle see p82. Those planning on starting at Heddon-on-the-Wall (to avoid the industrial grittiness of Wallsend) should take Arriva's No 685 or Stagecoach's No 85 (see below).

Between Bowness-on-Solway and Carlisle

The main bus service is operated by Stagecoach (No 93, though one of the buses on Saturday is, for some obscure reason, the No 71). Note that on Sunday or Bank Holiday the only public transport option is a Taxi Bus (must be pre-booked) which runs twice a day, see p214 for details. Many people, particularly those for whom Bowness is the end of the trail and are thus a bit weary, find it a whole lot more appealing to treat themselves to a private cab back to Carlisle, which should cost about £30. Ask at The King's Arms in Bowness (see p196) for the number of a local taxi firm, as this should be the best price-wise, rather than someone from Carlisle (see p196).

There is now another option, a **shared taxi**, currently operated by Metro Taxi, leaving Bowness at 10.40am and 3pm from the King's Arms in Bowness (9.40am and 2pm from Carlisle Station for those heading in the other direction) and costing £6 per person. See p214 for details.

PUBLIC TRANSPORT – BUS SERVICES

Route no	Operator	From	To	Via	Frequency
685/85	ANE, SC	Newcastle	Carlisle	Heddon, Corbridge, Hexham, Haltwhistle, Greenhead & Brampton	Mon-Sat 1/hr
85	SC	Newcastle	Hexham	Heddon-on-the-Wall, Corbridge	Sun & bank hols 1/hr
10	GNE	Newcastle	Hexham	Corbridge	Mon-Sat 3/hr, Sun 1/hr
74	GNE	Newcastle	Hexham	Matfen, Halton & Errington Arms	Mon-Sat 5-6/day
X84/X85	GNE	Newcastle	Hexham	Heddon-on-the-Wall, Wylam & Corbridge	Mon-Sat 1/hr, Sun 2/day
X85	ANE	Newcastle	Hexham	Corbridge	Mon-Fri 3/day
888	WBC	Newcastle	Keswick	Corbridge, Hexham, Alston & Penrith	July to end Sep daily 1/day

Service	Operators				Frequency
AD122	GNE	Hexham	Walltown	Chesters, Housesteads, OnceBrewed, Vindolanda, Haltwhistle	mid Apr to late Sep Sat & Sun, late May to late Aug daily 3/day
685	SC	Hexham	Carlisle	Haltwhistle, Greenhead, Brampton	Sun 4/day
880	TVC, HS	Hexham	Bellingham	Acomb, Wall Village, Humshaugh & Wark	Mon-Sat 6-7/day,
185*	TC	Haltwhistle	Carlisle	Roman Army Museum, Greenhead, Gilsland, Brampton & Crosby-on-Eden	Mon-Sat 2-3/day
680*	TC, WBC	Nenthead	Carlisle	Brampton & Alston	Mon-Sat 1-2/day
94	SC	Carlisle	Brampton	Crosby-on-Eden	Mon-Fri 1-2/day
97	SC	Carlisle	Brampton	Walton & Laversdale	Wed & Fri 1/day
93/71	SC	Carlisle	Bowness-on-Solway	Beaumont, Burgh-by-Sands, Dykesfield, Drumburgh, Glasson & Port Carlisle,	Mon-Sat 4-5/day plus 2/day Fri & Sat

Operator contact details

ANE = Arriva North East (☐ www.arrivabus.co.uk); GNE = Go North East (☐ www.simplygo.com); HS = Howard Snaith (☎ 01830-520609, ☐ www.howardsnaith.co.uk); SC = Stagecoach (☐ www.stagecoachbus.com); TC = Telford's Coaches (☎ 013873-75677, ☐ www.telfordscoaches.com); TVC = Tyne Valley Coaches (☎ 01434 602217, ☐ www.tynevalleycoaches.co.uk); WBC = Wright Brothers' Coaches (☎ 01434-381200, ☐ www.wrightscoaches.co.uk).

* These services may be withdrawn during 2014, please check before travelling.

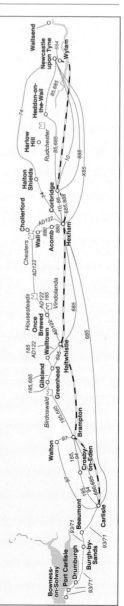

PLANNING YOUR WALK

By air
Newcastle Airport (see box p44) has frequent domestic flights from London (Heathrow, Gatwick), Aberdeen, Belfast, Birmingham, Bristol, Cardiff, Exeter, Southampton, Isle of Man and Jersey. The airport is 30 minutes from Central Station on the Tyneside Metro.

LOCAL TRANSPORT

With both a special Hadrian's Wall Country Bus service serving the middle section of the Wall, with good connecting bus services at either end and the Newcastle to Carlisle Hadrian's Wall Country rail line (the oldest coast-to-coast service in the country), public transport along the trail is surprisingly good. At Hexham and Haltwhistle the services dovetail neatly, with the buses calling in at the train stations. For further details visit the website 🖳 www.visithadrian swall.co.uk.

Hadrian's Wall Country Bus AD122
The Hadrian's Wall Country Bus, given the appropriate route number AD122, operates from Easter to late September on the central section of the wall, between Hexham and Walltown. As of 2014 the service is operated by Go North East and stops only at Hexham, Acomb, Chester, Housesteads, Once Brewed, Vindolanda, Milecastle Inn, Haltwhistle and Walltown with places to the east and west served by connecting services (see box p46 for details). Note also that only three services a day go all the way from Hexham to Walltown or vice versa, with an additional two in the afternoon travelling only between Hexham and Housesteads fort.

A one-day AD122 Rover ticket (£12/9/6/25 for adults/student/children/family ie two adults and up to three children under 16) permits unlimited travel on the AD122. Three-day tickets (£24/18/12/50) are also available. You can also buy an AD122 Rover Ticket + which includes travel on Go North East's services X84, X85 and Ten services between Newcastle and Hexham, and Tynedale Links services which go to Corbridge and Wylam (see 🖳 www.sim plygo.com/all-services/tynedalexpress).

Hadrian's Wall Country Rail Line (🖳 www.northernrail.org)
A Day Ranger ticket allowing unlimited day travel on rail services between Sunderland and Whitehaven (which encompasses Newcastle to Carlisle) is available on trains or from staffed stations for £19/9.50 adult/child.
● Newcastle to Carlisle via Hexham and Haltwhistle, daily 1-2/hr, 6-7/day stop at Brampton, Sunday services also call at Wylam & Corbridge
● Newcastle to Hexham via Wylam & Corbridge, Mon-Sat approx 1/hr

HADRIAN'S WALL

2

History

THE DECISION TO BUILD THE WALL

Though by far the most famous, Hadrian's Wall was in fact just one
of four Roman frontiers built between the subjugated south of what
is now called Britain and those tribes living in the northern part of the
island, known collectively as the Caledones. Since their invasion in
AD43, the Romans had at one time or another conquered just about
all the tribes living on the island of Britannia. But the area we now
call Scotland, once defeated, proved more difficult to keep under
control. Even a potentially decisive victory in AD84 somewhere north
of the Tay at a place they called Mons Graupius failed to quell the
ongoing insurrection by the Caledones.

Emperors came and went before the pragmatic Domitian (who
reigned AD81-96) decided that maintaining a grip over all of the
island would ultimately require too many troops; troops that could be
more usefully employed in other parts of the empire. It was thus
decided to draw a line across the island and establish a border to separate the controllable south from those 'lawless' lands to the north.
Initially that boundary was drawn to watch over the glens – the main
gateways into and out of the Highlands – a border known as the
Gask Frontier. However, as more and more troops were withdrawn
from Britannia to fight in other parts of the Empire, the border by
necessity receded south to the area now known, appropriately
enough, as the Borders.

Soon after his accession, Emperor Trajan (AD97-117) decided to
move the border still further south, choosing as his frontier the
Stanegate (though this was not what the Romans called it), the
east–west road that ran between the Roman settlements of Carlisle
and Corbridge. Built during the governorship of Agricola in AD80,
the Stanegate was an important trade route that needed protecting.
Trajan's troops set about building a line of turf and timber forts to
guard the Stanegate, including Vindolanda (see p161) and Corbridge
Roman Town (p136).

HADRIAN BUILDS HIS WALL

Having completely transformed the soldiers, in royal fashion, he made for Britain, where he set right many things and – the first to do so – drew a wall along a length of eighty miles to separate barbarians and Romans. **Aelius Spartianus**, *The Augustan History*

During Trajan's reign, his fortified border was used less as a defensive barrier than as a launchpad for incursions into Scotland; an *attacking* border, if you like. His successor and adopted son, Hadrian (AD117-138), however, saw it as more of a traditional border; as both a defensive barrier and a physical marker for the northern limit of his territories. Following a tour of his dominions in AD122, Hadrian ordered the refortification of Trajan's border with the building of a wall to the north of it along the line of the Whin Sill ridge, a geological fault running across the centre of Britain. This wall was to extend beyond the limits of the Stanegate, to stretch across the entire island. And thus the Wall that we know today began to take shape.

The building of the Wall was something of an organic process, evolving as the geology and political climate dictated. This is best illustrated by the curious size of the foundations, which for much of the first half of the walk (from Newcastle west to the River Irthing, which was the first section to be built) are far too broad for the wall that was eventually built upon them, suggesting, of course, that the Romans initially had plans to construct a much bigger barrier. The materials used in the Wall's construction changed too, depending on where it was built. In the east of the country, a core of rubble and puddled clay was used, whereas a limestone mortar core was prevalent in the middle of the country and in the western half of the country an all-turf wall was built (though this, too, was later converted to stone sometime in the second half of the second century AD as the infrastructure improved and the supply of building materials to the line of the Wall became more efficient).

To carry out all this construction, three legions were employed: the Second Augusta from Caerleon in South Wales, the Twentieth Valeria Victrix from Chester and the Sixth Victrix from York. It was their task to clear the ground

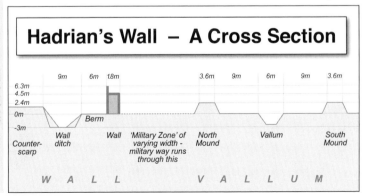

of trees and scrub where necessary and quarry, transport and organise the estimated 25 million facing stones that were used in the Wall, each approximately ten inches long, six inches high and twenty inches deep (25cm by 15cm by 50cm respectively). These were then set into the core of the Wall. As a measure of the legions' efficiency, an experiment was conducted recently in which

---

❏ Hadrian's Wall ... or is it?

It should be stated here that there are some who believe that the refortification of Trajan's turf-and-timber wall by Hadrian actually took place *before* the latter visited Britain. The history of the Wall is full of minor controversies like this because, as you'll see when you read this book and other accounts, much of the history of Hadrian's Wall is still open to conjecture. Indeed, up until the 19th century or so, it was actually known as the **Wall of Severus** after the emperor who ruled at the beginning of the 3rd century AD. It was just prior to Severus' reign, in AD197, that the Wall was overrun for the first time, leading to an extensive overhaul and rebuilding of the Wall between AD205 and 208 – which explains why, until archaeological discoveries proved conclusively otherwise, the Wall was originally attributed to Severus. Indeed, it was only in the 1839 and the publication of *History of Northumberland* by **John Hodgson**, a local vicar, that people began to accept that the Wall might be Hadrian's baby after all. In the book, produced in six volumes over more than twenty years, the reverend wrote a lengthy footnote in the final volume presenting all the evidence he'd amassed that the Wall was Hadrian's – and nobody has convincingly argued against his theory ever since. Unfortunately, Hodgson's health was failing him after working for so many years on a loss-making book, and he died while this final volume was being printed.

While on the one hand people may find it astonishing that nobody knew who was responsible for such a massive feat of civil engineering, on the other hand it's perhaps not that surprising: there are no contemporary accounts of the construction of the Wall that have yet been discovered, with the earliest mentions having been written in the late 4th century, over 150 years later (such as that by Spartianus, as quoted opposite). What's more, these later authors weren't beyond rewriting history if it suited them. It is believed, for example, that Severus' son, Caracalla, could have been one of the sources for the rumour that his father was the originator of the Wall and not Hadrian. He and Severus had spent three years in northern Britain, and particularly Caledonia, trying to conquer the whole island without success. In 211, the emperor himself was killed at York and Caracalla had to retreat back to Rome with his tail between his legs. However, in later texts this was portrayed as a victory, such as this example from the late 4th century:

'... *after driving out the enemy, he* [Severus] *fortified Britain, as far as it was useful, with a wall led across the island to each end of the Ocean.*'
Aurelius Victor, *Liber de Caesaribus*

One can only assume, therefore, that this and all the other histories written at this time that claim the Wall for Severus were using the same deceitful source, namely Caracalla or one of his followers, who wanted to present the campaign as a success.

All of which goes to prove just how difficult it is to compile an accurate chronology of the Roman Empire in Britain. So with the following account of the Wall's construction and history, it's worth bearing in mind that not all of it should be taken as gospel but merely as a version of events currently accepted by the majority of Wall experts. Furthermore, don't be surprised if some of the 'facts' written here are contradicted by accounts in other books.

a section of the Wall was rebuilt using some original facing stones. It conclud-
ed that a gang of 80 men needed 32 wagons and 64 oxen to keep it supplied
with enough lime, water and stone to build the Wall. Yet despite all the effort
required, the original construction took as little as six years to complete.

It's a level of efficiency that becomes even more impressive when one considers the sheer enormity of the Wall (or *Vallum Aelium* as the Romans may
have called it, Aelium being Hadrian's family name). An estimated one ton of
stone had to be dragged up for every single yard of it. Stretching from the
Solway Firth to the North Sea, the Wall was 80 Roman miles long (73 modern
miles) and stood at around 6m (20ft) high and just under 3m (10ft) thick. And
just to ensure the security of the Wall, a 6m (20ft) **ditch** (Hadrian's ha-ha, perhaps?) was dug on the northern 'Scottish' side along its length (though not, it
must be said, around many of the crags, where the crags themselves were considered an adequate defence). A typical Roman defence, this ditch would probably have had a 'false floor' under which sharp spikes would have been con-
cealed. Spikes were also placed in the **Berm**, the flat area between the ditch and
the Wall.

Such manifold defences are impressive. Yet even so, Hadrian's Wall could
act as an effective barrier only if it was sufficiently manned. So while the bulk
of the men continued to be stationed in the old forts built by Trajan along the
Stanegate road, **milecastles** (see box p114) with a capacity for 32 men were
built along the entire length of the Wall at intervals of, as their name suggests,
one Roman mile (the equivalent of a thousand paces); thus there were a total of
80 milecastles in all. And evenly spaced between each one were two **turrets** or
observation posts, 161 all told along the Wall's entire length and always made
of stone, regardless of the material of the Wall draped between them. Each was
capable of holding 10 men. Estimates suggest that it would have taken just $2^{1}/_{2}$
minutes to run from one fort to the next, so messages could have been relayed
along the Wall speedily.

Improving the Wall

Just a couple of years after the wall was finished the defences were strength-
ened, possibly in response to pressure from either the Caledones to the north of
the Wall or the Brigantes – whose territory the Wall crossed. Specifically, a
series of **16 forts**, each housing 500 to 1000 men, was constructed at irregular
intervals along the Wall. These, in many cases, replaced the forts along the
Stanegate, which were either converted into supply bases or abandoned altogether. The Wall was extended at its eastern end too, beyond Pons Aelius to
Segedunum (see p99).

In addition, 50 to 100 yards (46-91m) south of the Wall two 10ft (3m) high
walls of earth were constructed, with a 10ft (3m) deep, 120ft (36m) wide ditch
between them. This earthwork is known as the **Vallum** which, confusingly,
means 'wall' in Latin; the name was given by the Venerable Bede, an 8th-
century monk and early English historian who was the first to write about the
Wall's dimensions. (Incidentally, Bede wrote his *Ecclesiastical History of the
English People* at his monastery in Jarrow, a building that was constructed, at

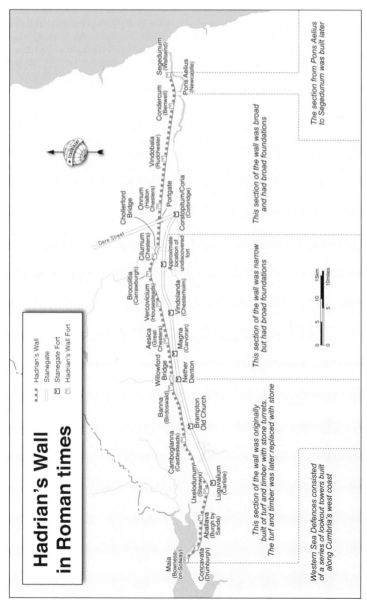

Hadrian's Wall
in Roman times

Legend:
- Hadrian's Wall
- Stanegate
- Stanegate Fort
- Hadrian's Wall Fort

The section from Pons Aelius to Segedunum was built later

This section of the wall was broad and had broad foundations

This section of the wall was narrow but had broad foundations

This section of the wall was originally built of turf and timber with stone turrets. The turf and timber was later replaced with stone

Western Sea Defences consisted of a series of lookout towers built along Cumbria's west coast

Forts (east to west):
Segedunum (Wallsend), Pons Aelius (Newcastle), Condercum (Benwell), Vindobala (Rudchester), Onnum (Halton Chesters), Portgate, Corstopitum/Coria (Corbridge), Cilurnum (Chesters), Chollerford Bridge, Dere Street, Brocolitia (Carrawburgh), Vercovicium (Housesteads), Aesica (Great Chesters), Vindolanda (Chesterholm), Magna (Carvoran), Willowford Bridge, Nether Denton, Banna (Birdoswald), Brampton Old Church, Camboglanna (Castlesteads), Uxelodunum (Stanwix), Luguvalium (Carlisle), Aballava (Burgh by Sands), Concavata (Drumburgh), Maia (Bowness-on-Solway)

Approximate location of undiscovered fort

Scale: 0 5 10 15km / 5 10miles

HISTORY

least in part, from stones taken from the Wall.) Nobody is completely sure what the Vallum is for; as it is on the south side of the Wall it is unlikely to have been a defensive barrier; nor, with both the Stanegate and, later, the Military Way (see p58) nearby, would it have made much sense to construct a road here. Recent theories have suggested that the Vallum marked the border between the civilian territory and a sort of 'military no-go zone' surrounding the Wall. Another suggestion is that it was used to stop conscripted British soldiers, forced against their will to serve the Romans along the Wall, from running away.

The character of the Wall had now changed. From a lengthy but fairly flimsy construction whose primary purpose was a lookout from which to keep an eye on the locals, the Wall now became a defensive, heavily fortified barrier; while the number of soldiers stationed on the Wall went from a relatively measly 3000 to a much more intimidating 15,000 – a 500% increase in manpower. As a result, it is estimated that around 10% of the entire imperial Roman army was based in Britain, even though the island accounted for only 4% of their total territory.

It should be noted here that although Roman soldiers built the Wall, it was Rome's auxiliary legions who actually manned it. These soldiers were recruited from various parts of the empire – on the Wall alone you'll come across evidence of auxiliary legions from Belgium, Germany, Spain, Iraq, Syria and elsewhere. These auxiliary soldiers were not officially Roman citizens, at least not until they had served a certain length of time (usually about 25 years, the minimum term of service for an auxiliary) in the army and had retired.

THE WALL POST-HADRIAN

Whatever the original intentions of Hadrian, the defensive obligations of the Wall soon became rather secondary to more mundane yet lucrative duties. Following Hadrian's death in AD138 his successor, Antoninus Pius, decided to push the Empire's frontier further north once more, to a line stretching from the Clyde to the Firth of Forth. Not to be outdone, Antoninus fortified his new border with a 'Wall' of his own (AD142-4), the **Antonine Wall**, made of turf. So, just 10 years after the completion of Hadrian's Wall, its primary purpose as a border-cum-defensive-barrier was all but finished. The character of Hadrian's original fortifications changed too. Some forts, such as Housesteads, no longer on the front line, were left to languish and developed more into trading posts than military positions. Others, however, such as Corbridge, two miles south of the Wall, prospered as supply bases for the Roman troops stationed further north along Antoninus's border.

Markets were established near all the forts and the local tribe, the Brigantes, soon set up small villages, called *vici* (singular: *vicus*), in the shadow of the Wall to take advantage of the trading opportunities afforded them by having the world's first professional army, staffed by regularly paid, full-time soldiers. The new, non-military character of these forts continued even after the Antonine Wall was abandoned, about AD160, just 20 years after its inception, having been repeatedly overrun. *(continued on p58)*

❏ THE ROMANS IN BRITAIN

It took the Romans a while to reach Britain. Expanding in every direction from their base on the west coast of what we now call Italy, conquering the cold, windswept island in the top left-hand corner of the known world was never really a priority for them. And even when the Romans did eventually decide to invade, it wasn't the beauty of the land or the treasures it contained that lured them here. Instead, it could be said that the invasion was instigated by the whim of one man who was looking for a way to impress his friends and fellow citizens and strengthen his political position at home.

That man was Julius Caesar, and the year was 55BC. At that time Julius Caesar was one of a triumvirate, along with Pompey and Crassus, vying for supreme power in Rome; and the best way to improve your standing at home at that time was to win a battle abroad. So casting his eye around for a suitably easy yet seemingly impressive land to conquer, Julius hit upon Britannia.

Iron-age Britain was a dynamic society of hillforts and nascent towns characterised by a grid of streets each flanked with houses, places of worship, forges and workshops, and each populated by traders, craftsmen, warriors and druid priests. Metalwork was the Briton's signature craft, whether for vanity and decoration, such as the beautiful brooches that now sit in museums across the land, or for more belligerent purposes, such as horned helmets, swords and spears. The Romans described the country as 'uncivilised', but to them that simply meant that the inhabitants didn't live in cities.

To Caesar, Britain was the perfect victim for his invasion. He knew it wasn't the land of popular imagination, a land peopled by a barbaric yet united race that would fight tooth and nail to defend their homeland. Instead, he surmised that it was inhabited by a disparate set of tribes who were too busy with their own internecine squabbles to care too much about foreigners arriving on their shores, and whose squabbling would make them easy to divide, conquer and rule. Unfortunately, things didn't quite pan out the way Caesar had imagined. Firstly, the weather – that most fickle of British facets – intervened. Storms across the channel smashed much of Caesar's army before it had even caught sight of land; those troops that did make it across found the locals would not stand and fight, as the Romans had hoped, but preferred instead to engage in guerrilla warfare, which hardly seemed fair at all. Thus their first invasion in 55BC was abandoned almost as soon as it had begun. A second campaign the following year was only slightly more successful: though they managed to get across the Channel in greater numbers this time, the might of the Roman Empire reached only as far as the Thames at Brentford – which, as anybody who's been to Brentford recently will agree, is a poor return for all that effort. Confronted with the might of the Catuvellauni tribe, the Romans were forced to retreat with their imperial tail between their legs, the only trophies they had to show for their invasion being a couple of tributes and taxes paid by a few piddling little tribes in southern England.

Claudius and the conquest

So it was left to one of Julius Caesar's successors, the divine Emperor Claudius, finally to invade and occupy in AD43, using a massive force of some 40,000 men. The disparate tribes of Britain in the 1st century AD were no match for the professionalism and discipline of the Roman legions. The Romans knew this; so, too, did many of the British tribes, or at least the smarter ones who, rather than engaging the imperial legions in battle – a route that could lead only to certain defeat and possible annihilation – opted instead to live in peace and relative freedom, albeit under the rule of Rome, and enjoy the advantages that acquiescence brings.

(continued overleaf)

HISTORY

❏ THE ROMANS IN BRITAIN

(continued from p55) Thus, for the first decade or two, things went pretty much to plan for the empire. True, the west and north of the island still lay beyond their control. But the tribes in that portion of Britain which they *had* conquered seemed to find living under the Romans to be no bad thing, and played the part of meek and obedient subjects rather well. And they probably would have done for much longer too, had Nero not ascended to the imperial throne in AD54. Corrupt and oppressive, Nero's brutal administration caused the Britons to rise up against their rulers. The leader of this revolt was Boudicca (aka Boadicea), queen of the Iceni tribe, who rampaged through the province in AD60 destroying key Roman settlements one by one as she went, including Colchester (Camulodunum), London (Londinium, where thousands of Romans were massacred) and St Albans (Verulamium). Though the uprising was soon quashed the entire affair had exhausted both sides. Boudicca, witnessing the slaughter of her own troops at the final battle, took her own life and now lies buried, so it is said, under Platform 10 of London's King's Cross Station.

What's more, further upheaval back in Rome forced the empire to rethink its ambitions, and a halt to its expansionist policy in Britain was called – even though the west and north still remained unconquered and alive with the enemies of Rome and its empire.

The accession of Vespasian in AD68 saw a return to stability and a consequent reinvigoration of Rome's ambitions to subjugate the British Isles; just a decade later Rome was again launching successful campaigns into the lands we now know as Wales, Cumbria and Scotland, under the rule of the new governor, Gnaeus Julius Agricola. Of the three regions, it was Scotland (then called Caledonia) that proved the most stubborn and even after a decisive victory against the Caledones at Mons Graupius (believed by some historians to be Bennachie in Aberdeenshire) the survivors were able to flee and regroup in the relative safety of the Highlands.

Recognising the difficulty of flushing the Caledones out from their remote base, the Emperor Domitian opted instead for a policy of containment, building a line of fortifications known as the **Gask Frontier**, which ran south-west to north-east across Perthshire in Scotland. The idea of the frontier was to watch over the Scottish glens – the main exit and entry points into the Highlands – thereby effectively placing the Caledones under house arrest. Yet even this newer, more realistic strategy was soon deemed to be too ambitious and, as other parts of the empire came under attack from various tribes, the decision was made to withdraw one of the four legions stationed in Scotland and to pull back from the Gask Frontier.

Trajan and expansion

With the death of Domitian (possibly at the hands of his wife) in AD96, and the brief reign of Nerva, who ruled for less than two years, Marcus Ulpius Traianus, or Trajan, a career soldier, was anointed emperor in AD98. As his military background would suggest, Trajan's style was aggressive and focused largely on the continuing expansion of Rome's borders. Indeed, the empire was never larger than it was under his reign, as Armenia, Romania and Mesopotamia were brought under his rule.

Once again, however, in order to achieve these victories Trajan was forced to reduce his army's presence in Scotland, and in order to do this the empire's northern frontier was once again redrawn further south. This time a road known as the Stanegate (Saxon for 'Stone Road') was chosen as the frontier. Built in AD80 to link the towns of Corbridge and Carlisle, the road cut across the two main military routes heading north, one on either side of the Pennines.

To suggest that Trajan ignored Britain, however, is wrong. Indeed, his unquenchable ambition simply would not allow him to be content with only half the island. So, while it is true that under his reign the northernmost boundary of his empire receded south into what we now know as England, Trajan did not view this Stanegate Frontier as a defensive border but more of an offensive one, as a base from which to launch further raids into Scotland. Indeed the Stanegate road became an essential military line of communication, enabling the Romans to move troops quickly across the Pennines from one major north–south road to the other. To guard the road, forts and watchtowers were placed at intervals along the Stanegate – the forerunner, of course, to Hadrian's Wall and its forts.

As for the land to the south of the Stanegate, Trajan was content to continue with what was known as the Flavian policy (the Flavians being the imperial dynasty that preceded Trajan and included Emperor Vespasian): allowing Roman culture and society to influence the development of the province, so that in time Britain would come to identify more closely with its masters and therefore, hopefully, be less inclined to rebel.

Hadrian and his Wall

With the death of Trajan in AD117, another Spanish military man and a relative of Trajan, Publius Aelius Hadrianus, was chosen as heir. Though no less competent, militarily speaking, than Trajan, where the latter was consumed by an ambition to push back the frontiers of his empire, Hadrian was content to adopt a more defensive approach and protect all the gains made in his predecessor's reign. This change in policy heralded a period of almost 100 years of continuous peace; it also, of course, led to the building of one of the greatest military constructions of them all: a wall of stone along the empire's northernmost border, a frontier that up until now had been defended merely by hastily built turf and timber forts and watchtowers.

The end of Roman Britain

The Romans survived in Britain for almost another 400 years after Hadrian, until the start of the 5th century. Indeed, it's fair to say that they did more than just survive: they positively prospered. And so, too, did their subjects, who found that the Roman way of doing things, particularly when it came to matters of architecture, road-building, cooking, drinking, trading, educating and organising society in general, was often the best way (see box p58). Far from an extended swansong, the last 200 years of Roman rule saw some of the empire's greatest achievements in Britain, including Bignor Villa in Sussex. In fact, some historians have even gone as far as to declare that, by the time the Romans departed, Britain was one of the most 'Romanised' of its territories, and its people the most prosperous and peaceful.

So what drove the Romans out from this most compliant of provinces? The truth is that nothing did, or at least nothing within Britain itself. Instead, as the Empire crumbled and its borders were attacked from all sides, the Romans found themselves unable to hold on to all their territories; just as Britain was one of the last places to succumb to Roman rule, so it became one of the first to be dispensed with when the going got tough.

As they withdrew, other invaders filled the vacuum. In particular, the Anglo-Saxons from across the North Sea, Picts from northern Scotland and invaders from Ireland all penetrated Roman Britain's borders. Attempts to restore some sort of Roman law and order went on for the next two centuries or so. But by then, the Golden Age of Roman Britain was well and truly over.

HISTORY

(continued from p54) After this, Hadrian's Wall remained the definitive limit of the Roman Empire for the next 200 years. In addition, a second road, the **Roman Military Way**, was built around AD160 between the Stanegate and the Wall, often along the northern earthwork of the Vallum (which by now had been largely decommissioned). Such a road would be vital for the rapid transport of troops along the Wall and eventually replaced the Stanegate as the primary artery adorning the neck of Britain.

It would be wrong, therefore, to think of the Wall purely as a means of defence, a place to shelter from the spears of the Barbarians to the north. Because, whatever Hadrian's original intention for his Wall, it had evolved to become more of a checkpoint, a place to watch the comings and goings of the locals as they crossed the border, and to collect tolls and customs duties from the traders.

Severus's restoration

That is not to say that the Wall had entirely forsaken its military duties; indeed, following a successful breach by invaders sometime around the end of the 2nd

---

❏ Life in Roman Britain

Though the number of Roman troops who occupied Britannia was relatively small compared to the total population, their influence was all-pervasive. Roman cities sprouted on England's green and pleasant land, filled with quintessentially Roman buildings – basilicas, villas, baths and forums – that employed the latest Roman construction methods, exuded an architectural style that was intrinsically Roman, and were all crowded with local people who dressed in the Roman style, spent Roman money, measured distances in Roman miles (the word itself derived from the Latin for 1000 paces, the Roman mile being slightly shorter than the modern

Over the heather the wet wind blows,
I've lice in my tunic and a cold in my nose.

The rain comes pattering out of the sky,
I'm a Wall soldier, I don't know why.

The mist creeps over the hard grey stone,
My girl's in Tungria; I sleep alone.

Aulus goes hanging around her place,
I don't like his manners, I don't like his face.

Piso's a Christian, he worships a fish;
There'd be no kissing if he had his wish.

She gave me a ring but I diced it away;
I want my girl and I want my pay.

When I'm a veteran with only one eye
I shall do nothing but look at the sky.
WH Auden, *Roman Wall Blues*

one) and ate Roman food. Nor did Roman influence end there, for towards the end of their empire the descendants of many who had prospered under Roman rule even began to worship Roman gods and speak Latin as a first language!

And you can't blame them; without deriding the traditional British culture that had thrived before the invasion, life under the Romans certainly seemed a more comfortable affair. Rough, muddy tracks became sleek metalled roads. Buildings, previously made of timber, thatch and mud now became imposing, stone-made constructions with such novel features as windows and columns, with indoor plumbing and warmth provided by underfloor heating rather than the dangerous and unhealthy open hearth. The Romans brought with them a complete change in the organisation of

century AD, it was decided to restore, renovate and refortify Hadrian's Wall. This took place at the beginning of the 3rd century under the reign of Emperor Severus. Amongst the improvements was a rebuilding of the Wall using a super-hard white mortar which allowed it to be much narrower than before. The Wall had never looked so good, nor so impregnable; it's been estimated that 3,700,000 tons (30,138,000kg) of stone was used in its construction. Indeed, so comprehensive was the renovation that the original construction of the Wall was for over 1500 years wrongly ascribed – and even named after! – Severus; prior to conclusive proof that the Wall was built during the reign of Hadrian, it had always been assumed that Hadrian had ordered the construction of the Vallum only and that it was Severus who had built the actual Wall (see box on p51).

AFTER THE ROMANS

Unfortunately, after the Romans had gone their greatest monument on these shores suffered. Though it had been overrun only three or four times (nobody is sure exactly how many) since its original construction, when the Empire crum-

---

British society, from the family-based 'clan' system so popular among the 'primitive' tribes to a highly stratified civil and military structure.

Other innovations that were introduced include canals, water mills, factories and even such basics as new cereals and vegetables. And when they went they took much of their technology with them, including glass-making (the secret of which wasn't rediscovered until the 13th century), lighthouses (reintroduced in the 19th century), lavatories and central heating (commonplace again only in the 20th century).

Indeed, so pervasive was their influence that their currency became the legal tender of Britain just as it was across the rest of the empire, and Latin became the *lingua franca* of traders in this remote northern outpost. Furthermore, as the merchants and traders of Britain learned Latin, so they learned the advantages of literacy and the written record. Nor was that the only benefit reaped by the traders of the occupied provinces. The fact that there were now thousands of foreign troops on their land was in itself a business opportunity and soon local villages were springing up near Roman strongholds to take advantage.

Of course, while Britain enjoyed great prosperity, it was still forced to play the part of the conquered; because while there was some integration and mixing of the two sides – an integration that grew the longer the Romans remained in Britain – there was still very much an 'us and them' mentality on both sides. For the Romans, inevitably, there was a sense of snobbery when it came to discussing the Brits, whom the former frequently came to sneer at as the Britunculli – a translation of which would be something like 'wretched little Brits'. The Brits, too, while happy to adopt much that was good about the Roman way of life, still identified themselves first and foremost with their tribes. The Brigantes occupied the region that today we think of as northern England (Lancashire, Yorkshire, Cumbria and parts of Derbyshire) while the Hadrian's Wall region was shared with the Carvetii. But the 'independence' of these tribes depended to a large extent on their obedience to Rome: the more supine the tribe, the greater the control they had over their affairs, with the more compliant even allowed to establish their own governing body, able to wield at least partial power over the affairs of their territory.

HISTORY

bled and the troops were withdrawn in AD409 the Wall was subjected to all manner of depredations and indignities. For one thing, local landowners started to remove the stone for their own purposes. Hexham Abbey (see p138) was just one beneficiary of this pilfering, with the crypt constructed entirely of Wall stone. And where the locals left the Wall untouched, the elements took their toll as wind and rain gradually wore down the remaining structure. Today, only around ten miles of the Wall are still visible.

And so it stood for centuries, forlorn and neglected if not exactly ignored. Soon it even lost its duty as a boundary between countries as the border gradually drifted north and the country beyond – now called 'Scotland' after the Scots tribe from Ireland who migrated centuries after the Romans had left – shrank.

Interest in the Wall was first revived, at least in print, in 1600 with the publication of *Britannia* by William Camden, headmaster of Westminster School in London, who attempted to explain the form, function and construction of the Wall. His work was built on a century later by the Rev John Horsley and the publication of *Britannia Romana*, in which, of course, the Wall featured heavily.

The General wades in

Horsley's work revived great interest in the Wall amongst the reading public but it was not enough to prevent further damage being visited upon it during the Jacobite Uprising. In 1745, Bonnie Prince Charlie smashed his way from Scotland down through Carlisle and on to Derby before turning back. The ease with which he was able to advance so far had much to do with the fact that his adversaries, General Wade and his men, were hunkered down in Newcastle waiting to ambush him there, having assumed that Charlie would choose the eastern road for his advance. As a result of Charlie's success, Wade's troops constructed the Military Road (the modern B6318) across the Pennines to enable the swift movement of troops from one side of the country to the other. (This Military Road should not be confused with the Romans' Military *Way* – see p58 – though this lies nearby and performed much the same job almost 1700 years earlier.) To build this road, the Royal forces of George II removed sections of the Wall to pave their new highway. In fact, not only did they plunder the Wall for building material, they even built their road on top of it! (It should be noted that, though Wade is most associated with this road, it was actually built three years *after* his death.)

The Wall's modern pioneers

Once peace had returned to Britain, Camden's and Horsley's works encouraged others to look at the Wall anew. Among them was the shopkeeper William Hutton who in 1802 walked from his home in Birmingham to the Wall, walked along it and back, and then walked all the way home again – a total journey of about 600 miles (966km). Taking 35 days to complete, it was an impressive feat by any standards, particularly when one considers that he was 78 years old at the time and wore the same pair of socks for the entire walk! The product of his adventure was a book, *The History of the Roman Wall which crosses the Island of Britain from the German Ocean to the Irish Sea, Describing its Antient* [sic] *State and its Appearance in the Year 1801* – a title almost as long as the Wall

'Wall of Severus, near Housetead [sic], Northumberland' (19th century engraving)

itself – in which his love of Severus' Wall (as it was still called) and his interest in its history shines through. John Hodgson and John Collingwood Bruce (whose *Wallet Book of the Roman Wall*, printed in 1863 and later renamed *Handbook to the Roman Wall*, was still being published over 100 years later) also contributed to our knowledge with texts on the history and archaeology of the Wall and it was Hodgson who first definitively proved that the Wall was built during Hadrian's reign and not Severus'.

Then there was John Clayton, a Newcastle town clerk in the late 19th century, who bought four of the Wall forts and to whom we owe a great debt of gratitude; without his excavation and restoration work much of the Wall still extant would have been lost. That's not to say Clayton's work is unanimously admired today. In particular, his attempts to rebuild much of the Wall, taking great liberties and using largely non-Roman methods and materials, make more than one modern archaeologist weep; Clayton preferred to rebuild without mortar, so in effect the sections of Wall he rebuilt resemble a 'modern' drystone wall, still common around northern England, rather than the original Roman Wall. Clayton's efforts may have ensured that there is more of the Wall visible today but it can also be argued that what we are looking at is not really the Roman Wall at all but a 19th-century reconstruction, with almost none of the Wall's original inner core remaining. Nevertheless, to the layman, Clayton's work is vital, the miles he 'reconstructed' helping us to imagine what the Wall must have looked like when first built.

HISTORY

The work of Clayton was continued in the 20th century by individuals such as FG Simpson (of Stead & Simpson shoeshop fame), Eric Birley and Sir Ian Richmond, and later by bodies such as the National Trust, English Heritage and the Tyne and Wear Museums Service, organisations who concentrated less on the Wall and more on its accompanying forts and other buildings.

A proper survey of the Wall, recording every surviving remain and ruin, was conducted in 1985 to ensure there was a complete record of what exactly the authorities had in their care. And then, in 1987, UNESCO announced that the Wall was to become a World Heritage Site, thereby placing it alongside such wonders as the magnificent ruined city of Petra in Jordan, the awe-inspiring Pyramids of Giza in Egypt, Cambodia's mesmerising temples at Angkor Wat, Peru's fabled lost city of Machu Picchu, the architectural dream that is India's Taj Mahal and that other Great Wall, the one in northern China. The establishment in 2003 of a national trail running along the entire length of the Wall has once more brought it into the spotlight, and its instant success should ensure that millions more will enjoy the Wall's grandeur for years to come.

❏ **Visiting the forts – a walker's view**

To many or even most people on the Hadrian's Wall path, the various forts and museums are little more than milestones on the trail: places to tick off as they pass by rather than places to actually stop at and visit. However, some of our readers – many not even particularly interested in Roman history (or at least not before the trail) – write in to tell us how much they enjoyed the various museums on the way. The following from Jane Johnson was one such letter:

'To get an idea of the Roman remains we decided it would be good to have visited the sites before commencing the walk, establishing their location as well as those of the Roman roads. We camped for a week, basing ourselves at Haltwhistle; this enabled us to visit Chesters, Vindolanda (5hrs), Corbridge etc as well as the smaller off route places such as the bridge abutment across from Chesters. From Haltwhistle it was an easy train ride to Newcastle to visit the sites along the West Road and the Great North Museum: Hancock with its new displays.

We didn't do the actual walk until the following year but even with the gap in time we really appreciated having been to the main sites as we had some knowledge of things. Before setting off we spent two nights in Newcastle to see the rest of the sites around there. Arriving at the station in the early afternoon we hopped on the metro to South Shields to reach Arbeia, well worth visiting, before settling in to the city.

The next day we went to Segedunum and then did the short walk back to the city (not the most inspiring start to a walk!) leaving a 10-mile stretch to Heddon on the second day. This means you can visit Segedunum and walk the first five miles without baggage. What an easy start to the walk. Both Arbeia and Segedunum are great, especially having the reconstructions as they give an idea of the size of buildings. We wanted to stay in B&Bs for the actual walk and used a baggage transfer company to take our bags. Of course all this could be done in about two weeks' holiday if you have both the time and finance.'   **Jane Johnson**

While Jane's itinerary may be a bit extreme for some tastes, her email is at least further testimony that it is worth visiting some of the forts on the way.

MINIMUM IMPACT & OUTDOOR SAFETY

3

Minimum impact walking

In April 2005 Britain was given a rude awakening by UNESCO, when it threatened to have Hadrian's Wall placed on their 'in danger' list of World Heritage sites. The warning was something of a national embarrassment, for at the time there were only 29 out of the total 600 World Heritage sites on this list and only one in the so-called 'developed world' (Cologne Cathedral in Germany).

Thankfully, the threat seems to have abated somewhat since 2005; the Wall (which is now entered as part of the 'Frontiers of the Roman Empire' which also covers the Antonine Wall) has stayed off the 'in danger' list, which now numbers 44 sites out of a total of 981 (including the nearby Maritime Mercantile City in Liverpool).

UNESCO's concern about the Wall arose largely because of the huge and sudden influx of walkers trekking alongside the Wall. The thousands of people who have trekked along the National Trail since it opened (on 23 May 2003) have left their mark on the area, eroding the land and endangering the archaeological sites that are as yet unexcavated (and the majority of the Wall and its fortifications remain unexcavated; indeed, according to one expert only about 5% of the Wall and it accompanying buildings have been examined!). The soil in this part of the world is particularly thin and the climate rather damp. Combine this with thousands of pairs of boots and you have the recipe for some serious erosion. Vegetation is trampled, exposing not just the soil but also, over time, archaeological deposits.

Nor is the Wall itself exempt from the depredations of walkers: in 2004, a team of 800 Dutch bankers walked *on* the Wall between Steel Rigg and Housesteads as part of a team-building exercise, sparking fury amongst conservationists and historians alike. To be fair to the bankers, they have returned since and abided by the Hadrian's Wall Code of Respect much more closely – see box pp64-5 – splitting their group up into more manageable sizes and keeping off the Wall itself!

The controversy is only exacerbated by the fact that there was so much opposition to the creation of the path in the first place, particularly amongst historians worried about protecting the Wall. Their fears were allayed only when they received assurances that the Wall and its earthworks would be protected; unfortunately, the resources just haven't been available to protect it properly.

Though some may blame the authorities for the current crisis, accusing them of inadequate preparation and provision, this doesn't mean we as trekkers can't do our bit as well. The Hadrian's Wall Code of Respect, known as **Every Footprint Counts**, helps visitors minimise their impact on the trail. But the preservation of the Wall, while of overriding importance, should not be the only concern of walkers. The whole area is affected, economically, socially and culturally, by the arrival of walkers. By following a few simple guidelines while walking the trail, you can minimise your impact on it and have a positive effect on the local communities and the environment hereabouts.

ECONOMIC IMPACT

Rural businesses and communities in Britain have been hit hard in recent years by a seemingly endless series of crises. Most people are aware of the country code; not dropping litter and closing the gate behind you are still as pertinent as ever. But in light of the economic pressures that local countryside businesses are under, there is something else you can do: buy local.

❏ **Caring for the Wall – the Hadrian's Wall Code of Respect**

Overriding all other concerns about caring for the natural environment is the need to protect the Wall itself, and all the forts, milecastles, turrets, earthworks and ditches that go to make up the Roman defences – whether excavated or still buried beneath the soil. With these considerations uppermost, the following code – known as **Every Footstep Counts** – has been formulated and endorsed by government agencies, English Heritage, the National Trust, local authorities, farmers, conservation and user groups concerned with the Wall.

● **Don't climb or walk on the Wall** Please don't walk on the Wall or climb it for a better view or to take a photograph of yourself, no matter how tempting.

● If walking only part of the trail, **consider following a circular route** or setting off from a place other than the usual starting points. This will limit the general wear and tear.

● **Don't walk the Wall in winter** The ground (and the unexcavated archaeological sites still buried within it) is more fragile and liable to damage then. Again, consider a nearby circular walk or visit one of the off-Wall Roman sites instead, such as Corbridge or Vindolanda. This is why the passport scheme runs only from May to October.

● Visit the Roman forts along the way, which will help to relieve the pressure suffered by the Wall itself.

● Stay and eat locally and use local services when visiting the Wall; that way the local economy will benefit from your visit.

● Keep to waymarked and signposted paths and trails only.

● Keep dogs under close control and on a lead when walking through fields with sheep; on National Trust land this is compulsory. Only let go of the lead if you're threatened by a farm animal.

● Never light fires, and take litter away with you.

Support local businesses

Look and ask for local produce to buy and eat; not only does this cut down on the amount of pollution and congestion that the transportation of food creates (the so-called 'food miles'), but also ensures that you are supporting local farmers and producers; the very people who have moulded the countryside you have come to see and who are in the best position to protect it. If you can find local food which is also organic so much the better.

It's a fact of life that money spent at local level – perhaps in a market, or at the greengrocer, or in an independent pub – has a far greater impact for good on that community than the equivalent spent in a branch of a national chain store or restaurant. While no-one would advocate that walkers should boycott the larger supermarkets, which after all do provide local employment, it's worth remembering that businesses in rural communities rely heavily on visitors for their very existence. If we want to keep these shops and post offices, we need to use them.

ENVIRONMENTAL IMPACT

A walking holiday in itself is an environmentally friendly approach to tourism. The following are some ideas on how you can go a few steps further in helping to minimise your impact on the environment while walking the Hadrian's Wall Path.

- Use public rather than private transport whenever you can, particularly the Hadrian's Wall Country bus.
- Leave all farm gates as you find them.

In addition to the above rules, there are some other important guidelines that need to be followed to minimise the damage trekkers do to the archaeological deposits.

- Camping is allowed only on official sites. Don't 'wild camp' near the Wall.
- If the path resembles a worn line in the grass, walk alongside it to avoid exacerbating the erosion. In other words, **keep on the grass**! This is one of the most important rules – and also one of the most unusual, for on most trails you are usually told to stick to the path to prevent widening of the trail and the spreading of erosion. However, Hadrian's Wall is, of course, not your usual path and the authorities' main concern is not to preserve the state of the path but to protect the as-yet unexcavated archaeological treasures that lie beneath. This is why the path is a green sward, as it was felt that this was one of the best surfaces to protect the unexcavated treasures. But if that protective layer is eroded away, those treasures are put in danger. The erosion mats that have been placed on some of the muddier parts do a reasonable job but they can't be 100% successful. So avoid walking on a worn or eroded part of the trail and **walk side by side, not in single file**.
- Similarly, don't walk on any nearby ridge or hillock. Just as the trail cuts a delicate path through the Wall's numerous unexcavated mounds so you should avoid treading on any raised ground.
- If you find anything that might conceivably be of historical or archaeological interest on the trail, report your find(s) to a Wall guardian, trail officer or possibly a nearby museum. Do not, whatever you do, keep the find for yourself as a keepsake.
- Do not chip off a bit of stone or other matter from the Wall as a souvenir.

Use public transport whenever possible

Public transport along the Wall is not bad (though it can be infrequent), with most places served by at least one bus or train a day. Public transport is preferable to using private cars as it benefits everyone: visitors, locals and the environment.

Never leave litter

Leaving litter shows a total disrespect for the natural world and others coming after you. As well as being unsightly, litter kills wildlife, pollutes the environment and can be dangerous to farm animals. Please carry a degradable plastic bag so you can dispose of your rubbish in a bin in the next village. It would be very helpful if you could pick up litter left by other people too.

● **Is it OK if it's biodegradable?** Not really. Apple cores, banana skins, orange peel and the like are unsightly, encourage flies, ants and wasps and ruin a picnic spot for others. Using the excuse that they are natural and biodegradable just doesn't cut any ice. When was the last time you saw a banana tree in England?

● **The lasting impact of litter** A piece of orange peel left on the ground takes six months to decompose; silver foil 18 months; a plastic bag 10 years; clothes 15 years; and an aluminium can 85 years.

Respect all wildlife

Care for all wildlife you come across along the path; it has as much right to be there as you. As tempting as it may be to pick wild flowers, leave them in place so the next people who pass can enjoy them too. Don't break branches off or damage trees in any way. If you come across wildlife, keep your distance and don't watch for too long. Your presence can cause considerable stress, particularly if the adults are with young, or in winter when the weather is harsh and food is scarce. Young animals are rarely abandoned. If you come across young birds, keep away so that their mother can return.

Outdoor toiletry

Public toilets are marked on the trail maps in this guide and you will also find facilities in pubs, cafés and campsites along the trail. As a result, there shouldn't be any need to 'go' outdoors. This is very important. Normally, when caught short outdoors and with no public facilities nearby, considerate trekkers would dig a small hole in the ground in which to bury their excrement. However, as previously mentioned many of Hadrian's Wall's treasures are as yet unexcavated. For this reason, **it is forbidden to dig anywhere near the Wall**! And this point cannot be emphasised enough.

● **Toilet paper, tampons and sanitary towels** These take a long time to decompose, whether buried or not, and are easily dug up by animals and may then blow into water sources or onto the path. The best method for dealing with any of these is to **pack it out**. Put the used item inside a paper bag which you then place inside a plastic bag (or two if you're worried about ruptures). Then simply empty the contents of the paper bag at the next toilet you come across and throw the bag away.

Wild camping
Wild camping is not allowed along the Wall and, with the number of campsites serving the trail, there's no need to either.

ACCESS

Britain is a crowded cluster of islands with few places where you can wander as you please. Most of the land is a patchwork of fields and agriculture and the environment through which the Hadrian's Wall Path marches is no different. However, there are countless public rights of way, in addition to the main trail, that criss-cross the land.

This is fine, but what happens if you feel a little more adventurous and want to explore the moorland, woodland and hills that can also be found near the walk?

Right to roam
The Countryside & Rights of Way Act 2000 (CRoW), or 'Right (or Freedom) to Roam' as dubbed by walkers, came into effect in full on 31 October 2005 after a long campaign to allow greater public access to areas of countryside in England and Wales deemed to be uncultivated open country. This essentially means moorland, heathland, downland and upland areas. Some land is covered by restrictions (ie high-impact activities such as driving a vehicle, cycling and horse-riding are not permitted) and some land is excluded, such as gardens, parks and cultivated land. Full details are given on the Countryside visitors page of the Natural England website (🖥 www.naturalengland.org.uk).

With more freedom in the countryside comes a need for more responsibility from the walker. Remember that wild open country is still the workplace of farmers and home to all sorts of wildlife. Have respect for both and avoid disturbing domestic and wild animals.

The Countryside Code
The countryside is a fragile place which every visitor should respect. The Countryside Code (see box) was revised in part because of the changes brought about by the CRoW Act (see above). While it is just common sense, do make sure you are aware of the code – and adhere to it.

> ### ❑ The Countryside Code
>
> **Respect other people**
> ● Consider the local community and other people enjoying the outdoors
> ● Leave gates and property as you find them and follow paths unless wider access is available
>
> **Protect the natural environment**
> ● Leave no trace of your visit and take your litter home
> ● Keep dogs under effective control
>
> **Enjoy the outdoors**
> ● Plan ahead and be prepared
> ● Follow advice and local signs
>
> There's more on each point at
> 🖥 www.naturalengland.org.uk/
> ourwork/enjoying/countrysidecode

Other points to consider on the Path
● **Keep to paths across farmland** Stick to the official path across arable or pasture land, though do bear in mind the Hadrian's Wall Code of Respect (see p64).

● **Use gates and stiles to cross fences, hedges and walls** The path is well supplied with stiles where it crosses field boundaries. On some of the side trips you may find the paths less accommodating. If you have to climb over a gate because you can't open it always do so at the hinged end.

● **Walk side by side and on healthy grass** In other words don't walk in single file and don't walk on worn areas.

● **Help keep all water clean** Leaving litter and going to the toilet near a water source can pollute people's water supplies.

● **Take special care on country roads** Drivers often go dangerously fast on narrow winding lanes. To be safe, walk facing the oncoming traffic and carry a torch or wear highly visible clothing when it's getting dark.

● **Protect wildlife, plants and trees** Care for and respect all wildlife you come across. Don't pick plants, break tree branches or scare wild animals. If you come across young birds that appear to have been abandoned leave them alone.

● **Make no unnecessary noise** Enjoy the peace and solitude of the outdoors by staying in small groups and acting unobtrusively.

Outdoor safety

AVOIDANCE OF HAZARDS

Though the Hadrian's Wall Path passes through some pretty wild countryside, the good waymarkings, proximity of the B6318 (the so-called Military Road) and the A69 highways to the south and the lack of any major highlands, fells or mountains mean that it is unlikely you're going to get lost or come to grief on the trail. Indeed, perhaps the biggest threat to your life is provided by the roads which cut across the path, particularly on the section between Heddon-on-the-Wall and Chollerford, and there's already been one memorial erected by the Robin Hood pub to a walker who was hit and killed by a vehicle on this road.

That said, there are a number of hazards that beset trekkers on even the easiest trails. But with good planning and preparation these can be avoided. This information is just as important for those out on a day walk as for those walking the entire Hadrian's Wall. In addition to the points listed below, always make sure you have suitable **clothes** (see p36) to keep you warm and dry whatever the conditions and a spare change of inner clothes. Carrying plenty of **food and water** is vital too. A **compass**, **whistle**, **torch**, **map** and **first-aid kit** should be carried; see p38. The **international distress signal** is six blasts on the whistle or six flashes with a torch.

Safety on the Hadrian's Wall Path

Sadly every year people are injured walking along the trail, though usually it's nothing more than a badly twisted ankle. The most dangerous section is from

Sewingshields to Walltown, where the unpredictable weather leads trekkers to their doom – though with a road never far away, there's nothing too serious to worry about. Abiding by the following rules, however, should minimise the risks:

● Avoid walking on your own if possible.
● Make sure that somebody knows your plans for every day you are on the trail. This could be a friend or relative whom you have promised to call every night or the B&B or hostel you plan to stay in at the end of each day's walk. That way, if you fail to turn up or call, they can raise the alarm.
● If the weather closes in suddenly and fog or mist descends while you are on the trail, particularly on the moors or fells, and you become uncertain of the correct trail, do not be tempted to continue. Just wait where you are and you'll find that mist often clears, at least for long enough to allow you to get your bearings. If you are still uncertain and the weather does not look like improving, return the way you came to the nearest point of civilisation and try again another time when conditions have improved.
● Always fill your water bottle or pouch at every available opportunity and ensure you have some food such as high-energy snacks.
● Always carry a torch, compass, map, whistle and wet-weather gear with you.
● Wear strong sturdy boots with good ankle support and a good grip, not trainers.
● Be extra vigilant with children.

Dealing with an accident
● Use basic first aid to treat the injury to the best of your ability.
● Work out exactly where you are. If possible leave someone with the casualty while others go to get help. If there are only two people, you have a dilemma. If you decide to get help, leave all spare clothing and food with the casualty.
● In an emergency dial ☎ 999 or ☎ 112.

WEATHER FORECASTS

The trail suffers from extremes of weather so it's vital that you always try to find out what the weather is going to be like before you set off for the day. Many B&Bs and tourist information centres will have pinned up somewhere a summary of the weather forecast. You can get an online forecast through 🖥 www .bbc.co.uk/weather or 🖥 www.metoffice.gov.uk. Pay close attention to it and alter your plans for the day accordingly. That said, even if the forecast is for a fine sunny day, always assume the worst and pack some wet-weather gear.

BLISTERS

It is important to break in new boots before embarking on a long trek. Make sure the boots are comfortable and try to avoid getting them wet on the inside. Air your feet at lunchtime, keep them clean and change your socks regularly. If you feel any hot spots, stop immediately and apply a few strips of zinc oxide tape and leave on until it is pain free or the tape starts to come off.

If you have left it too late and a blister has developed you should surround it with 'moleskin' or any other blister kit to protect it from abrasion. Popping it can lead to infection. If the skin is broken keep the area clean with antiseptic and cover with a non-adhesive dressing material held in place with tape.

HYPOTHERMIA, HYPERTHERMIA & SUNBURN

Also known as exposure, **hypothermia** occurs when the body can't generate enough heat to maintain its normal temperature, usually as a result of being wet, cold, unprotected from the wind, tired and hungry. It is usually more of a problem in upland areas such as on the moors. Hypothermia is easily avoided by wearing suitable clothing, carrying and eating enough food and drink, being aware of the weather conditions and checking the morale of your companions.

Early signs to watch for are feeling cold and tired with involuntary shivering. Find some shelter as soon as possible and warm the victim up with a hot drink and some chocolate or other high-energy food. If possible give them another warm layer of clothing and allow them to rest until feeling better.

If allowed to worsen, strange behaviour, slurring of speech and poor coordination will become apparent and the victim can quickly progress into unconsciousness, followed by coma and death. Quickly get the victim out of any wind and rain, improvising a shelter if necessary. Rapid restoration of bodily warmth is essential and best achieved by bare-skin contact: someone should get into the same sleeping bag as the patient, both having stripped to their underwear, putting any spare clothing under or over them to build up heat. Send urgently for help.

Hyperthermia occurs when the body generates too much heat, eg heat exhaustion and heatstroke. Not ailments that you would normally associate with the north of England, these are serious problems nonetheless. Symptoms of **heat exhaustion** include thirst, fatigue, giddiness, a rapid pulse, raised body temperature, low urine output and, if not treated, delirium and finally a coma. The best cure is to drink plenty of water.

Heatstroke is more serious. A high body temperature and an absence of sweating are early indications, followed by symptoms similar to hypothermia such as a lack of coordination, convulsions and coma. Death will follow if treatment is not given instantly. Sponge the victim down, wrap them in wet towels, fan them and get help immediately.

Sunburn can happen, even up here and even on overcast days. The way to avoid it is to stay wrapped up but that's not really an option. What you must do, therefore, is to wear a hat and smother yourself in sunscreen (with a minimum factor of 15); apply it regularly throughout the day.

Don't forget your lips, nose, the back of your neck and even under your chin to protect you against rays reflected from the ground.

THE ENVIRONMENT & NATURE

4

Conservation

GOVERNMENT AGENCIES AND SCHEMES

Natural England

Natural England (www.naturalengland.org.uk) is the single body responsible for identifying, establishing and managing: National Parks, Areas of Outstanding Natural Beauty, National Nature Reserves and Sites of Special Scientific Interest.

The highest level of landscape protection is the designation of land as a **national park** which recognises the national importance of an area in terms of landscape, biodiversity and as a recreational resource. At the time of writing there were nine national parks in England (plus the Norfolk and Suffolk Broads which apparently have the same 'status' but aren't actually national parks. The Hadrian's Wall Path passes through one: the 1049 sq km Northumberland National Park (www.northumberlandnational park.org.uk), England's most remote national park, and an area that contains some of the best-preserved parts of the Wall. But there is an extra dimension to that designation in Northumberland National Park – the sky. In December 2013, the park was awarded the title of **Northumberland Dark Sky Park** (see box p152).

The second level of protection is **Area of Outstanding Natural Beauty** (AONB), of which there are 33 wholly in England (plus the Wye Valley which straddles the English-Welsh border) covering some 15% of England and Wales. The only AONB on the trail is the exquisite Solway Coast (www.solwaycoastaonb.org.uk), west of Carlisle, though the trail also brushes the northern edge of England's second largest AONB, North Pennines (www.northpennines .org.uk), which begins just to the south of the road running between Brampton and Hexham. Their primary objective is conservation of the natural beauty of a landscape.

Other levels of protection include: **National Nature Reserves** (NNRs), of which there are 224 in England, including Greenlee Lough NNR, the largest freshwater lake in Northumberland, situated north of Housesteads in Northumberland National Park; Muckle

Moss NNR, a 'mire' or peat bog close by between Stanegate and Vindolanda; Drumburgh Moss NNR, south of the trail and the hamlet of the same name; and South Solway NNR just south of Bowness at the western end of the walk. The last two combined are both lowland raised bogs – peat bogs – and together form the **South Solway Mosses Special Area of Conservation** (SAC). Overlapping many of the NNRs are **Sites of Special Scientific Interest** (SSSIs). These range in size from little pockets protecting wild flower meadows, important nesting sites or special geological features, to vast swathes of upland, moorland and wetland. On the trail there are several (the following descriptions all assume you are heading west along the trail): Close House, Riverside, the riverbank area by the Tyne before you head onto the golf course; Brunton Bank Quarry, to the north of the path just past Planetrees; Roman Wall Loughs, Roman Wall Escarpments and Muckle Moss which together form one large SSSI stretching from just east of Sewing Shields to Cawfields Quarry; Alolee to Walltown (beginning about a kilometre west of Chesters fort and stretching for a couple of kilometres along the Wall from the crags at Walltown); the Tipalt Burn that crosses the path at the lovely Thirlwall Castle; the River Eden and its tributaries (first encountered at the River Irthing, west of Gilsland; White Moss, Crosbymoor (on the way into Crosby-on-Eden); and the Upper Solway Flats and Marshes, Drumburgh Moss, Glasson Moss and Bowness Common at the far western end of walk.

❏ **Campaigning and conservation organisations**

These voluntary organisations started the conservation movement in the mid-19th century and are still at the forefront of developments. Independent of government but reliant on public support, they can concentrate their resources either on acquiring land which can then be managed purely for conservation purposes, or on influencing political decision-makers by lobbying and campaigning.

● **English Heritage** (🖳 www.english-heritage.org.uk) Organisation whose central aim is to make sure that the historic environment of England is properly maintained and it is responsible for nearly all the Roman forts along the Wall that are open to the public – though in one notable instance shares this duty with....

● **National Trust** (NT; 🖳 www.nationaltrust.org.uk) A charity that aims to protect, through ownership, threatened coastline, countryside, historic houses, castles and gardens, and archaeological remains for everybody to enjoy. In particular the NT cares for almost 750 miles of British coastline, over 250,000 hectares of countryside and 300 historic buildings, monuments, parks, gardens and reserves, including George Stephenson's birthplace in Wylam, Northumberland, Housesteads, and six miles of the Wall itself!

● The umbrella organisation for the 47 wildlife trusts in the UK is **The Wildlife Trusts** (🖳 www.wildlifetrusts.org). Two relevant to the Hadrian's Wall path are **Cumbria Wildlife Trust** (🖳 www.cumbriawildlifetrust.org.uk) and **Northumberland Wildlife Trust** (🖳 www.nwt.org.uk).

● **Royal Society for the Protection of Birds** (RSPB; 🖳 www.rspb.org.uk) The largest voluntary conservation body in Europe focusing on providing a healthy environment for birds and wildlife and with 200 reserves in the UK and over a million members.

❏ **The Hadrian's Wall Trust**

In 2012 Hadrian's Wall Heritage Ltd became a charitable trust (⌨ www.hadrians walltrust.org), funded by English Heritage and Natural England, with its principal aims being to '*protect the archaeology, conserve the landscape that surrounds it, promote understanding and access, and ... to contribute to the social and economic benefit of local and regional communities through sustainable tourism development and sense of place*'.

However, in March 2014 the Trust issued a press release announcing its decision to gradually wind down to closure over the course of the year, owing to '*significant financial constraints*'. The press release ends by saying '*We are working together to produce a strategy that will ensure the core responsibilities of the Trust can be sustained and the legacy of its fine work preserved for the future.*'

At the time of writing the Trust was still operating their 'Adopt a Stone' scheme (⌨ www.adoptastone.co.uk), launched in 2012, where people are invited to adopt virtual stones in a virtual Hadrian's Wall and the National Trail. Every penny of this money goes into conserving the Wall and the National Trail. In return, adopters get a personal message on their virtual stone and an e-certificate. You can also sponsor a turret or milecastle too! Sponsoring a stone can cost as little as £3 though there are options for larger donations and monthly payments too.

Flora and fauna

Northumberland and Cumbria are England's two 'wildest' counties so, as you would probably expect, much of the nation's native flora and fauna is more abundant here than elsewhere. Furthermore, given the variety of habitats that you pass through on the trail, from woodland and grassland to heathland, moor and bog, the variety of flora and fauna present is also commensurately greater.

The following is not in any way a comprehensive guide – if it were, you would not have room for anything else in your rucksack – but merely a brief run-down of the more commonly seen flora and fauna on the trail, together with some of the rarer and more spectacular species.

MAMMALS

One of the great attractions of walking any long-distance trail in Britain is the opportunity it affords of seeing a native animal in its natural environment, and the Hadrian's Wall trail is no different. That said, spotting the wildlife is another matter. Many of Britain's native species are nocturnal and those which aren't are often very shy and seldom encountered. Then of course there are those – the otter, for example, or the water vole – that are few in number anyway and sightings are always very rare.

Nevertheless, with a bit of luck and patience, on the quieter parts of the trail you may well be rewarded with a sighting or two of something fluffy. One crea-

THE ENVIRONMENT & NATURE

ture that you will definitely see along the walk is the **rabbit** (*Oryctolagus cuniculus*). It was actually the Romans who brought the first rabbits to Britain. Timid by nature, most of the time you'll have to make do with nothing more than a brief and distant glimpse of their white tails as they race for the nearest warren at the sound of your footfall. Because they are so numerous, however, the laws of probability dictate that you will at some stage during your walk get close enough to observe them without being spotted; trying to take a decent photo of one of them, however, is a different matter.

Incidentally, rabbits and Romans have a shared history as the Romans brought rabbits with them to use as the main ingredient in gourmet dishes. And now, 2000 years later, the descendants of those first rabbits are said to be one of the main threats to the Wall, their burrows destroying its foundations from below ground just as the boots of trekkers damage them from above. The situation is said to be so serious, some scientists are calling for a reintroduction of myxomatosis, the disease that wiped out 99% of the rabbit population in the 1950s. If you're lucky you may also come across **hares** (*Lepus europaeus*), often mistaken for rabbits but they are much larger, with longer bodies, ears and back legs.

Northumberland and Cumbria play host to a number of creatures that are found in few other places in England. In particular, there's the **red squirrel** (*Sciurus vulgaris*), which I have seen hanging around the trees near Birdoswald Fort. Elsewhere in the country this small, tufty-eared native has been usurped by its larger cousin from North America, the **grey squirrel** (*Sciurus carolinensis*), but in the north of England and Scotland the red squirrel maintains a precarious foothold. Fears for their survival on these shores have prompted the establishment of Red Alert, a charity aimed at protecting the species. For more information see 🖳 www.rsst.org.uk.

Two other creatures that are subject to long-term protection programmes are the otter and the water vole. Previously persecuted because it was (wrongly) believed to have an enormously detrimental effect on fish stocks – indeed, it was hunted with dogs up until 1977 – the **otter** (*Lutra lutra*) is enjoying something of a renaissance thanks to some concerted conservation efforts. At home both in saltwater and freshwater, they are a good indicator of a healthy unpolluted environment and are said to be well established on the banks of the North Tyne in Northumberland National Park.

As for the **water vole** (scientifically known as *Arvicola terrestris*, but better known as 'Ratty' from Kenneth Grahame's classic children's story *Wind in the Willows*), this is another creature, like the red squirrel, that's fallen foul of an alien invader, in this case the **mink** (*Mustela vison*) from North America which has successfully adapted to the British countryside after escaping from local fur farms. Unfortunately, the mink not only hunts water voles but is small enough to slip inside their burrows. Thus, with the voles afforded no protection, the mink is able to wipe out an entire riverbank's population in a matter of months. Incidentally, this is another reason why protecting the otter is important: they kill mink.

Other creatures you might see include the ubiquitous **fox** (*Vulpes vulpes*), now just as at home in the city as it is in the country. While generally considered nocturnal, it's not unusual to encounter a fox during the day too, often lounging in the sun near its den.

Another creature of the night that you may *occasionally* see in the late afternoon is the **badger** (*Meles meles*). Relatively common throughout the British Isles, these sociable mammals with their distinctive black-and-white striped muzzles live in large underground burrows called setts, appearing around sunset to root for worms and slugs.

One creature that is strictly nocturnal, however, is the **bat**, of which there are 17 species in Britain, all protected by law. Your best chance of spotting one is at dusk while there's still enough light in the sky to make out their flitting forms as they fly along hedgerows, over rivers and streams and around street lamps in their quest for moths and insects. The commonest species in Britain is the **pipistrelle** (*Pipistrellus pipistrellus*).

In addition to the above, keep a look out for other fairly common but little-seen species such as the carnivorous **stoat** (*Mustela erminea*), its diminutive cousin the **weasel** (*Mustela nivalis*), the **hedgehog** (*Erinaceus europaeus*) – these days, alas, most commonly seen as roadkill – and any number of species of **voles**, **mice** and **shrews**.

Finally, a surprisingly large number of trekkers encounter deer on their walk. Mostly this will be the **roe deer** (*Capreolus capreolus*), a small native woodland species, though it can also be seen grazing in fields. As with most creatures, your best chance of seeing one is very early in the morning, particularly in Northumberland National Park: there are said to be 6000 in Kielder Forest alone! Britain's largest native land mammal, the **red deer** (*Cervus elaphus*), is rarely seen on the walk though it does exist in small pockets in Cumbria.

REPTILES AND FISH

The **adder** (*Vipera berus*) is the only common snake in the north of England, and the only poisonous one of the three species in Britain. They pose very little risk to walkers – indeed, you should consider yourself extremely fortunate to see one, providing you're a safe distance away. They bite only when provoked, preferring to hide instead. The venom is designed to kill small mammals such as mice, voles and shrews, so deaths in humans are very rare but a bite can be extremely unpleasant and occasionally dangerous to children or the elderly. You are most likely to encounter them in spring when they come out of hibernation and during the summer when pregnant females warm themselves in the sun. They are easily identified by the striking zigzag pattern on their back. Should you be lucky enough to encounter one, enjoy it but leave it undisturbed.

Salmon (*Salmo salar*) thrive in the clean waters of Northumberland National Park.

BIRDS

The woods, moorland and hedgerows along the Hadrian's Wall trail provide homes for a wealth of different species.

While Northumberland is famed for its birdlife, in order to appreciate its richness it's often necessary to leave the trail, either by heading to one of the offshore islands or visiting the forest at Kielder. The former is one of the best birdwatching venues in Britain and the latter's not bad either, though in Kielder it's fair to say that often you can't see the birds for the trees. Nevertheless, the area is particularly rich in raptors, including **sparrowhawks** (*Accipiter nisus*), **goshawks** (*Accipiter gentilis*), **merlins** (*Falco columbarius*), **peregrines** (*Falco peregrinus*) and **kestrels** (*Falco tinnunculus*).

At the northern end of Kielder Water, Bakethin Reservoir has been declared a nature reserve and attracts **ospreys** as well as more common residents including wildfowl and gulls. The conifer forests at Kielder play host to the **crossbill** (*Loxia curvirostra*), while the deciduous, lower areas of the North Tyne Valley are popular with the **pied flycatcher** (*Ficedula hypoleuca*) and **redstart** (*Phoenicurus phoenicurus*).

THE ENVIRONMENT & NATURE

Occasionally, some of these species may be glimpsed on the trail but in the main it's the usual 'garden' species that dominate: the **great tit** (*Parus major*), **coal tit** (*Parus ater*), **blue tit** (*Parus caeruleus*), **blackbird** (*Turdus merula*), **mistle thrush** (*Turdus philomelos*) and **robin** (*Erithacus rubecula*).

You may also see but are more likely to hear the continuous and rapid song of the **skylark** (*Alauda arvensis*). They tend to move from moorland to lower agricultural land in the winter. Just bigger than a house sparrow, they have brown upper parts and chin with dark flakes and a white belly.

LAPWING/PEEWIT
L: 320MM/12.5"

SKYLARK
L: 185MM/7.25"

As for Cumbria, the AONB (Area of Outstanding Natural Beauty) along the Solway Firth at the western end of the trail is renowned as a haven for birdlife. The most famous, or at least the most voluble, inhabitant is the **barnacle goose** (*Branta leucopsis*). The goose is actually only a winter visitor, as it flees its nesting sites on the cliffs of Svalbard, Norway, to enjoy Cumbria's milder climate. Up to 30,000 of the birds arrive in November, heading back to Norway in mid-April.

Other species you might encounter on this shore-line include **ducks**, **swans**, **ringed plovers** (*Charadrius hiaticula*), **oystercatchers** (*Haematopus ostralegus*) and **lapwings** (*Vanellus vanellus*). The latter is black and white with iridescent green upper parts and is approximately the size of a pigeon or tern. Its most dis-tinctive characteristic, how-ever, is the male's tumbling, diving, swooping flight pattern when disturbed, believed to be either a display to attract a female or an attempt to distract predators from its nest, which is built on the ground. Common in Solway, you can also find them on the moors in Northumberland.

CURLEW
L: 600MM/24"

One of the most common birds seen on the path is the **pheasant** (*Phasianus colchicus*). The male is distinctive thanks to his beautiful long, barred tail feath-ers, brown body and glossy green-black head with red flashes, while the female is a dull brown. Another way to distinguish them is by the distinctive strangu-lated hacking sound they make together with the loud beating of wings as they fly off. Another moorland favourite is the rare **black grouse** (*Tetrao tetrix*). Feeding on cotton grass and tree shoots, in spring they gather together in 'leks' – display grounds – where the males conduct a spectacular courtship display. Its much commoner relative, the **red grouse** (*Lagopus lagopus scoticus*), is one of the few birds that stays on the moors year-round.

Less common but still seen by most trekkers is the **curlew** (*Numenius arquata*). The largest of the British wading birds, it's the emblem of Northumberland National Park and lives on the moors there throughout spring and summer, returning to the coast in autumn. With feathers uni-formly streaked grey and brown, the easiest way to identify this bird is by its thin elongated, downward curving beak.

Other birds that make their nest on open moorland and in fields include the **redshank** (*Tringa totanus*), **golden plover** (*Pluvialis apricaria*), **snipe** (*Gallinago gallinago*), **dunlin** (*Calidris alpina*) and **ring ouzel** (*Turdus torquatus*).

BLACK GROUSE
L: 580MM/23"

THE ENVIRONMENT & NATURE

❏ **Oak leaves showing galls**
Oak trees support more kinds of insects than any other tree in Britain and some affect the oak in unusual ways. The eggs of gall-flies cause growths known as galls on the leaves. Each of these contains a single insect. Other kinds of gall-flies lay eggs in stalks or flowers, leading to flower galls, growths the size of currants.

TREES

In the main, the Wall passes through bleak moorland bereft of any plantlife that can rise higher than the carpet of heather, though there are patches of woods and forest along the way, particularly in the Northumberland National Park and towards the western end of the trail in Cumbria. Indeed, woodland in Cumbria is estimated to cover a surprisingly large 65,000 hectares, or 9.5% of the land in the county, though a storm at the beginning of 2005 which blew down 500,000 trees probably reduced these figures. Even more surprising, Cumbria's woodland cover has actually *increased* over the past two decades. Conifer woodland makes up the majority, though there's also a fair bit of broadleaf woodland. Popular species include willow, oak, beech and maple.

Oak woodland is a diverse habitat and not exclusively made up of oak. Other trees that flourish here include **downy birch** (*Betula pubescens*), its relative the **silver birch** (*Betula pendula*), **holly** (*Ilex aquifolium*) and **hazel** (*Corylus avellana*) which has traditionally been used for coppicing (the periodic cutting of small trees for harvesting).

Hazel (with flowers)

Further east there are some examples of limestone woodland. **Ash** (*Fraxinus excelsior*) and oak dominate, along with **wych elm** (*Ulmus glabra*), **sycamore** (*Acer pseudoplatanus*) and **yew** (*Taxus baccata*). The **hawthorn** (*Crataegus monogyna*) also grows along the path, usually in isolated pockets on pasture. These species are known as pioneer species and play a vital role in the ecosystem by improving the soil. It is these pioneers – the hawthorn and its companion the **rowan** (*Sorbus aucuparia*) – that

Ash (with seeds)

THE ENVIRONMENT & NATURE

you will see growing alone on inaccessible crags and ravines. Without interference from man, these pioneers would eventually be succeeded by longer-lived species such as the oak.

In wet, marshy areas and along rivers and streams you are more likely to find **alder** (*Alnus glutinosa*). Finally, in the Northumberland National Park there are a few examples of the **juniper** tree (*Juniperus communis*), one of only three native British species of conifer, the blue berries of which are used to flavour gin.

Alder (with flowers)

FLOWERS
Spring is the time to come and see the spectacular displays of colour on the Hadrian's Wall Path, when most of the flowers are in bloom. Alternatively, arrive in August and you'll see the heathers carpeting patches of the moors in a blaze of purple flowers.

Woodland, hedgerows and riverbanks
From March to May **bluebells** (*Hyacinthoides non-scripta*) proliferate in some of the woods along the trail, providing a wonderful spectacle. The white **wood anemone** (*Anemone nemorosa*) – wide open flowers when sunny, closed and drooping when the weather's dull – and the yellow **primrose** (*Primula vulgaris*) also flower early in spring. **Red campion**

Juniper (with berries)

(*Silene dioica*), which flowers from late April, can be found in hedgebanks along with **rosebay willowherb** (*Epilobium angustifolium*) which also has the name fireweed due to its habit of colonising burnt areas.

In scrubland and on woodland edges you will find **bramble** (*Rubus fruticosus*), a common vigorous shrub responsible for many a ripped jacket thanks to the sharp thorns and prickles. **Blackberry** fruits ripen from late summer to autumn. Fairly common in scrubland and on woodland edges is the **dog rose** (*Rosa canina*) which has a large pink flower, the fruits of which are used to make rose-hip syrup.

In streams or rivers look out for the white-flowered **water crow-foot** (*Ranunculus penicillatus pseudofluitans*) which, because it needs unpolluted, flowing water, is a good indicator of the cleanliness of the stream.

Other flowering plants to look for in wooded areas and in hedgerows include the tall **foxglove** (*Digitalis purpurea*) with its trumpet-like flowers, **forget-me-not** (*Myosotis arvensis*) with tiny, delicate blue flowers, and **cow**

THE ENVIRONMENT & NATURE

parsley (*Anthriscus sylvestris*), a tall member of the carrot family with a large globe of white flowers which often covers roadside verges and hedgebanks.

Perhaps the most ubiquitous plant on the trail, however, is none of the above – nor is it even a British native. **Himalayan balsam** (*Impatiens glandulifera*) is a tall plant that can reach to well over head height and produces pink flowers with pods that 'explode' when squeezed, scattering their seeds. Introduced in 1839, it particularly enjoys riverbanks where it thrives, often suffocating out any other plant.

Heathland and scrubland

There are three species of heather. The most dominant is **ling** (*Calluna vulgaris*) with tiny flowers on delicate upright stems. The other two species are **bell heather** (*Erica cinera*) with deep purple bell-shaped flowers and **cross-leaved heath** (*Erica tetralix*) with similarly shaped flowers of a lighter pink, almost white colour. Cross-leaved heath prefers wet and boggy ground. As a result, it usually grows away from bell heather which prefers well-drained soils.

Heather is an incredibly versatile plant which is put to many uses. It provides fodder for livestock, fuel for fires, an orange dye and material for bedding, thatching, basketwork and brooms. It is still sometimes used in place of hops to flavour beer and the flower heads can be brewed to make good tea; it is also used in the production of some varieties of honey. It is incredibly hardy and thrives on the denuded hills, preventing other species from flourishing. Indeed, at times highland cattle are brought to certain areas of the moors to graze on the heather, allowing other species a chance to grow.

Not a flower but worthy of mention is the less attractive species **bracken** (*Pteridium aquilinum*), a vigorous non-native fern that has invaded many heathland areas to the detriment of native species.

Grassland

There is much overlap between the hedge/woodland-edge habitat and that of pastures and meadows. You will come across **common birdsfoot-trefoil** (*Lotus corniculatus*), **Germander speedwell** (*Veronica chamaedrys*), **tufted** and **bush vetch** (*Vicia cracca* and *V. sepium*) and **meadow vetchling** (*Lathyrus pratensis*) in both. Often the only species you will see in heavily grazed pastures are the most resilient.

Of the thistles, in late summer you should come across the **melancholy thistle** (*Cirsium helenoides*) drooping sadly on roadside verges and hay meadows. Unusually, it has no prickles on its stem.

The **yellow rattle** is aptly named, for the dry seedpods rattle in the wind, a good indication for farmers that it is time to harvest the hay.

Other widespread grassland species include **harebell** (*Campanula rotundifolia*), delicate yellow **tormentil** (*Potentilla erecta*), which often spreads onto the lower slopes of mountains along with **devil's-bit scabious** (*Succisa pratensis*). Also keep an eye out for orchids such as the **fragrant orchid** (*Gymnadenia conopsea*) and **early purple orchid** (*Orchis mascula*).

Herb-Robert
Geranium robertianum

Meadow Cranesbill
Geranium pratense

Heartsease (Wild Pansy)
Viola tricolor

Lousewort
Pedicularis sylvatica

Red Campion
Silene dioica

Common Dog Violet
Viola riviniana

Germander Speedwell
Veronica chamaedrys

Heather (Ling)
Calluna vulgaris

Harebell
Campanula rotundifolia

Early Purple Orchid
Orchis mascula

Bell Heather
Erica cinerea

Foxglove
Digitalis purpurea

Gorse
Ulex europaeus

Meadow Buttercup
Ranunculis acris

Marsh Marigold (Kingcup)
Caltha palustris

Bird's-foot trefoil
Lotus corniculatus

Water Avens
Geum rivale

Tormentil
Potentilla erecta

Primrose
Primula vulgaris

Ox-eye Daisy
Leucanthemum vulgare

Cotton Grass
Eriophorum angustifolium

Common Ragwort
Senecio jacobaea

Hemp-nettle
Galeopsis speciosa

Cowslip
Primula veris

Rowan (tree)
Sorbus aucuparia

Dog Rose
Rosa canina

Forget-me-not
Myosotis arvensis

Scarlet Pimpernel
Anagallis arvensis

Self-heal
Prunella vulgaris

Thrift (Sea Pink)
Armeria maritima

Ramsons (Wild Garlic)
Allium ursinum

Common Hawthorn
Crataegus monogyna

Sea Campion
Silene maritima

Bluebell
Hyacinthoides non-scripta

Yarrow
Achillea millefolium

Hogweed
Heracleum sphondylium

Common Vetch
Vicia sativa

Honeysuckle
Lonicera periclymemum

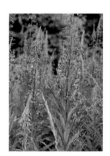

Common Fumitory
Fumaria officinalis

Spear Thistle
Cirsium vulgare

Common Knapweed
Centaurea nigra

Rosebay Willowherb
Epilobium angustifolium

Colour photos (following pages)

● **C5**: The splendid remains of Milecastle 39 (see p157) displaying the classic playing card shape, with Crag Lough in the distance.

● **C6** Looking east towards Housesteads Fort (behind the trees) from Cuddy's Crags; note the 'Clayton Wall' here – named after John Clayton (see p61) who 'restored' it in the 1800s.

● **C7 Top**: The unique arched gateway of Milecastle 37 (see p155). **Middle left**: The well-designed and well-preserved communal latrines at Housesteads Fort (see p154; photo © Bryn Thomas). **Middle right**: A mock-up of the turf-and-timber Wall at Vindolanda (see p161). **Bottom**: The extensive ruins of the Roman baths (see p130) at Chesters Fort.

● **C8 Top**: The granary at Housesteads Fort (see p154). **Bottom**: Walltown Crags (see p169). For many people, this is their favourite section of the Wall.

● **C9 Top**: It's difficult to get lost on the long, straight road through the marshes to Drumburgh – and plenty of signs should you go astray! **Bottom**: Don't miss the impressive falls at Cam Beck (see p185), near the bridge just a few metres off the path.

● **C10 Top**: The brooding remains of Thirlwall Castle (see p172), constructed in the 14th century largely from Roman Wall stones. **Bottom**: Just a couple of the locals you'll meet along the way.

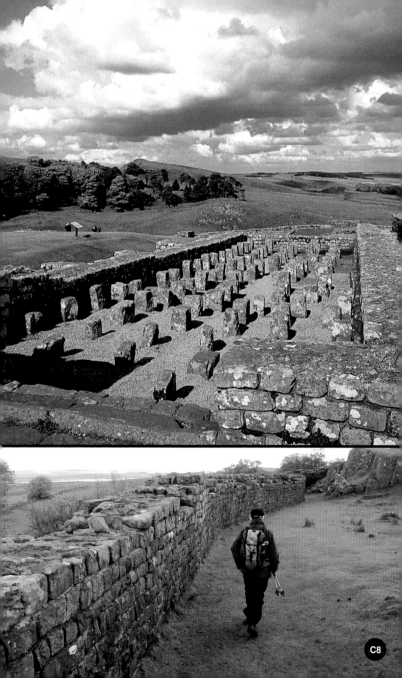

NEWCASTLE

City guide

Either a fittingly epic place to begin an epic walk, or the perfect venue for a post-trek knees-up, Newcastle is a grand city and, especially following its recent regeneration, a surprisingly attractive one too.

Arriving by train, the first thing you'll see as you cross the Tyne is an untidy jumble of roofs, a messy skyline that belies the uniform elegance of much of the town centre with its stylish Classical 19th-century façades interspersed here and there with the latest in cutting-edge municipal architecture. Yet Newcastle is like that, a city that is forever defying those who dismiss it as merely a city of brown ale and the Blaydon Races, fun-runs and football. As the starting point for a major trek it's ideal: functional, convenient, with great amenities and plenty to keep you occupied round-the-clock. The Great North Museum: Hancock, see pp91-2, is also the perfect introduction to the Wall and its history (and like just about every other museum and gallery in the city, it's free), while if you are coming to the end of your Hadrian's Wall odyssey and Newcastle is your last stop, there couldn't be a better place to celebrate than the revamped Quayside, home to numerous bars, bistros and a buzzing nightlife.

ARRIVAL

Most visitors alight at Newcastle's **Central Station** and it's hard to imagine a more appropriate place to arrive in this city. Built in 1850, the station stands in the heart of a metropolis that will forever be associated with George Stephenson (see box p110), the 'Father of the Railways' who was born in nearby Wylam, and which thrived on the back of the railways in the glory days of the late 19th century. The terminus, lying just to the north of the River Tyne, has its own metro station and three ATMs on platform two.

The **National Express coach station** stands a five-minute walk to the west on St James Boulevard.

The **ferry terminus** is 7 miles (11km) east of the city centre; the nearest metro station is Percy Main, a 20-minute walk away (or 5

(Opposite) Top: Newcastle's BALTIC Gallery from the 'Winking Eye' Millennium Bridge. **Bottom**: George Stephenson, the father of the railways, grew up in a cottage by the now disused railway track on the way in to Wylam. It can be visited (see p110).

minutes on Go North East's bus R19). From Percy Main it's 15-20 minutes by metro to Central Station. It's much easier, however, to catch Go North East's bus No 327 (£3 one way) which waits for disembarking passengers outside the ferry terminal before conveying them to Neville St in front of Central Station. Going the other way, the bus departs from Central Station $2^{1/4}$ and $1^{1/4}$ hours before the ferries to Amsterdam are scheduled to depart. The bus also calls in at Newgate St and the YHA hostel (now closed) on Jesmond Rd.

The **airport** (see box p44) lies 25 minutes away from the city centre by metro and that is the best way into the city. However, if you prefer bus, Stagecoach's X78 stops on the road outside the airport and goes to Eldon Square Bus Station.

TRANSPORT

Within the city

Newcastle, or at least its centre, is a fairly compact place and the chances are you'll be walking for most of the time. The main local **bus** station (Eldon Square) is in front of the branch of John Lewis on Percy St, with a second, Haymarket, a few metres to the north. However, one of the most useful bus services for getting to the start of the walk is Stagecoach's No 22 which goes to Wallsend Metro (daily 3/hr) from the Central Station.

There is also a pretty efficient **metro** (underground) service connecting most parts of the city, which runs daily from approximately 5am to midnight. A metro map can be found in most brochures and, of course, in the stations themselves. You'll probably use it to get to and from your hotel, as well as to the start of the walk at Wallsend.

Fares (£1.70-3.20 single) depend on the distance travelled. Alternatively, you may wish to buy a **Day Saver pass** (£2.60-4.50 depending on the number of zones covered), which enables unlimited travel on the metro and the Shields Ferry. Or there's the **Day Rover pass** (£6.90), which allows unlimited one-day access on all metro, ferry and bus lines. Incidentally, don't be tempted to jump on the metro without a ticket, no matter how lax the ticket checking seems to be; the fine for those caught is £20 and it's a bit daft for what is, after all, a pretty inexpensive service.

The **Shields Ferry** – useful for Arbeia, see pp93-4, a steep but shortish stroll away – costs £1.50 one-way and runs daily every half-hour from 6.15am (Mon-Wed to 7.45pm, Thur-Sat to 10pm, Sun to 5.45pm).

General information about all public transport in and around Newcastle can be found on Nexus (💻 www.nexus.org.uk), the organisation responsible for all public transport in Tyne and Wear.

Further afield

There are also lots of bus services from Newcastle to places on or near the route. Arriva's/Stagecoach's No 685 goes to Carlisle, Arriva's No X85 goes to Hexham, Go North East's Nos 10 and 74 also go to Hexham and Wright's No 888 goes to Keswick. Most of these services stop at a number of places en route; see pp46-8 for further information.

SERVICES

Tourist information

The **main tourist information centre** (TIC; ☎ 0191-277 8000, 🖳 www.new castlegateshead.com; Mon-Sat 9.30am-5.30pm, Sun 10am-4pm), at 8-9 Central Arcade on Market St, lies in the heart of the city centre. Packed to the gills with souvenirs and schedules, brochures and books, timetables and tours covering just about all Northumberland's and Tyneside's attractions (and indeed often further afield). There are also information points and kiosks throughout the city including at the bus station and the railway station.

Other services

You'll have no trouble finding a **bank/ATM** in the city centre: they're everywhere. There are also **post office** branches including one in WH Smith on Northumberland St and a second, Barras Bridge Post Office, 50 metres east of Haymarket metro on St Mary's Place.

There are several **outdoor/camping/trekking** shops in town, including Start Outdoors on Grainger St, and a Black's in the Eldon Square shopping centre. There's also Wild Trak on St Andrew St near Chinatown. For **chemists** there's Boots, with branches all over the city, including outside both Monument and Haymarket metro stations, and a big one in the Eldon Square shopping centre.

WHERE TO STAY

Most places do not accept one-night bookings on a Saturday night. As they say around here, that's just being canny.

Hostels

Remember that if you book in advance you may well be able to get a room in a hotel such as the Travelodge for about the same price as you would pay to stay in a hostel dormitory. The city has lost its YHA youth hostel, which has of course served to bolster the popularity of the two other hostels in town. The 177-bed *Albatross* (see map p85; ☎ 0191-233 1330, 🖳 www.albatrossnewcas tle.com; 2-12-bed dorms; WI-FI), on Grainger St, was always slightly better value anyway, with free toast, tea and coffee, kitchen, free wifi and a satellite TV and pool table in the comfy lounge. There's a vaguely antipodean feel to this place but it's none the worse for that. The cost of a bed depends on when you stay and the size of the dorm (the bigger the dorm, the less you pay) but expect to pay £16.50-22.50 per person (the higher prices tending to occur at weekends); there are also a few twin rooms (£22.50-24.50pp). The other option is *Eurohostel* (☎ 08454-900 371, 🖳 www.euro-hostels.co.uk/newcastle; shared dorms for up to 10 people; private rooms for 1-14 people!; WI-FI) at 17 Carliol Square, another central place with a dorm bed from just £16 including continental breakfast, private rooms from £29 per person. There's also a kitchen you can use to cook your meals – and a good-value bar menu for those who can't be bothered.

(cont'd on p86)

NEWCASTLE-UPON-TYNE

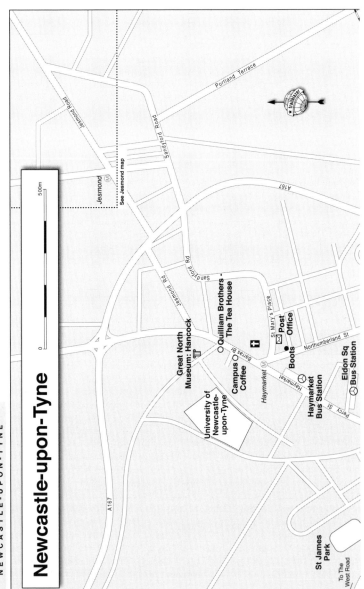

NEWCASTLE-UPON-TYNE

Key locations on the map:

New Bridge St
To Segedunum
BALTIC Centre for Contemporary Art
Gateshead Millennium Bridge
Malmaison
The Sage
South Shore Road
Newcastle Central Travelodge
Pitcher & Piano
Melbourne Street
River Tyne
City Road
See Quayside map
Eurohostel
Quayside
Bridge
A167
Tyne Bridge
Swing Bridge
Laing Art Gallery
High Level Bridge
Pilgrim St
Dean St
Hadrian's Wall Path
Post Office & WH Smith
Grey St
Monument
HSBC
The Close
Hadrian's Wall I plaque
Barclays
TIC
Collingwood St
Centurion Café
Copthorne
Start Outdoors
Grainger St
Clayton St
Big Mkt
Great Mkt
Albatross
Mark Toney's
Eldon Sq
Eldon Sq Shopping Centre
Newgate St
Central Station
Gallowgate
Wild Trak
CHINATOWN
Gate Cinema Complex
Scrumpy Willow
Black Swan Courtyard
County Hotel
Neville St
Central Station
Stowell St
Westgate Rd
Fujiyama
Boulevard
Westgate Rd
St James Boulevard
Discovery Museum
Westmoreland
Coach Station (National Express)
Forth Banks
St James Boulevard

Accommodation in and around Jesmond

If it's a B&B you're after, the chances are you're going to end up in the Jesmond area to the north of the town centre. On Osborne Ave, on the corner of Manor House Rd, *Avenue Guest House* (☎ 0191-281 1396, 🖥 www.avenuenew castle.co.uk; 4S/3T/3D/1F, all en suite; WI-FI) is another great choice, a long-established place with well-appointed rooms. B&B costs £42.50 for a single, £65 for two sharing, while the family room is £80.

Jesmond Park Hotel (☎ 0191-281 2821, 🖥 www.jesmond-park.co.uk; 6S/3T/4D/5F, some en suite; 🐾; WI-FI), 74-76 Queens Rd, is a smart place just down from *Francesca* pizzeria (see p90). Its exterior is unimposing and though called a hotel it manages to combine the efficiency and standard of service of a big hotel with the cosiness of a simple B&B. B&B costs £35-45 for a single, £62.50-72.50 for two sharing, or £95-120 for three/four adults in a family room.

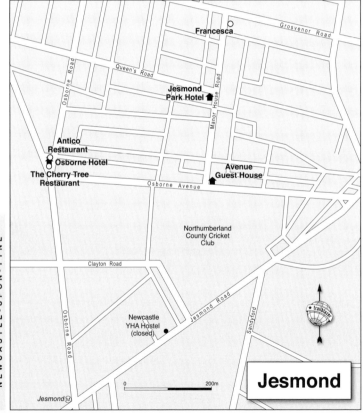

> ❏ **Where to stay: the details**
> In the descriptions of accommodation in this book, ♥ means at least one room has a bath; 🐾 signifies that dogs are welcome in at least one room but always by prior arrangement, an additional charge may also be payable; WI-FI means wi-fi is available in the property, though not always (reliably) in every room.

Finally, there's ***Osborne Hotel*** (☎ 0191-281 3385, 🖥 www.theosborne hotel.co.uk; 14S/3T/4D/2D, T or F, all en suite; ♥; WI-FI) at 13-15 Osborne Rd. A large hotel where rates are £47.50 for a single, £75 for two sharing and £95-120 for a family room. They also run *Antico* restaurant (see p90) next door.

Other accommodation in Newcastle

For potentially the best deal in the city you could try the ***Newcastle Central Travelodge*** (see map p85; ☎ 0871-984 6164; 🖥 www.travelodge.co.uk; 203D or F, all en suite, ♥; 🐾 £20; WI-FI 1 hr/£5, 24 hrs/£10). Part of a nationwide chain, Newcastle's version sits right in the heart of the city just a minute from the Tyne and the path. However, it has some annoying little rules (no check-in before 3pm, for example, unless the room is available and you pay £10 extra – and they won't pick up or take in luggage from baggage carriers for their guests). But if you book at least 21 days in advance you may be able to get one of their smart, clean rooms for as little as £21 during the week, which represents very good value indeed. Breakfast (a buffet with hot and cold food) costs £7.65. Parking is available for £5 for 24 hours.

The Premier Inn Newcastle Quayside (☎ 0871-527 8804, 🖥 www.pre mierinn.com; 100 rooms, all en suite; ♥; WI-FI) by the foot of the Tyne Bridge on Lombard St is even more central and offers similar deals from £29 for a double, though bring earplugs if you've got a room overlooking the quayside. Car parking is available for £7 a night if pre-booked.

County Hotel (see map p85; ☎ 0871-376 9029, 🖥 www.thistle.com; 114 rooms, all en suite, ♥; WI-FI), opposite the Central Station entrance on Neville St, is in a 19th-century building. As with many of Newcastle's hotels of this calibre, their tariff depends on demand and can be as low as £70 but rack rates are usually more than twice this, which gives you some idea of which ballpark they're playing in.

Vermont Hotel (see Quayside map, p101; ☎ 0191-233 1010, 🖥 www.ver mont-hotel.com; 101 rooms, all en suite; ♥; WI-FI), up by Castle Keep (see p93), is a grand-looking place in a central yet quiet location. The rooms are equipped with all the gubbins you'd expect – satellite TV and mini-bar. The hotel offers 24-hour room service and has a couple of bars as well as a fitness centre. As with County Hotel the rates change every day; the receptionist explained that you're looking at rates from £110 up to £330 for a suite. A full English breakfast costs £11.95 and a continental breakfast is £8.95 per person.

The ***Copthorne Hotel*** (see map p85; ☎ 0191-222 0333, 🖥 www.millenni umhotels.co.uk; 156 rooms, all en suite, ♥; 🐾 if small; WI-FI) sits in a great location on The Close, right on the Tyne (and the Hadrian's Wall Path!) and just a couple of minutes west of the fun at the Quayside. Ugly as sin on one side, the side facing the water is better and the interior is fine, with rooms (every one of which overlooks the water) equipped with everything you'd expect from a hotel of this standard. There's also a pool, gym and more than one restaurant. Rates start at £100 for a single/double but the actual cost depends on availability and when you book.

Perhaps at the top of the pile, however, is the *Malmaison* (see map p85; ☎ 0191-245 5000, 🖳 www.malmaison.com/hotels/newcastle; 122 rooms, all en suite, ➹; 🐾 by prior arrangement; wi-fi), a sophisticated place housed in the old Co-operative building on the Quayside overlooking the Millennium Bridge. The chic, dark reception has the décor and ambience of the pop-star Prince's boudoir and it's fair to say that this place won't be to everyone's taste – though I found the staff to be the friendliest in the city. Wi-fi and cable TV are just a couple of the facilities. Weekday rack rates are £160-375, though weekend rates are far more reasonable. A continental breakfast costs £14.95 and a full English is £15.95.

Finally, I must mention *Hadrian Lodge Hotel* (off Map 1, p101; ☎ 0191-262 7733, 🖳 www.hadrianlodgehotel.co.uk; 9S/5T/10D/1D, T or F, all en suite; ➹; wi-fi), on Hadrian Rd, close to the start of the walk in Wallsend. It's a bit out of the way but the metro (Hadrian Rd stop – it's right opposite) is just across the road and while this hotel is nothing fancy, it's reasonable value at £45 for a single, £59 two sharing a room, or £80-110 for the family room. The rate includes a continental breakfast; there is an additional charge of £5.95 for a full English. If you've driven up you may be interested to know that the car park is once again £5 per day – and their website suggests you may, by prior arrangement, be able to leave your car there for the entire duration of your walk.

WHERE TO EAT AND DRINK

The food in Newcastle is sometimes breathtakingly good value. Lunchtimes in particular are very inexpensive, with all manner of enticing deals offered by the restaurants and bars. In my opinion, if Newcastle is the last stop at the end of your walk, it's the best place to put on those pounds you've lost along the trail.

Cafés and bakeries   [see map pp84-5]
For a break and a cup of tea in the centre of town, *Centurion Café* (daily 10am-late), at the station, is perfectly acceptable and does some decent sandwiches, as does *Campus Coffee* (Mon-Sat 7.30am-5pm in term time, to 4pm otherwise), just by the university on Barras Bridge. Nearby, *Quilliam Brothers – The Tea House* (☎ 0191 2614861; 🖳 www.quilliambrothers.com; Mon-Fri 8am-1am, Sat 9am-1am) is a new place that hosts film evenings, an art gallery and live music evenings – as well as purveying some of the finest tea known to man and some decent food too. Stotties (buns) with various fillings are served with roast potatoes and salad and start at only £4.95. It's all rather splendid. Its nearest rival is *Scrumpy Willow and The Singing Kettle* (☎ 0191-221 2323; Mon-Sat

10am-8pm, Sun 11am-4pm), at 89 Clayton St, a friendly little place where all dishes are homemade using local and organic ingredients where possible and, as you'd probably expect of such an establishment, there's a good vegetarian selection. Their full English breakfast costs £6.90, the veggie/vegan option is £5.65.

If it's a hot day, don't miss the chance to sample the ice cream at *Mark Toney's* (☎ 0191-232 7794; Mon-Sat 7.30am-8pm, Sun 9.30am-8pm), next to Albatross on Grainger St. They also do an all-day breakfast, home-made soups, sandwiches and quiches.

Chinatown
Less of a 'town' than a single street, **Stowell St**, Chinatown (see map pp84-5) is nevertheless chock full of restaurants, most offering some sort of special deal, and a couple of all-you-can-eat places that are ideal for that end-of-trek blowout.

Starting by the elaborate oriental gate at the northern end of Stowell St, the first place you come to is *China Town Express* (Sun-Wed noon-11.30pm, Thur-Sat noon-2am), a no-nonsense Chinese café that offers 'happy hour' meals (5-7.30pm) for £5.30, or £5.80 with a starter. Perhaps its biggest recommendation, however, comes from its customers, a large proportion of whom are Chinese – always a good sign. Come here for dinner before 6pm or you'll be queuing.

King Neptune (☎ 0191-261 6657; daily noon-1.45pm, Mon-Fri 6-10.45pm, Sat 5.30-11pm, Sun 6-10.30pm) describes itself as a seafood specialist though has a full à la carte menu. Their Diamond Banquet (£37.80pp) with lobster as a starter will leave you feeling as stuffed as that horse in the museum at Segedunum.

Further on, the large *Lau's Buffet King* (☎ 0191-261 8868; daily 11.45am-10.30pm) is in deadly rivalry with its equally cavernous neighbour over the road, *No 1 Oriental Buffet* (☎ 0191-261 5787; daily 11.45am-10.30pm). Both offer all-you-can-eat 60-dish buffets starting at £6.45, the price rising according to what time of day you eat (with the cheapest time being before 4pm, 4-6pm £6.95, after 6pm £9.25, Saturday £9.95). As with all these places, some of the dishes can be unexceptional, to say the least, but for value they're hard to beat.

Finally, opposite the end of the street on Bath Lane, *Fujiyama* (☎ 0191-233 0189; Mon-Sat noon-2pm & 6-11pm, Sun noon-3pm & 6-11pm) is a Japanese teppanyaki restaurant which seems expensive after the all-you-can-eat excesses of Stowell St. Nevertheless, the food is delicious and the set menus at £18.10 seem fair value.

Quayside   [see map p90]
There are several great **Indian restaurants** in the city, particularly in this area. The very fancy *Vujon* (☎ 0191-221 0601, 💻 www.vujon.com; Mon-Sat 11.30am-2pm, daily 5.30-11.30pm), on Queen St is a classy Indian restaurant with an unusual menu; try the chilli hot sea bass Goan style, where the fish is marinated in garlic, lemon rind and fresh herbs and served on garlic and pak choi (£14.90). My favourite, however, is *Rasa* (☎ 0191-232 7799, 💻 www.rasarestaurants.com; Mon-Sat noon-3pm, daily 6-11pm), though this could be because they do masala dosas (£6.95) – proof, in my opinion, that the

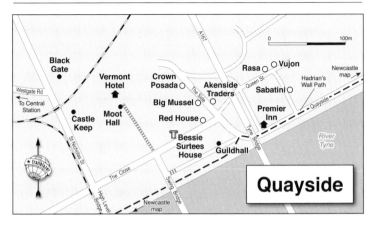

Indian gods not only exist but they love us and want us to be happy. Rasa is part of a chain but still highly recommended by many trekkers, with mains starting at about £7.95.

Just to the west on The Side are more choices: *Big Mussel* (☎ 0191-232 1057, 🖥 www.bigmussel.co.uk; Mon-Fri noon-2pm & 5.30-10.15pm, Sat noon-10.15pm, Sun noon-3pm & 5.30-10pm) is, as its name suggests, a seafood place specialising in mussel dishes (though vegetarian and poultry options are on the menu too); it has a variety of special offers with a large bowl of mussels just £9.50 before 7pm. *Sabatini* (☎ 0191-261 4415, 🖥 www.sabatinis.co.uk; Mon-Sat noon-10.30pm) is a pizza/pasta joint with happy hours (noon-6.30pm, to 5pm on Sat) when pizzas and pasta dishes are £6.50. Finally, down on The Close is the *Red House* (☎ 0191-261 1037, 🖥 www.theredhousecl.co.uk; Sun-Thur 11am-midnight, Fri & Sat to 1am) which deals in fantastic homemade butchers pies, mash and peas (£6.95).

Jesmond [see map p86]

Top of the list for value comes *Francesca* (☎ 0191-281 6586; Mon-Sat noon-2.30pm & 5-9.30pm), a long-established pizzeria that's been serving the residents of this smart suburb for over 25 years. They don't take bookings and you often have to queue, such is the popularity of this great little place, though it's worth the wait; the food is cheap and plentiful, with most pasta and pizzas around £4.50-5.95; for the indecisive there's a half-pizza-half-pasta option for £6.95. Slightly more upmarket, *Antico* (☎ 0191-281 2990, 🖥 www.anti corestaurant.com); daily noon-2pm & 5-10pm), run by Osborne Hotel (see Where to stay) next door, has a reasonable wine list and smarter décor, though still serves pizzas beginning at just £7.25.

Just the other side of the Osborne, *The Cherry Tree* (☎ 0191-239 9924, 🖥 www.thecherrytreejesmond.co.uk; Mon-Sat 9am-11.30pm, Sun 9am-9pm; food served Mon-Sat noon-2.30pm & 5-10pm, Sun noon-9pm) serves the best of

British food using delicious local and seasonal produce; it's not particularly cheap, but the menu changes regularly and the food – such as a divine fillet of sea bass for £14.75 – is often exquisite.

NIGHTLIFE

For most people, going out in Newcastle means heading to the Quayside to hit the bars and clubs there. It's beyond the scope of this book to provide a thorough review of each place. For an old-style, traditional pub in the Quayside try **Akenside Traders** or **Crown Posada**, on The Side (see Quayside map opposite). The **Pitcher & Piano**, part of the nationwide chain, is a typically smart affair with a great location by the Millennium Bridge, overlooking the water.

Finally, for more genteel entertainment, cross the river to **The Sage** (🖳 www.thesagegateshead.org), the giant slug-shaped glass auditorium and concert venue next to the BALTIC centre (see p94). Or you can see the latest Hollywood blockbuster at the **Gate Cinema** in the town centre – or something more thought-provoking at one of three independent **cinemas** in town: The Side (🖳 www.amber-online.com/sections/side-cinema), on the Quayside, Tyneside Cinema (🖳 www.tynesidecinema.co.uk), on Pilgrim St, and Star & Shadow (🖳 www.starandshadow.org.uk) in Byker/Ouseburn in front of the Tanners Pub.

WHAT TO SEE AND DO

There's so much to see and do in Newcastle; the following is a brief walking tour around the city's major highlights, with a bias towards those with a Roman or Wall connection. Further details of these attractions can be obtained from the tourist office (see p83), which organises walking tours of the city. Alternatively, you can take one of the **hop-on hop-off bus tours** (☎ 0191-228 8900, 🖳 www .city-sightseeing.com; daily from week before Easter to end Nov; £8) which visit all the major sites. The best place to get start is the railway station.

Great North Museum: Hancock

The first place any self-respecting Wall-walker should head is the rather clumsily titled Great North Museum: Hancock (☎ 0191-208 6765, 🖳 www.twmuseums.org.uk/greatnorthmuseum; Mon-Sat 10am-5pm, Sun 2-5pm; admission is free but a donation is appreciated), opened in May 2009 following a £26 million overhaul and which now houses the collections that were once scattered across various museums in the city, including the Museum of Antiquities and the Shefton Museum.

Occupying centre stage both on the ground floor and in Wall walkers' imaginations is the interactive model of Hadrian's Wall. Characters from Roman Briton discuss various topics – construction, religion, defence of the Wall etc – at the simple press of a button, while surrounding the model are various treasures dug up from the soil near the Wall and its accompanying forts. A highlight is an ivory folding knife in the shape of a gladiator found at South Shields. There's also a reconstruction of a Mithraeum (see box p148-9) which really gives you a flavour of what a secretive, strange and sinister religion this was. Apparently, the stone from which historians were finally able to determine that the Wall was Hadrian's construction and not that of his successor, Severus, will also be on display soon.

Perhaps the most impressive items, however, are the various pieces of jewellery. They include the gold Aemilia finger ring from Corbridge, dating back to between the 2nd and 4th centuries AD, which is believed to be one of the oldest Christian artefacts ever found on (or rather under) British soil. There's also a beautiful 3rd-century cameo of a bear on sardonyx, found in 1877, and a whole jewellery 'set' including brooch, necklace, bracelet and rings – all of which you would believe could have been made yesterday, such is their condition. The case on arms and weaponry is also enlightening, including as it does a highly decorated cheek piece from an auxiliary's cavalry helmet, again found in South Shields, and even a tiny segment of scale armour.

Other highlights include the model of the skeleton of *Tyrannosaurus rex* at the rear of the museum on the ground floor and the giant Japanese spider crab near the entrance. Overall, a very entertaining and educational morning's outing.

❏ The Swan Hunter Shipyard

Though not as venerable as the nearby Roman ruins of Segedunum, the Swan Hunter Shipyard, with its iconic, multicoloured cranes puncturing the skyline of north Tyneside, is nevertheless a vital part of the region's history. Unfortunately, it appears that that history has come to an end. In 2007, Swan Hunter's boss Jaap Kroes declared shipbuilding to be an industry with no future, and put the yard – and its cranes – up for sale. Sold to North Tyneside Council and One NorthEast in 2009, by 2013 it was being cleared up in preparation for development.

It was a huge body blow to both Wallsend and the city of Newcastle as a whole, an area that had suffered from more than its fair share of economic woes through the decades. Though it must be said that on this occasion the decision to close the site permanently wasn't entirely surprising, given its dramatic decline. Between 1993 and 2003 not one new ship was launched from Swan Hunter's yard, and a decision by the Ministry of Defence to hand over the work on an unfinished ship at Swan Hunter to the BAE Systems site at Govan in Glasgow in 2006 resulted in the shipyard being mothballed. Attempts to secure new contracts or change tack and become a breaking business both failed, and the managers were left with no choice but to lay off all but 10 of Swan Hunter's remaining 260 workers.

All of which seems a long way away from the time when Britain led the world in shipbuilding and the Tyne produced a staggering 25% of the world's ships. Many of the world's most famous and innovative vessels were created at Swan Hunter during the 20th century, including the Cunard liner *Mauretania*, a revolutionary steamship launched in 1906 that was, for a time, not only the world's largest ocean liner but also its fastest.

In recent years, however, the stories coming out of the Swan Hunter shipyard tended to be about job cuts and industrial disputes as the yard struggled to make its mark in the new globalised market. Jaap Kroes's decision to invest in the shipyard in 1995 brought a glimmer of hope and for a while, as several refurbishment contracts rolled in, it appeared as if the good times were back once more. But when the *Lyme Bay* was taken to Scotland to be fitted out, it was the first time a ship had left Swan Hunter unfinished, and many then saw the writing on the wall.

Castle Keep/Castle Garth [see map p90]

Perhaps better and more precisely known as the **Castle Keep** (🖳 www.castle keep-newcastle.org.uk; Mon-Sat 10am-5pm, Sun noon-5pm, last admission 4.15pm; £4), these are the most visible remains of the New Castle, the edifice that gave the city its name. Built during the reign of Henry II (1168-78), this New Castle was established on the foundations of Castle Garth, built in 1080 by William the Conqueror's eldest son Robert Curthose.

The Keep itself, and the **Black Gate**, on the northern side of the railway tracks, that was part of the same fortifications, are probably of only minimal interest to the Wall walker. However, one case in the Keep's museum section does have a few Roman artefacts, including fragments of a figure of Mercury. There are also details of the extent of the original Roman fort which was built to guard the bridge nearby. This bridge was **Pons Aelius** (*Pons* being Latin for 'bridge', Aelius being Hadrian's family name), which stretched across the Tyne in approximately the same location as the small Swing Bridge that you see today. It was from this bridge that the Roman fort took its name; a bridge that would have been about 700ft long (210m) and 18ft (5.4m) wide and the most impressive of the three main bridges the Romans built to cross the Tyne (the others were at Corbridge and Chollerford). In the 19th century, two altars were found in the water near the site of the bridge, though there's nothing left there today. Having noted the extent of the Roman fort, pop upstairs to the roof to get a better idea of its size and layout, and for good rooftop views of the city, its river and bridges.

Arbeia [off Map 1, p101]

☎ 0191-456 1369, 🖳 www.twmuseums.org.uk/arbeia; Apr-Oct Mon-Fri 10am-5pm, Sat 11am-4pm, Sun 2-5pm; Nov-Mar closed; admission free

Though not strictly a Wall fort, being on the other side of the Tyne and four miles further east of the end of the Wall at Segedunum, Arbeia was, nevertheless, an important part of the whole military set-up in Britain and anybody with a taste for all things Roman should seriously consider a visit. Though it seems a long way on the map, it's fairly straightforward to get to. Take the metro to South Shields, descend to Ocean Rd (not the bus station), turn right and walk for ten minutes past Asda, cross the roundabout and then take a left up Baring St past Vespasian (!) and Trajan (!!) streets, Claudius Court (!!!) and the Arbeia Unisex Hair Studio (!!!!). The fort lies opposite Hadrian (!!!!!) Primary School.

The name *Arbeia* means 'Place of Arabs' after the soldiers from Tigris, in what is now modern-day Iraq, who were garrisoned here in the 4th century. The history of the fort goes back further than this, however, having been built c AD163 under Emperor Marcus Aurelius to keep an eye on the sea and river. That changed in AD208 when Emperor Septimius Severus converted it into a granary and supply base for his troops campaigning in Scotland (see p58-9). Though Severus was killed in York just three years later and his Scottish assault ended soon after, the fort continued to supply the troops along the Wall for up to two centuries afterwards.

Because of its purpose as a storeroom, granary and unloading bay for imports arriving up the Tyne from overseas, Arbeia doesn't follow the classic playing-card layout of your average Roman fort (about which, see box p102).

NEWCASTLE-UPON-TYNE

Nevertheless, some great finds have been dug up by archaeologists, who are still painstakingly excavating the site today. Many of these finds can be seen in the reception, including some incredible carved ringstones. The inhumation (burial) room opposite is also enlightening, showing how the Romans interred their dead.

Outside, two Roman buildings have been reconstructed. The **West Gate** provides great views over the site, though in all honesty it is probably not an exact replica of how the gate would have looked. Nevertheless, it is impressive, and contains some useful information on the history of the site.

Of more interest, however, are the barracks at the south-eastern corner that offer a telling glimpse into the rudimentary living conditions of the average soldier in South Shields at the time. Walk around the back of the barracks and you'll find the bright murals of the **Commanding Officer's House**, the exact designs of the murals taken from original Roman designs.

The South Bank: BALTIC Centre for Contemporary Art and The Sage
The regeneration of Newcastle's city centre is a thing of wonder. From a run-down and slightly sleazy area of the city, the waterfront is now the most photographed part of the metropolis; its dilapidated, crumbling constructions spruced up and given a new lease of life or replaced by some breathtaking works of modern architecture. From being the shame of the city, the waterfront is now a place to be celebrated.

Perhaps the most impressive manifestation of this regeneration is the **BALTIC Centre for Contemporary Art** (☎ 0191-478 1810, 🖳 www.baltic mill.com; galleries open daily 10am-6pm, Tue from 10.30am), once a disused grain warehouse, now a world-class centre for contemporary art. It's a delight and, like most of the museums and galleries, is free, though some of the exhibitions charge and you probably won't find it easy resisting the temptation to eat in one of the cafés, including the rooftop restaurant, or to buy something from the BALTIC's gift shop. Nearby is the glass **Sage** building (see p91), an international music venue designed by architect Norman Foster that's been variously described as a glass wave, a blister or a giant slug.

The Tyne bridges   [see Map 3, p105]
Where once there was just one bridge across the Tyne in the area we now know as Newcastle – the Roman Pons Aelius that remained until 1248 – today there are seven bridges within reasonable distance of each other in the city centre.

The most eyecatching is also the one furthest east, the **Millennium Bridge**, which, despite the name, was formally opened in May 2002 by the Queen. One of the smallest (126m long and just 50m above water) this footbridge, also known as the **Winking Eye**, is one of the most revolutionary and even has its own cleaning mechanism: when the bridge is raised the rubbish collects in special receptacles which are then emptied.

Heading west, the next bridge is the impressive **Tyne Bridge**, opened in 1928 by George V and looking for all the world like its contemporary, the Sydney Harbour Bridge. After that we come to the comparatively small **Swing Bridge**, built on the site of the Roman Pons Aelius in 1876. As its name might suggest, it rotates through 90 degrees to allow ships to pass through. After this there's the oldest and most impressive of Newcastle's seven crossings, the **High**

Level Bridge, built by Robert Stephenson, the son of George (see box p110), and opened by Queen Victoria in 1849. The **Queen Elizabeth II Bridge**, which carries the Metro, comes next, followed by the **King Edward VII Bridge**, built in nearby Middlesbrough and another railway bridge. Finally, **Redheugh Bridge** (pronounced 'Red-yuff') was built on the site of two previous bridges and was opened in 1983 by the late Diana, Princess of Wales.

Other attractions in Newcastle

Bessie Surtees House (see map p90; 🖥 www.english-heritage.org.uk; Mon-Fri 10am-4pm, closed 24 Dec-7 Jan & Bank hols; free) sits in the heart of Quayside at 41-44 Sandhill. The name is not strictly correct, for there are in fact *two* merchants' houses here dating back to the 16th and 17th centuries, one of which is a rare example of Jacobean domestic architecture. The name comes from one of the inhabitants, who eloped with John Scott, who later became Lord Chancellor of England. There's not much to see inside, just three rooms, the main one empty save for a few photos of the house in days gone by. The main attraction is, perhaps, the giant fireplace, the exquisitely carved overmantel bearing a date of 1657.

   Laing Art Gallery (☎ 0191-232 7734, 🖥 www.twmuseums.org.uk/laing, see map p85; Tues-Sat 10am-5pm, Sun 2-5pm; free but donations appreciated), on New Bridge St, is the city's oldest gallery, having welcomed visitors for well over a hundred years. The collection includes both contemporary works and paintings from the 18th and 19th centuries.

   The **Discovery Museum** (☎ 0191-232 6789, 🖥 www.twmuseums.org.uk/discovery; see map p85; Mon-Fri 10am-4pm, Sun 11-4pm; free) is the region's biggest free museum (though donation boxes are situated around the museum), housing a wealth of scientific and technological material as well as displays on social history, regimental militaria and costumes.

❏ **The West Road – the real Wall route**
Most people know that Hadrian's Wall did not follow the river, as the trail does, but originally ran through the heart of Newcastle. However, you'd struggle to find much in the way of evidence to back this up. There's a **plaque** near Central Station (head east past the George Stephenson statue and you'll find it on your right, under the Westgate Road sign on the wall of Neville Hall, before the Literary and Philosophical building), which says that the route of the Wall went under the building. And on Westgate Rd, in the small **Black Swan courtyard** by a pottery, you'll find some stone foundations unearthed in 1985 by the potter himself, David Fry, that have been interpreted as belonging to a milecastle (though it must be pointed out that it doesn't actually lie where the milecastle around here would have been). Both these 'sights' are marked on the map on pp84-5. However, apart from these two examples, and some of the stones of Castle Garth which were once part of the Wall's fabric, Hadrian's Wall is virtually invisible in Newcastle.

   Virtually ... but not totally; travel up West Rd, for example, which follows the line of the Wall through the western half of the city, and you'll find a few more sights with Roman connections.

(cont'd overleaf)

❏ **The West Road – the real Wall route** (*cont'd from p95*) These sights on West Rd are probably not going to feature heavily in any photo album of your trek because, to put it succinctly, they're not the most scintillating of Roman treasures. Nevertheless, there is something charming about finding a temple to an obscure god sitting next to 48 Broombridge Ave; and of finding the best-preserved Vallum crossing of the entire Wall at the end of an unassuming cul-de-sac, and having to knock on the door of No 26 to get the key. Furthermore, there's something delightfully incongruous about the decent chunk of Wall, complete with its own turret, that lies prone and in resigned silence next to the traffic and pollution of the A186, one of the city's main thoroughfares.

Nor, so rumour has it, are they the only ruins on this multicultural artery. Amongst the road's cafés and colleges, the tanning salons and takeaways is, so it is said, yet more evidence of those busy Romans, including, according to one report, a large Wall stone next to an air pump in a garage forecourt. I don't suggest for a moment you hike the length of the road just to see if you can spot some more for yourself – leave that to the archaeologists, Wall buffs, guidebook writers and other slightly obsessive sorts who like that sort of thing – but it is interesting to see that, no matter how much you try to cover it with more modern constructions, you just can't keep a good Roman wall down for long.

For this reason, however, a trip up West Rd can be recommended to anyone with a taste for the absurd as well as the antique. Your chariot for the West Rd tour should be Stagecoach North East bus No 39 or 40; buy one of the Day Rover passes (see p82) as you'll be hopping on and off several times to view the sites. The bus leaves very regularly from Eldon Sq Bus Station (make sure it's heading to Denton, not Wallsend) goes past St James Park and onto the A186 (West Rd). After ten minutes or so, and having passed the hospital, look out on your right for West Gate Community College and the TV mast after it. Jump out at the bus stop here (just before the mast) and head down Weiner Rd (which lies right by the bus stop), taking the first right onto Westholme Gdns, then the first left onto Broombridge Ave. Before the first house on the left is the **Antenociticus Temple**, complete with a platform on which a statue of the god stood, flanked by a couple of replica altars (as with most treasures, the real altars, along with the head and limbs of the statue that were found, are now in Newcastle's Great North Museum: Hancock). Antenociticus himself was probably worshipped by the Vangiones from the upper Rhineland region who lived in the nearby Benwell Fort (see below); as is usual, the soldiers built their temples away from the fort, considering the latter no place for holy sites. The current residents of Broombridge Ave do not, it is believed, still worship at this site. The next site is within easy walking distance. This is a **Vallum crossing** that would have led to the entrance to **Benwell Fort**, of which this is the only bit left above ground. The crossing can be found at the bottom end of the noose-shaped cul-de-sac known as Denhill Park. As with all the sites on this road, the Vallum crossing is owned by English Heritage, who provide a fair artist's impression of how it must have looked in its heyday.

Jumping back on the bus, about 1500m further west and just before the main intersection with the A1, is a fairly broad and impressive piece of Wall lying serenely beyond the pavement to the left of the road. Halfway along its length is a foundation that gives the whole ruin its name: **Denton Turret**. As is usual with all the forts along the Wall, the turret would have been manned by around ten men. An inscription recovered from the site suggested that it was built by the First Cohort of the Second Legion of Augusta. Presumably, the soldiers who manned the turret would have walked back to their abode at Benwell. But by good fortune there's a bus stop on the other side of the road to take you back into town.

NEWCASTLE-UPON-TYNE

Using this guide

The trail guide has been described from east to west and divided into six different stages. Though each of these roughly corresponds to a day's walk, do not assume that this is the only way to plan your walk. There are so many places to stay en route that you can pretty much divide up the walk wherever you want.

On p31 are tables to help you plan an itinerary. To provide further help, practical information is presented on the trail maps, including walking times, places to stay, camp and eat, as well as shops where you can buy supplies, taps (for drinking water), phone boxes and public toilets. Further service details are given in the text under the entry for each settlement.

TRAIL MAPS

Scale and walking times

The trail maps are to a scale of 1:20,000 (1cm = 200m; $3^1/_8$ inches = one mile). Walking times are given along the side of each map and the arrow shows the direction to which the time refers. The black triangles indicate the points between which the times have been taken. **See box below on walking times**.

The time-bars are a tool and are not there to judge your walking ability. There are so many variables that affect walking speed, from the weather conditions to how many beers you drank the previous evening. After the first hour or two of walking you will be able to see how your speed relates to the timings on the maps.

Up or down?

The trail is shown as a dotted line. An arrow across the trail indicates the slope; two arrows show that it is steep. Note that the arrow points towards the higher part of the trail. If, for example, you are walking from A (at 80m) to B (at 200m) and the trail between the two is short

---

❏ **Important note – walking times**
Unless otherwise specified, **all times in this book refer only to the time spent walking**. You will need to add 20-30% to allow for rests, photography, checking the map, drinking water etc. When planning the day's hike count on 5-7 hours' actual walking.

and steep, it would be shown thus: A– – –>> – – – – B. Reversed arrow heads indicate downward gradient.

Accommodation

Accommodation marked on the map is either on or within easy reach of the path. Many B&B proprietors based a mile or two off the trail will offer to collect walkers from the nearest point on the trail and take them back next morning.

Details of each place are given in the accompanying text. The number of **rooms** of each type is given at the beginning of each entry, ie: **S** = Single, **T** = Twin room, **D** = Double room, **F** = Family room sleeping three or more. Note that many of the family rooms have a double bed and one/two single beds thus in a group of three or four, two people would have to share the double bed but it also means the room can be used as a double or twin.

Rates quoted for B&B-style accommodation are **per person (pp)** based on two people sharing a room for a one-night stay; rates are usually discounted for longer stays. Where a single room **(sgl)** is available the rate for that is quoted if different from the rate per person. The rate for single occupancy **(sgl occ)** of a double/twin may be higher, and the per person rate for three/four sharing a triple/quad may be lower. At some places the only option is a **room rate**; this will be the same whether one or two people (or more if permissible) use the room. See p29 for more information on rates.

The text also mentions whether the bedrooms have a **private bathroom** (usually en suite but it may be just outside the room) or a shared bathroom. Most of these have only a shower. In the text ☕ signifies that at least one room has a bathroom with a **bath**, or access to a bath, for those who prefer a relaxed soak at the end of the day. Also noted is whether the premises have WI-FI (WI-FI), if **dogs** (🐾 – see also p220) are welcome, if packed lunches (Ⓛ) are available and the associated charges.

Other features

Features are marked on the map when pertinent to navigation. In order to avoid cluttering the maps and making them unusable not all features have been marked each time they occur.

The trail guide:
Wallsend to Bowness-on-Solway

WALLSEND TO HEDDON-ON-THE-WALL   [MAPS 1-8]

Getting to the start of the walk

There are a number of ways of getting to the start of the walk. Most people choose to use public transport (see box p46-8) and jump out at Wallsend Metro or the adjacent coach station (which is helpfully signed in Latin – *Raedarum publicarum statio* – someone in charge of signage at the city council clearly has a sense of humour). From there you can walk across the road to the Asda supermarket for some last-minute supplies or straight towards the Tyne and Segedunum.

SEGEDUNUM [see Map 1, p101]
☎ 0191-236 9347; 🖳 *www.twmuseums.org.uk/segedunum; Apr-Oct daily 10am-5pm, Nov to mid Dec & mid Jan to Mar Mon-Fri 10am-3pm, Sat 11am-2pm; £5.25/3.25/free adults/concs/children*
Nestling adjacent to the Swan Hunter shipyard (see box p92), which itself is replete with history, Segedunum is a fantastic introduction to the kind of Wall fort that will become oh-so-familiar as you progress along the trail.

Translating as 'Strong Fort', Segedunum is the last Wall fort heading east; instead of continuing from here to the sea, the Wall took a sharp turn south at this point, heading off from the fort's south-eastern corner through the now-defunct Swan Hunter shipyard and down to the water's edge. You can see a little bit of this Wall by the side of the trail at the very start of the walk, just outside the fence that surrounds Segedunum.

At first it seems strange that the Wall doesn't actually cover the entire breadth of the country. After all, what is the point of building a wall right across an island if you're not going to finish the job, thereby allowing the locals to sneak around one end? But with Arbeia Fort (see pp93-4) guarding the river's mouth from the other side of the Tyne and this fort watching over the land to the east on this side, it's fair to say that little could cross undetected from one side – of either the Tyne or the Wall – to the other. In fact, Segedunum was actually something of an afterthought; originally, the Wall terminated at Pons Aelius (see p93) and only later did they decide to extend it a further three miles east to Segedunum.

Today, little remains of the original Roman fort which would have held 600 men. The Saxons proved pretty efficient at carting off the masonry for their own building projects, such as Bede's monastery at Jarrow; Newcastle's Great North Museum: Hancock has proved equally efficient at appropriating much of the remainder to fill their display cases (this is, after all, the most excavated of all the Wall forts).

But what makes the fort here so appealing is not so much what the Romans left behind but the way the little that has survived has been presented. From the 35m-high viewing tower, which provides great views over the site, to the clear information boards and the reconstructed bath-house, this fort is an object lesson in how history should be told. And whilst some may complain at the slightly child-centric **galleries**, with their games and quizzes designed to keep young minds interested, many will find it stimulating and useful and the reconstructed cavalry barrack (complete with horse!) gives a fair idea of what living conditions were like on the Wall. Upstairs in the Strong Place Gallery (Strong Place being a translation of Segedunum) is the history of the location of the fort, including exhibits from its time as a coal mine and as part of the Swan Hunter Shipyard.

Highlights of Segedunum include the aforementioned **Panorama Tower**, where you get a better idea of just how large the fort was (note that the fort originally covered the large paved area to the north of the main road too, which today is outside the official site). The **Roman baths** are good, too, though if you've seen other Roman baths you may well be disappointed by the rather plain, undecorated look of this one. There's a reason for this: Roman baths along the Wall, including this one (which would not have stood originally on this spot but outside the fort, near where the *Ship Inn* is today), would have been for the use of soldiers rather than Roman civilians and as such would have been less fancy than the average mosaic-floored *balineum* of popular imagination. Still, it's done as authentically as possible using recreated Roman cement, *opus signinum*, for the floors, and there are frescoes on the walls. Outside, there's a small Roman-style medicinal **herb garden**. One other highlight is the only **stone toilet seat** surviving from Roman Britain.

Don't forget to visit the reconstructed Wall, either, which lies outside the site on the north-west corner; accurate, as far as I know, though some have quibbled about the crenellations, which may be a mere embellishment to make it look more like a military construction. Following the demolition of a scaffolding yard that lay to the north of this reconstructed wall, the remains of another Roman construction has been found, though its exact purpose has yet to be determined. One place that is open to public gaze, however, is **B Pit**, an old colliery shaft discovered during the Segedunum excavations. Incidentally, while we're on the subject of collieries and coal, the coal industry – the making of Wallsend – was another thing that the Romans brought to the area, having been the first to mine it here. As such, the Romans could be said to have been the first to bring coals to Newcastle!

The route

From the entrance to Segedunum, turn right and head down Station Rd, which runs along the back of Segedunum's reception and museum. A path runs east–west above Station road; this is the start of the trail. Before you begin, however, don't forget to stamp your passport at the Segedunum reception or, if they're closed, at the box by the rear entrance to the museum or at Asda across the road. (Both Segedunum and Asda also sell the passport, badge and certificate.)

This **15-mile (24km; 4³/₄-5hrs)** first stage begins by the only remaining piece of the Wall that originally ran down from the fort to the Tyne, and which now stands just over the railings outside the fort grounds. As the easternmost part of the Wall still in existence, this is an appropriate place to begin. Through all of Newcastle, by the way, the trail is called **Hadrian's Way** for some reason and this is what you'll see on the signs. Heading west, the path you are following was originally an old railway track, an extension of the Blyth and Tyne Railway. By the side of the trail are the abutments of old bridges and the ironmongery of various parts of the railway, now finding secondary employment as resting posts.

It must be said that, though not without interest, this is not the most auspicious start to a trail. It's not the way the trail leads through the industrial heart of the city that disappoints; if you're in the right frame of mind a short walk through an entirely man-made landscape can be as diverting as any country romp. But hemmed in by warehouses and the backs of housing estates, there's little industry, or indeed anything to see. Unfortunately, one or two trekkers have also been sub-

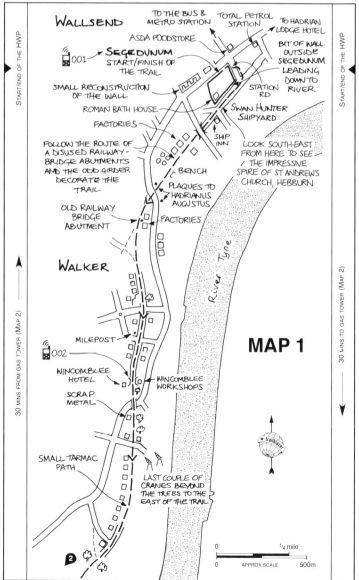

WALLSEND

TO THE BUS & METRO STATION

TOTAL PETROL STATION

TO HADRIAN LODGE HOTEL

ASDA FOODSTORE

001 → SEGEDUNUM START/FINISH OF THE TRAIL

BIT OF WALL OUTSIDE SEGEDUNUM LEADING DOWN TO RIVER

SMALL RECONSTRUCTION OF THE WALL

STATION RD

ROMAN BATH HOUSE

SWAN HUNTER SHIPYARD

FACTORIES

SHIP INN

FOLLOW THE ROUTE OF A DISUSED RAILWAY-BRIDGE ABUTMENTS AND THE ODD GIRDER DECORATE THE TRAIL

LOOK SOUTH-EAST FROM HERE TO SEE THE IMPRESSIVE SPIRE OF ST ANDREW'S CHURCH, HEBBURN

BENCH

PLAQUES TO HADRIANUS AUGUSTUS

OLD RAILWAY BRIDGE ABUTMENT

FACTORIES

WALKER

River Tyne

MAP 1

MILEPOST

002

WINCOMBLEE HOTEL

WINCOMBLEE WORKSHOPS

SCRAP METAL

30 MINS TO GAS TOWER (MAP 2)

SMALL TARMAC PATH

LAST COUPLE OF CRANES BEYOND THE TREES TO THE EAST OF THE TRAIL

2

★ trailblazer

0 — ¼ mile

0 — APPROX SCALE — 500m

jected to insults and threats from local kids on both this stretch and the one that leads across Denton Dene (see Map 5, p108) and have written to say that they felt threatened in these areas. We should, I suppose, be thankful that the abuse has so far been just verbal and that these incidents, as unpleasant as they are, are still quite rare. If nothing else, at least you are getting the worst of the trail out of the way now – and it will also make you appreciate the rest of the trek more.

Crossing roads and following the signposts, eventually the path passes a school and a gas tower, drops away from the railway track and heads down to the water's edge and the **Walker Riverside Park** (an appropriate name for a park at the start of a national trail).

❏ The layout of the Wall forts

The fort at Segedunum is pretty typical of the design of all Wall forts along the trail. Often described as '**playing-card shaped**' (ie rectangular with rounded corners), the layout varied little from one to the next. At its centre were the **headquarters**, the *Principia*, the heart and brains of the fort. It was here that justice was dispensed, plans formulated, men paid and ceremonies, both secular and religious, performed. Sometimes, as with Segedunum, a **shrine** was housed within this building under which, in a small safe-room underneath, the money to pay the soldiers' wages would be stashed. The commanding officer's house, or *praetorium*, where he lived with his family and servants, stood next door, usually to the east of the HQ, while the **hospital** and other public buildings sat to its west. Often you'd find the fort's **granary** here too, one of the most interesting buildings, architecturally, of the whole fort. The granary's sides were buttressed to help the walls withstand the pressure created by all that grain being housed within it, while the floor itself was raised to allow air to circulate, thus preventing the grain at the bottom of the heap from going mouldy. The granary would have had a porch, too, to stop the grain getting wet when it was being unloaded from the carts. There's a particularly good granary, complete with the porch pillars, at Corbridge.

Flanking these buildings to north and south were the barracks. **Cavalry barracks** are distinguishable from the infantry barracks by a recess or ditch hewn into the floor – dug to collect the horse's urine and prevent it from seeping into the cavalry officer's quarters next door. Segedunum has fine examples of these. Usually, three men and three horses would share one of these 'apartments' and there would be about nine apartments to each barrack. **Infantry barracks** were much simpler affairs, housing about five men to a room. At the end of each barrack were the living quarters of the *decurian*, the man in charge of the barrack. The fort at Arbeia has recreated a block of infantry barracks. Scattered amongst these buildings were others, such as the **public latrines**, of which Housesteads has a particularly fine example.

As with Segedunum, the whole fort would often lie on both sides of the Wall, with its northern end extending beyond the Wall's line into 'barbarian' territory. There would usually be more gates on the northern side than the southern side, too, to allow the soldiers to charge out quickly to meet their barbarian foes.

Other buildings associated with the fort would lie outside its walls, including religious buildings such as **temples** (witness the Mithraeum outside Brocolitia, for example), and **public baths** (the ruins at Chesters have a great example of these). A **civilian settlement**, or *vicus*, would often grow up around the Wall, too, peopled with retired soldiers from the fort, their children (who automatically became Roman citizens when their father did), wives (who *didn't*), traders and locals.

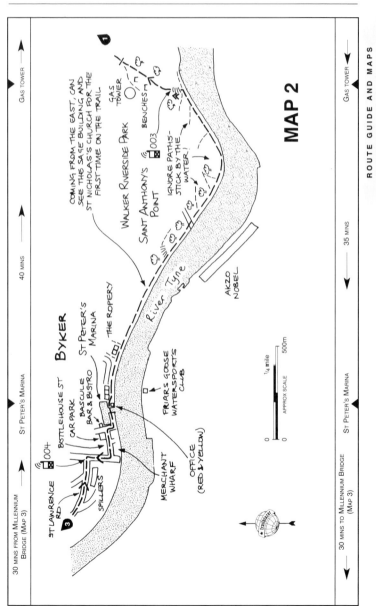

MAP 2

St Lawrence Rd

Byker

Bottlehouse St

Car Park

Bascule Bar & Bistro

St Peter's Marina

The Ropery

Spillers

Merchant Wharf

Office (Red & Yellow)

Friars Goose Watersports Club

Akzo Nobel

River Tyne

Saint Anthony's Point

Walker Riverside Park

Benches

Gas Tower

Coming from the east, can see the safe building and St Nicholas's church for the first time on the trail.

Ignore paths – stick by the water!

1/4 mile

500m

APPROX SCALE

30 mins from Millennium Bridge (Map 3) — St Peter's Marina — 40 mins — Gas Tower

30 mins to Millennium Bridge (Map 3) — St Peter's Marina — 35 mins — Gas Tower

From peaceful **St Anthony's Point** (Map 2), the path plots a westward course through the smart **St Peter's Marina** and on to the very heart of the city, past such modern Tyneside icons as BALTIC and the **Millennium Bridge** (Map 3) – the first of the city's seven bridges. (Incidentally, look out for seals swimming in the Tyne. I saw one just down from St Peter's Marina, while another trekker wrote to say that he watched one swimming by the bridge at Wylam!). To your right as you march through the town centre is the Castle Keep (see p93 and map p90), situated on the site of the Roman fort of Pons Aelius; note how, less than two hours into the walk, you've already encountered two of the Wall's 17 Roman forts! Though the milecastles and turrets were evenly spaced out along the Wall, the forts were not, being built instead at strategic points along it – in this case, to overlook one of the two Wall bridges to cross the Tyne. This bridge would have stood where the Swing Bridge now stands though, alas, nothing remains today.

After the seventh and final Tyne bridge, Redheugh, the trail continues, hugging the river through mile after mile of business parks and industrial estates. This is Armstrong country (see box p106) and his crest can be seen at various points along the trail.

The dominant architectural feature of this section, however, lies across the river on the south bank. These are the **Dunston Coal Staithes** (Map 4), which were used to load coal from the collieries onto the colliers – the ships that would transport the cargo south to London and elsewhere.

Negotiating a rather charmless section to cross the A695, you join yet another disused railway-turned-footpath, this one originally running between **Scotswood** (Map 5), Newburn and Wylam. Though located in the midst of a veritable spaghetti bolognaise of major traffic arteries, factory showrooms and noisy warehouses, the walk itself is pleasant enough, the worst industrial excesses hidden behind a screen of trees.

Crossing the A191 to **Denton Dene**, the trail continues to seek out the city's greener elements amidst the noisy urban sprawl, hopping from one green space to the next like a frog leaping from lilypad to lilypad. Rejoining the disused railway at the end of a cul-de-sac, Ottringham Close, the path finally takes on a more peaceful aspect, though with the suburbs of Lemington and Newburn just a few metres away, you're never far from either civilisation or traffic. Note the **Lemington Glass Cone** (Map 6) ahead and to the left of the trail, and no, your eyes aren't deceiving you: it *is* made of brick. This late 18th-century cone derives its name, of course, from its former purpose as a furnace for making glass. Almost opposite, the *café* (Mon-Fri 9am-3pm) in the Lemington Centre (☎ 0191-264 1959, 🖥 www.lemingtoncentre.co.uk) is a nice (and very cheap) little stop serving snacks and lunches.

Crossing the old toll road at **Newburn** you come to *The Boathouse* (☎ 0191-229 0326; food served Mon-Sat noon-6pm, Sun noon-4pm). Look on the wall for the flood markers; the height of the water in 1771 is particularly impressive. The old toll road also marks the unofficial limits of the city, at least as far as Wall walkers are concerned, as you finally leave the hullabaloo of

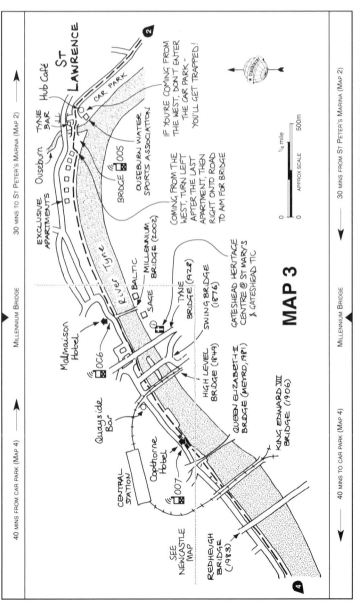

ST LAWRENCE

Hub Café

TYNE BAR

CAR PARK

Ouseburn

BRIDGE 005

OUSEBURN WATER SPORTS ASSOCIATION

EXCLUSIVE APARTMENTS

River Tyne

BALTIC

MILLENNIUM BRIDGE (2002)

SAGE

IF YOU'RE COMING FROM THE WEST, DON'T ENTER THE CAR PARK – YOU'LL GET TRAPPED!

COMING FROM THE WEST, TURN LEFT AFTER THE LAST APARTMENT, THEN RIGHT ONTO ROAD TO AIM FOR BRIDGE

TYNE BRIDGE (A2&)

SWING BRIDGE (1876)

GATESHEAD HERITAGE @ ST MARY'S & GATESHEAD TIC

MAP 3

Malmaison Hotel

OC6

Quayside Bar

Copthorne Hotel

007

CENTRAL STATION

SEE NEWCASTLE MAP

HIGH LEVEL BRIDGE (1849)

QUEEN ELIZABETH II BRIDGE (METRO, 1981)

KING EDWARD VII BRIDGE (1906)

REDHEUGH BRIDGE (1983)

30 MINS TO ST PETER'S MARINA (MAP 2)

MILLENNIUM BRIDGE

40 MINS FROM CAR PARK (MAP 4)

30 MINS FROM ST PETER'S MARINA (MAP 2)

MILLENNIUM BRIDGE

40 MINS TO CAR PARK (MAP 4)

0   ¼ mile
APPROX SCALE
0   500m

ROUTE GUIDE AND MAPS

Newcastle behind to enter the delightful **Tyne Riverside Country Park**. It's a lovely way to wind down at the end of the first stage, a pleasant and peaceful riparian stroll with dog-walkers, joggers, butterflies, swans and the first truly mature trees on the trail as company. There's also a **Visitor Centre**, and while its opening hours are limited (generally weekends and school holidays), it shares the building with toilets and sinks that have potable water.

ROUTE GUIDE AND MAPS

❑ **William Armstrong – the forgotten man of the Industrial Revolution**

However high we climb in the pursuit of knowledge we shall still see heights above us, and the more we extend our view, the more conscious we shall be of the immensity which lies beyond.   **William Armstrong**

Though something of a local hero, William Armstrong's star has faded when compared to the lustre of his near contemporary, George Stephenson (see box p110). Yet the impact of both men on the history of Newcastle, Britain, and the wider world was equally enormous.

Born in 1810 in Pleasant Row, in the Shieldfield area of Newcastle, William George Armstrong's first calling was as a solicitor, a vocation in which he showed enough talent and ambition to become a partner in a legal practice in the city. Yet throughout this time Armstrong's first love was not the law of man but the immutable laws of science and, in particular, engineering. Indeed, he used to give lectures at Newcastle's Lit and Phil Society on this very subject, and it wasn't long before he was turning his hand to constructing the machines he talked about. His first major project was a hydro-electric generator, which he unveiled to the world in 1842. Switching from hydro-electrics to hydraulics, just four years later Armstrong was persuading a number of wealthy local businessmen to back his plans to develop hydraulic cranes, which would be powered with the assistance of the Whittle Dene Water Company, a firm that he himself had helped to set up a few years previously. (You'll pass Whittledene Reservoir on the trail.) The result of all this endeavour was the Newcastle Cranage company, based at Elswick, which later became known as Armstrong's Factory – as mentioned in the song *Blaydon Races*. The manufacture of cranes became the cornerstone both of his industrial empire and of the Industrial Revolution itself; Isambard Kingdom Brunel was just one of his regular customers.

Yet Armstrong wasn't finished yet; with the advent of the Crimean War Armstrong became involved in the development of arms, manufacturing an 18lb breach-loading gun that was sold all over the world. Indeed, such was the popularity of his weapons that *both* sides in the American Civil War were armed with Armstrong's artillery! He also developed an interest in bridges, constructing Newcastle's Swing Bridge and much of London's Tower Bridge.

There were, of course, considerable financial benefits to his success. By 1850 over 300 men were employed in Armstrong's Elswick factory, bringing unprecedented prosperity to the area. (The modern incarnation of his company, Vickers, formerly Vickers Armstrong, still operates in the area and lies just off the path; see Map 4.) The country at large also benefited, with Armstrong gifting his patents to the British government, an ostensibly selfless act which was nevertheless rewarded with a knighthood. His success also enabled him to own most of Jesmond Dene, as well as a magnificent mansion at Cragside. But as was typical of the man, despite the riches, he continued to invent, even though he became less involved in the company that he founded. It maybe comes as no surprise, therefore, to find that Cragside has a place in history as the first house in the world to be lit by hydro-electric power.

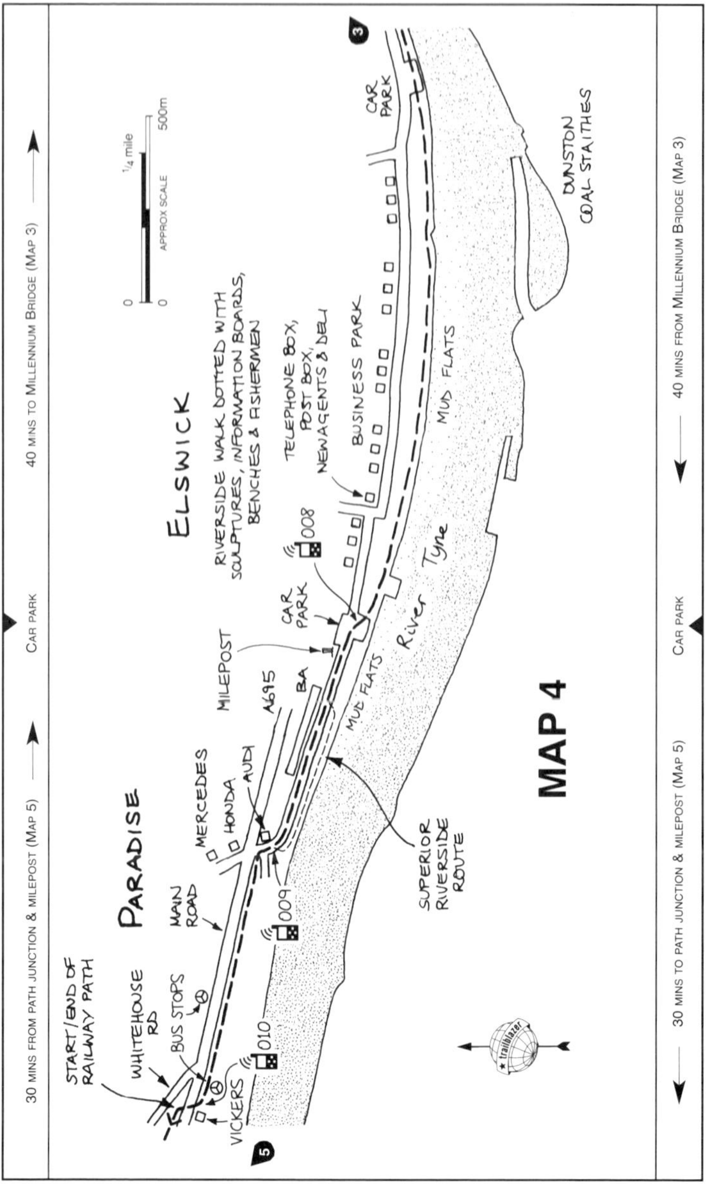

MAP 4

ELSWICK

PARADISE

RIVERSIDE WALK DOTTED WITH SCULPTURES, INFORMATION BOARDS, BENCHES & FISHERMEN

TELEPHONE BOX, POST BOX, NEWSAGENTS & DELI

BUSINESS PARK

River Tyne

MUD FLATS

DUNSTON COAL STAITHES

CAR PARK

CAR PARK

MILEPOST

A615

BA

SUPERIOR RIVERSIDE ROUTE

START/END OF RAILWAY PATH

WHITEHOUSE RD

MAIN ROAD

MERCEDES

HONDA

AUDI

BUS STOPS

VICKERS

008

009

010

¼ mile

500m

APPROX SCALE

30 MINS FROM PATH JUNCTION & MILEPOST (MAP 5)

40 MINS TO MILLENNIUM BRIDGE (MAP 3)

CAR PARK

30 MINS TO PATH JUNCTION & MILEPOST (MAP 5)

CAR PARK

40 MINS FROM MILLENNIUM BRIDGE (MAP 3)

trailblazer

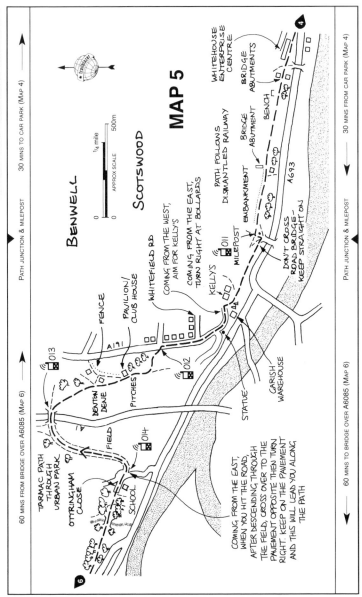

MAP 5

BENWELL

SCOTSWOOD

30 MINS TO CAR PARK (MAP 4)

PATH JUNCTION & MILEPOST

60 MINS FROM BRIDGE OVER A6085 (MAP 6)

WHITEHOUSE ENTERPRISE CENTRE

BRIDGE ABUTMENTS

PATH FOLLOWS DISMANTLED RAILWAY

BENCH

BRIDGE ABUTMENT

EMBANKMENT

A693

DON'T CROSS ROAD BRIDGE – KEEP STRAIGHT ON

COMING FROM THE EAST, TURN RIGHT AT BOLLARDS

COMING FROM THE WEST, AIM FOR KELLY'S

WHITEFIELD RD

PAVILION/ CLUB HOUSE

FENCE

A191

KELLY'S

MILEPOST

GARISH WAREHOUSE

STATUE

DENTON DENE

PITCHES

FIELD

TARMAC PATH THROUGH URBAN PARK

OTTRINGHAM CLOSE

SCHOOL

COMING FROM THE EAST, WHEN YOU HIT THE ROAD, AFTER DESCENDING THROUGH THE FIELD, CROSS OVER TO THE PAVEMENT OPPOSITE THEN TURN RIGHT. KEEP ON THE PAVEMENT AND THIS WILL LEAD YOU ALONG THE PATH

013

012

011

014

1/4 mile

0

500m

0

APPROX SCALE

30 MINS FROM CAR PARK (MAP 4)

PATH JUNCTION & MILEPOST

60 MINS TO BRIDGE OVER A6085 (MAP 6)

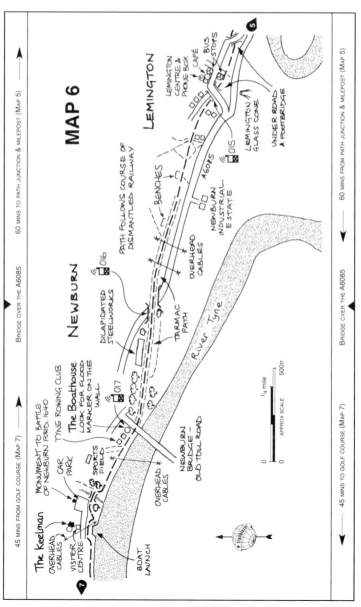

MAP 6

45 MINS FROM GOLF COURSE (MAP 7) ——→

The Keelman

OVERHEAD CABLES

VISITOR CENTRE

7

BOAT LAUNCH

MONUMENT TO BATTLE OF NEWBURN FORD, 1640

CAR PARK

SPORTS FIELD

The Boathouse
LOOK FOR FLOOD MARKER ON THE WALL

Tyne Rowing Club

017

NEWBURN BRIDGE – OLD TOLL ROAD

OVERHEAD CABLES

BRIDGE OVER THE A6085

NEWBURN

DILAPIDATED STEELWORKS

TARMAC PATH

016

River Tyne

60 MINS TO PATH JUNCTION & MILEPOST (MAP 5) ——→

PATH FOLLOWS COURSE OF DISMANTLED RAILWAY

BENCHES

OVERHEAD CABLES

NEWBURN INDUSTRIAL ESTATE

A6085

015

LEMINGTON

LEMINGTON CENTRE & PHONE BOX

CAFÉ

BUS STOPS

5

LEMINGTON GLASS CONE

UNDER ROAD & FOOTBRIDGE

60 MINS FROM PATH JUNCTION & MILEPOST (MAP 5)

APPROX SCALE

¼ mile

500m

0

0

45 MINS TO GOLF COURSE (MAP 7)

BRIDGE OVER THE A6085

trailblazer

Those who don't want this initial stage to end may like to consider calling in at **The Keelman** (Map 6; ☎ 0191-267 1689, 🖳 www.keelmanslodge.co.uk; 8D/6D, T or F, all en suite; 🛏; WI-FI in the pub), behind the Visitor Centre. It's one of the best pubs on (or rather, just off) the route, a vast place with real ales and its own micro-brewery, **Big Lamp**. They serve **food** (Sun-Fri noon-9pm, Sat to 9.30pm) and, in case the attractions of the beer already outweigh those of the walk, they charge £65.50 for two sharing (£49.50 sgl occ) plus breakfast

---

❏ George Stephenson and the Wylam Waggonway

Born (on 9 June 1781) and raised on the eastern fringes of Wylam, right by the old Wylam Waggonway, it was perhaps inevitable that George Stephenson – who must, as a child, have watched the progress of those early horse-drawn waggons passing his house – would somehow be drawn into the industry. Indeed, his very first job was working on the waggonway, where he was hired as a boy to keep a neighbour's herd of cows off the tram road.

Lacking formal education and unable to read or write, Stephenson joined his dad at Killingworth Colliery, though it wasn't long before his fascination for machinery, combined with a single-minded nature and fierce ambition, was leading him in new directions. In 1812 he became enginewright at the colliery and less than a year later Stephenson had persuaded his manager to let him try his hand at building a railway engine. The result was *Blucher*, a slow and clumsy beast (it was said to do no more than 4mph) which nevertheless became the first engine to avoid using cog-and-rack pinions – a breakthrough that thrust Stephenson to the very forefront of steam technology at the relatively tender age of 32.

Sixteen locomotives later and in 1819 Stephenson, his reputation for engine building now unmatched, was asked to construct an eight-mile line from Hetton to Sunderland. It was his – and the world's – first major steam railway project. It was also the task that convinced Stephenson that steam railways, if they were to have a future, needed to be constructed on as level a ground as possible; the hilly terrain that separated Hetton from Sunderland meant that his locomotive could not complete the journey without significant help from fixed hauling engines to help it negotiate the steeper parts, which slowed down the engine's progress considerably.

Further success followed; on 27 September 1825 – a date now known as the Birth of the Railways – his invention, *Locomotion*, carried 450 passengers at 15mph (24km/h) between Darlington and Stockton along his own railway line. Several years later, in 1829, an updated version of *Locomotion*, built with the help of his son Robert and called *Rocket*, won a competition to find the fastest locomotive when it travelled at an average speed of 36mph (58km/h) from Liverpool to Manchester, the line for which Stephenson had become chief engineer. It became his most celebrated achievement and firmly established his reputation as 'Father of the Railways'. With his new-found fortune Stephenson bought Tapton House, a grand Georgian manor near Chesterfield, where he kept busy opening coal mines, ironworks and limestone quarries in the nearby area. It was at Tapton that he died, on 12 August 1848, aged 67.

Today, it's possible to visit Stephenson's childhood home (☎ 01661-853457, 🖳 www.nationaltrust.org.uk/main/w-georgestephensonsbirthplace; mid-Mar to end Oct Thur-Sun 11am-5pm; £2; free for NT members) at Wylam, which is now owned by the National Trust. The white-stone cottage is a simple miner's affair that's been furnished to reflect the typical living arrangements of the late 18th century (when Stephenson was born), with everybody living in the one room.

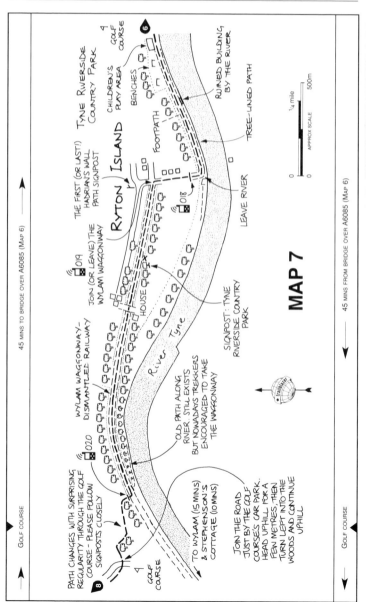

ROUTE GUIDE AND MAPS

45 MINS TO BRIDGE OVER A6085 (MAP 6)

GOLF COURSE

8 PATH CHANGES WITH SURPRISING REGULARITY THROUGH THE GOLF COURSE - PLEASE FOLLOW SIGNPOSTS CLOSELY

GOLF COURSE

WYLAM WAGGONWAY - DISMANTLED RAILWAY

020

TO WYLAM (15 MINS) & STEPHENSON'S COTTAGE (10 MINS)

OLD PATH ALONG RIVER STILL EXISTS BUT NOWADAYS TREKKERS ENCOURAGED TO TAKE THE WAGGONWAY

JOIN THE ROAD JUST BY THE GOLF COURSE'S CAR PARK. HEAD UPHILL FOR A FEW METRES, THEN TURN LEFT INTO THE WOODS AND CONTINUE UPHILL

River Tyne

SIGNPOST : TYNE RIVERSIDE COUNTRYSIDE PARK

MAP 7

019

JOIN (OR LEAVE) THE WYLAM WAGGONWAY

HOUSE

018

THE FIRST (OR LAST!) HADRIAN'S WALL PATH SIGNPOST

RYTON ISLAND

TYNE RIVERSIDE COUNTRY PARK

CHILDREN'S PLAY AREA

BENCHES

6

GOLF COURSE

FOOTPATH

LEAVE RIVER

TREE-LINED PATH

RUINED BUILDING BY THE RIVER

45 MINS FROM BRIDGE OVER A6085 (MAP 6)

0   ¼ mile
APPROX SCALE
0   500m

ROUTE GUIDE AND MAPS

(£7.95 full English, £4.95 continental). Breakfast is available from 7am for both residents and non-residents (from 8am on Sunday) but it must be booked in advance.

Otherwise, it's onwards and upwards, having forsaken the water's edge to join, briefly, the **Wylam Waggonway** (Map 7).

Thanks to the popularity of the trail, and the relative paucity of B&B options in Heddon-on-the-Wall, **Wylam**, 15-20 minutes along the Waggonway from the trail, is seeing an increasing number of trekkers looking for somewhere to stay on their first (or last) night.

WYLAM

Thankfully, there are a couple of decent accommodation options in the village, as well as a good place to eat.

There's also a **pharmacy**, a **post office**, a Spar **supermarket** (daily 6am-9pm) with an **ATM** and JA Stobo vegetable shop.

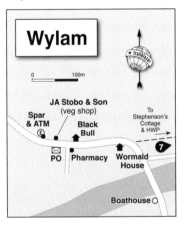

For **B&B** there's *Wormald House* (☎ 01661-852529, 🖳 www.wormaldhouse .co.uk; 2D/1T, all en suite; ●; ⓛ £5), the first place you come to as you reach the village from the trail. B&B costs £31-35. If prearranged they will pick you up at Heddon and drop you off the next morning.

Further up the hill, *Black Bull* (☎ 01661-853112, 🖳 www.blackbull-wylam.co.uk; 1S/3D/1D, T or F, all en suite; 🐾; WI-FI) has rooms starting from £25 for the single, £40 for two sharing and £60 for a family room. Note that they don't provide breakfast, nor do they accept debit/credit cards.

Finally, at the other end of town, just across the river, the *Boathouse* (☎ 01661-853431. 🖳 www.boathousewylam.info; Mon-Sat 11am-11pm, Sun noon-10.30pm; food served daily 11am-'late') is renowned for its award-winning cask ales (it regularly wins the CAMRA Northumberland Pub of the Year) with some good cheap fodder including local hand-made pies with mushy peas for £3.95.

Go North East's No X84 **bus** service calls here; see pp84-6 for further details.

It's a bit of an exhausting schlep to the top of the hill but **Heddon-on-the-Wall**, with its pubs, accommodation and, best of all, a great chunk of Hadrian's Wall on its outskirts, is a worthy reward at the end of a long but interesting first day.

HEDDON-ON-THE-WALL   [Map 8]

A fine place for a first night, Heddon-on-the-Wall lies at the culmination of a steep haul up from the River Tyne. As such, it marks the start of your Wall-walk proper (as opposed to the riverside meanderings you've enjoyed up to now) and, as if to emphasise that point, there's a **sizeable chunk of Wall** for you to savour, just a minute away from the path.

(cont'd on p114)

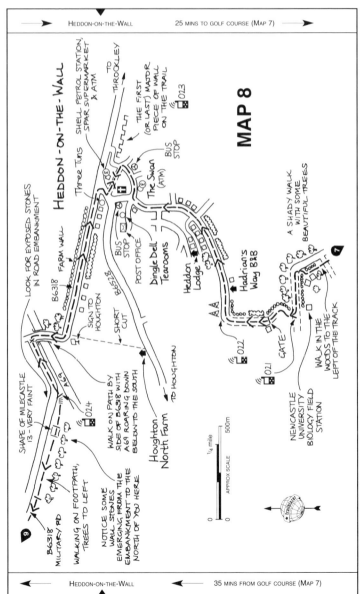

ROUTE GUIDE AND MAPS

HEDDON-ON-THE-WALL (*cont'd from p112*) You'll notice over the next few days that the Wall turns up in the unlikeliest of places, and it's no different here: lying parallel to the busy B6528, this portion is, at over 100m, the longest section of *broad* Wall remaining. As you'll see on the next stage, the Romans soon reduced their building ambitions, for although they still had the foundations for a broad Wall, west of here they built a narrow Wall on top of them. The flat circular platform that's incorporated into the Wall is a kiln that post-dates the Roman era.

As for Heddon itself, it's not a bad little place and is rather quaint in parts. It also has a few services for trekkers, including a **tearoom-cum-delicatessen**, the highly rated *Dingle Dell Tearooms* (Mon-Sat 9am-5pm), serving a range of local cheeses, meat, preserves and pickles; a **post office-cum-newsagent** (Mon-Sat 7am-6pm, Sun 7.15am-noon; post office Mon-Sat 7am-5.30pm) next door; a petrol station that doubles as a Spar **supermarket** (Mon-Sat 7am-9pm, Sun 8am-9pm); and **cashpoints** (one in the Spar and one in The Swan, both of which charge).

Heddon also has a couple of **pubs**. Of these, the *Three Tuns* (☎ 01661-852172, 🖥 www.thethreetunsheddon.co.uk; daily noon-11pm), on the B6528, is a great old

place, and where the spirit of the village now resides. It serves simple but tasty and very cheap pub grub (Mon-Sat noon-8pm, Sun noon-4pm) with most dishes less than £6. The preferred option of most trekkers is *The Swan* (☎ 01661-853161; food served daily noon-9.30pm; WI-FI), with some huge meals served at their contemporary carvery (£5.95 Mon-Sat, £9.45 on Sun/Bank Hols). They also do more standard pub fare as well as sandwiches. No dogs allowed inside.

For accommodation, before you even reach the village there's *Hadrian Way* (☎ 01661-853175, 🖥 www.hadrianway.co.uk; 1T or F en suite/1D or F/1D, 🛏; 🐾), with good views down the valley and rates £50-70 for two sharing, £25 for one person in the smaller double which is in the loft. *Heddon Lodge* (☎ 01661-854042 or ☎ 07802-660485; 🖥 www.heddonlodge.co.uk; 2D en suite/1D with private bathroom; 🛏; 🐾 £10; WI-FI), at 38 Heddon Banks, has some splendid accommodation surpassed only by the fantastic breakfasts, with ingredients sourced locally and organic where possible; rates are £42.50.

Though on the surface the layout of *Houghton North Farm* (☎ 01661-854364, 🖥 www.hadrianswallaccommodation.com; 22 beds in 6 rooms, 2 en suite; WI-FI) may resemble a hostel this really is a cut above

---

❑ **Milecastle numbers**

The **milecastles** built along the Wall have each been assigned their own unique figure – whether the milecastles can be seen today or not. The order runs from east to west, so the first milecastle on the Wall (which would have been near Segedunum in Newcastle) is called Milecastle 1, and so on up to Milecastle 80 at Bowness-on-Solway.

In addition to this designation, some of the more famous have been given their own name, such as the Grindon Milecastle (aka Milecastle 34). The Wall's **turrets** also have their own special number, each derived from the milecastle immediately to their west, with the turret closest to that milecastle given the letter A, and the next one to the west labelled B. So, for example, the turret immediately to the west of Milecastle 38 is known as Turret 38A, the next one to the west Turret 38B.

Note, by the way, that a number of these milecastles were destroyed soon after they were built: when it was decided to move the forts up to the Wall from the Stanegate (see p49), many were built on top of old milecastles or turrets. Cilurnum (Chesters) Fort, for example, was built on Turret 27A and remains of it can still be seen.

your average hostel or bunkhouse. There are six rooms: one sleeps two (2 beds) and three rooms sleep four (2 bunk beds); of the two en suite rooms one sleeps three (single bed and bunk bed); the other sleeps five (bunk above a double bed and a separate bunk bed). There's also a kitchen and dining area, free internet access, TV lounge and power shower to die for, as well as high standards of comfort and cleanliness. Rates

are £25-40pp but this does include a buffet-style continental breakfast. Furthermore, in spring, if you ask nicely, they may let you feed their pet lambs in the morning.

There are several **buses** between Heddon and either Newcastle or Hexham, including Arriva's/Stagecoach's No 685 & 85 services and Go North East's X84 & X85 services; see pp46-8 for further information.

HEDDON-ON-THE-WALL TO CHOLLERFORD [MAPS 8-16]
Introduction

Anyone glancing at the maps for this **15-mile (24km; 6¾-7hrs)** stage will find their heart sinking and probably conclude that this is a walk to be endured, not enjoyed. Why? Because most of the trail on this stage is owned by Northumberland Highway Department and throughout much of its length this walk is accompanied by one of its most important charges, the thundering B6318. Indeed, based on what the map is telling you, some of you may even decide to take the Corbridge–Hexham–Acomb deviation instead (see pp131-43), and rejoin the official trail again towards the end of the stage at Heavenfield. This deviation is even more attractive on a Monday, when a couple of eating places on the official trail are closed and the only places to get food are The Robin Hood Pub and Vallum Café, which lie opposite each other. But to put it succinctly, it would be wrong to do so, because this stage is packed with interest. For one thing, though the road is a constant companion, for most of this stage you'll be trekking slightly away from it in fields alive with livestock and other, wilder creatures of the British countryside such as hares, rabbits and a superb variety of birdlife including crows, lapwings, finches, swallows and, on the waters of Whittledene Reservoir, the great-crested grebe, tufted duck and dunlin. Indeed, there's even a birdhouse on one of the signposts by the reservoir (uninhabited, last time I looked).

Furthermore, permanent presence though it may be, the road is rarely an obtrusive one. (That said, sometimes you'll need to cross or at the very least walk alongside this very straight – and thus very fast – road, and outside the Robin Hood there's a memorial to a trekker who was hit by a vehicle on this stage, so you do need to exercise due caution throughout.) Bear in mind that the reason the trail follows the highway in the first place is because it is built right *upon* the Wall: the B6318 is merely the modern and more mundane moniker for the **Military Road**, built on top of the Wall on General Wade's orders in the 18th century to facilitate the rapid movement of his troops across the country in order to ward off incursions by Bonnie Prince Charlie and his followers. And though the Wall itself may not make much of an appearance until after St Oswald's (see p124), this allows its accompanying defences – the Vallum and, on the Wall's (and thus the road's) northern side, the Roman ditch – a chance to

ROUTE GUIDE AND MAPS

bask in the spotlight for a change; and it will be these, and the expansive views beyond, that will be occupying your attention today.

So, by all means, take the Corbridge–Hexham alternative if you prefer – it's a cracking walk – but not if your only reason for doing so is because you believe the official trail to be a bit duff. It's not. And my advice to those who are hoping to take the detour would be to take it and *then* come and do the proper trail. While those noble foot soldiers who intend to follow the official Hadrian's Wall Path faithfully should gird their loins and prepare themselves for an eventful march; just watch out for the chariots!

The route

The day begins as it means to continue: on the B6318 which starts behind the Three Tuns. It's not long before the first evidence of the Wall appears: as you enter a field following a diversion to cross the A69, stones from the Roman Wall lie where they emerged from the road embankment. Those with eagle eyes may be able to make out the platform outline of Milecastle 13, though it's extremely faint and you shouldn't worry if you can't make it out; there are plenty of better examples of milecastles to come.

More impressive tumescences appear just a few hundred metres further on in the next field. These are the subterranean remains of **Rudchester Fort** (aka Vindobala Fort; Map 9), once heavily pillaged by local farmers and the builders of the Military Road in the 18th century but now lying undisturbed beneath the soil of Rudchester Farm. Now owned by the local county council, there are hopes that this 4^1/$_2$-acre (1.8-hectare) fort will be re-excavated (it was last explored thoroughly in the 1930s) and developed properly one day – though what exactly is left after all these depredations remains to be seen.

The next few miles provide scant evidence that you are following a Wall, though other Roman constructions are evident. **B&B** is available at *Ironsign* (☎ 01661-853802, 🖳 www.ironsignfarm.co.uk; 3T, all en suite; 🛏; WI-FI; ⓁL; Mar-Oct) which charges £70 (sgl occ £50); if booked in advance they also do evening meals (£17.50 for three courses, made with ingredients sourced from the farm itself).

A little beyond Ironsign you cross the road to walk in the **Roman ditch**, the fortification that lay to the north of the Wall. This you follow almost all the way up to **Harlow Hill** (Map 10), a tiny, lonely little settlement whose most noticeable feature is its old church, now converted into a farmyard barn. There's a long-established **campsite**, *Belvedere* (☎ 01661-853869) with camping for £5 per person. The bacon sandwiches here have been described by more than one reader as excellent. A few yards up the hill, many of the buildings in the hamlet have been converted into the *Harlow Hill MXVI* (🖳 harlowhill-mxvi.co.uk). This describes itself as a unique holiday accommodation and leisure complex,

---

❏ **Walk side by side and on healthy grass** Don't walk in single file or on worn areas. Protect our heritage!

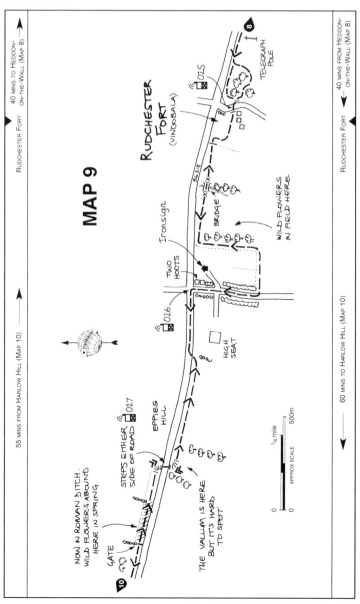

MAP 9

RUDCHESTER FORT (VINDOBALA)

B6318

Ironsign

TWO HOOTS

HIGH SEAT

EPPIES HILL

STEPS EITHER SIDE OF ROAD

GATE

NOW IN ROMAN DITCH. WILD FLOWERS ABOUND HERE IN SPRING

THE VALLUM IS HERE BUT IT'S HARD TO SPOT

WILD FLOWERS IN FIELD HERE

BRIDGE

TELEGRAPH POLE

trailblazer

¼ mile

500m

0

0

APPROX SCALE

though as you have to stay for a minimum of three days it's doubtful this is of much interest to the average trekker. A 'bistro-coffee shop' is planned on the site, however, so if it's open to the public it may be of interest to weary walkers in the future. The unusual name, by the way, refers to the fact that this was once the site of **Milecastle 16** (see box p114 for milecastles).

From here the trail continues in the ditch down to **Whittledene Reservoir**'s Great Northern Lake. With the Welton Burn feeding this reservoir and the Whittle Dene Aqueduct from Hollington Reservoir flowing into the Great Southern Lake at the southern end, this series of lakes rarely freezes over even in the depths of winter, and as such attracts birdlife year-round. Indeed, over

❑ Operation Nightingale

Walk past the entrance to the road leading to Albermarle Barracks in 2013 and you would have come across around a dozen men and women earnestly digging a large ditch parallel to the roadside. This, it turned out, was the latest manifestation of **Operation Nightingale**, a project founded in 2012 to help rehabilitate soldiers who had been injured during the conflict in Afghanistan by getting them to work at various archaeological sites around the country. The benefits are manifold: for one thing, the country's various archaeological digs benefit from the manual labour of some very fit and disciplined workers. Furthermore, many of the skills acquired by soldiers during their time in the army are of fundamental use in the field of archeology too, including surveying, geophysics, mapping and navigation. As for the soldiers themselves, the idea is that they benefit both by acquiring new skills (or adapting their existing ones to a non-military environment) and from the restorative effects of working as a team in some of the lovelier parts of Britain.

Perhaps surprisingly, the link between the British army and archaeology is not new at all, with some of the founding fathers of modern archaeology coming from the military including Lt-General Pitt Rivers, Brigadier Mortimer Wheeler, Col TE Lawrence (better known to you and me as Lawrence of Arabia) and OGS Crawford to name but four. The projects that Operation Nightingale have so far got involved with include the excavation of a 6th-century Anglo-Saxon cemetery on Salisbury Plain, during which a spear, shield, gold leaf brooches and beads (as well as 18 skeletons) were uncovered; and the excavation of a Roman villa/shrine and hypocaust in South Wales. As for the dig near Albermarle Barracks, the archaeologist overseeing the work, Nick Hodgson, who is based at Newcastle's Arbeia Fort, explained that they were interested in particular in an area of the Roman barrier known as the **Berm** – the flat bit of land between the defensive ditch and the Wall itself (the line of the Wall at that point, of course, being under the road). Nothing of particular interest has yet been uncovered according to the latest reports, though the team were hopeful that permission would be given for digs at other sites along the Wall; and with only an estimated 5% of the Wall thus far excavated and studied in detail, there are certainly plenty of possible locations for Operation Nightingale to continue its vital work.

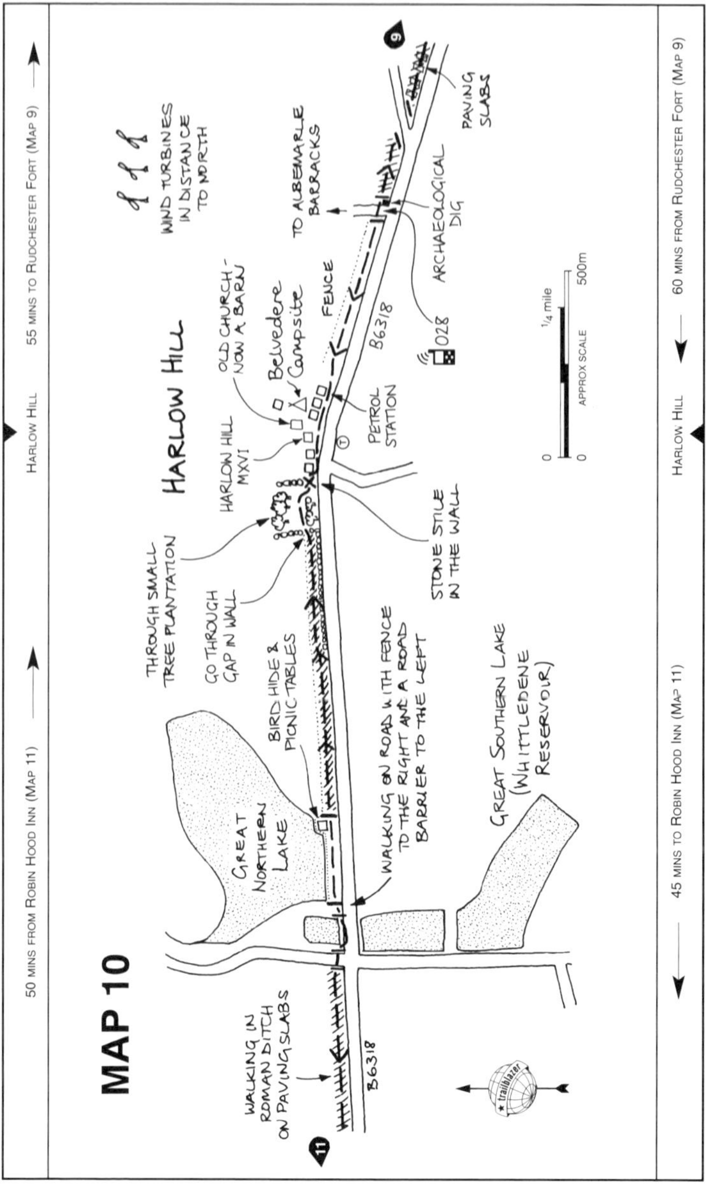

MAP 10

50 MINS FROM ROBIN HOOD INN (MAP 11)

HARLOW HILL

55 MINS TO RUDCHESTER FORT (MAP 9)

WIND TURBINES IN DISTANCE TO NORTH

HARLOW HILL

OLD CHURCH - NOW A BARN

HARLOW HILL MXVI

Belvedere Campsite

TO ALBEMARLE BARRACKS

PAVING SLABS

9

FENCE

ARCHAEOLOGICAL DIG

028

PETROL STATION

B6318

THROUGH SMALL TREE PLANTATION

GO THROUGH GAP IN WALL

BIRD HIDE & PICNIC TABLES

STONE STILE IN THE WALL

GREAT NORTHERN LAKE

WALKING ON ROAD WITH FENCE TO THE RIGHT AND A ROAD BARRIER TO THE LEFT

GREAT SOUTHERN LAKE (WHITTLEDENE RESERVOIR)

WALKING IN ROMAN DITCH ON PAVING SLABS

B6318

11

0   APPROX SCALE   500m

0   ¼ mile

45 MINS TO ROBIN HOOD INN (MAP 11)

HARLOW HILL

60 MINS FROM RUDCHESTER FORT (MAP 9)

ROUTE GUIDE AND MAPS

190 species of birds, as well as red squirrels and deer, have been spotted on or near the lakes. This gigantic series of reservoirs is more than just a nature reserve, however, for the reservoir pumps 25 million gallons of water a day to the treatment works. With picnic tables, a hide that could provide invaluable shelter from the rain, and views opening up north and south, it's a highly disciplined individual who resists taking a break here. After the reservoir, the path keeps to the north of the road until Robin Hood Inn (see below).

EAST WALLHOUSES (& AROUND)
[Map 11]

Exactly a mile to the north, and signposted off the trail, is **Matfen High House Farm** (☎ 01661-886192, 🖳 www.highhouse brewery.co.uk), part **tearoom/restaurant** (Sun-Tue 10.30am-5pm, Thur-Sat 10.30am-9pm), part farm and part **brewery**. You can find out exactly how beer is made on a tour (by appointment; £5pp) of the brewery, sample some at the Real Ale Bar, then buy a barrel or two of the product to take along the trail with you. 61), the man who, after Hadrian himself, is most associated with the Wall, was one of the previous owners of the farm. Across the yard, **Matfen High House B&B** (☎ 01661-886592, 🖳 www.matfen highhouse.co.uk; 1D/1T en suite, 1D/1T shared bathroom; 🛁; 🐾; WI-FI; Ⓛ from £4.50) dates back to 1735 and is said to serve 'fantastic' breakfasts. Rates are £30-40pp. They don't do evening meals, but do offer lifts to the Robin Hood Inn when the restaurant at Matfen High House Farm is closed.

There is also **Wellhouse Farm** (☎ 01661-842193, 🖳 www.wellhousefarm .uk; £6pp; 🐾) **campsite**, with 45 pitches, a toilet and shower block, a coin-operated washing machine and dryer, a mile to the south of the trail. It can be reached by continuing along the B6318 (while the path turns right into fields by East Wallhouses) then take the first left (see Map 11).

Robin Hood Inn (☎ 01434-672273, 🖳 www.robinhoodinn-militaryroad.co.uk), a pub dating back to 1752, is a favourite stop for trekkers with some hearty **food** (served Mon-Sat noon-9pm, Sun noon-6pm) and a **passport stamping point** (see box p38). **Campers** can pitch a tent at the back for £5 as long as they eat in the pub. However, there aren't any facilities. They also operate a **B&B** (1T/2D or F, 🛁; 🐾 £5; Ⓛ £5) with simple rooms sharing a bathroom for £30 per person (£45 sgl occ).

As an alternative to the pub, just a few minutes down the road is **Vallum Farm Tearoom** (☎ 01434-672652, 🖳 www.val lumfarm.co.uk; daily 10am-4.30pm), a licensed café with a great selection of cakes. As for the food, I can personally recommend the scones, and it can only be a matter of time before hymns are being written and sung in praise of their lemon drizzle cake. On a hot day their **ice-cream parlour** (daily 10am-5pm) could be just the ticket, as could a jug of Pimms (£6). Incidentally, the name is well chosen, for you can see the unmistakable undulations of the Vallum in front of the farmhouse. Across the courtyard is **David Kennedy @ Vallum** (☎ 01434-672406, 🖳 www.vallumfarm.co.uk; Mon-Sat 10am-5pm, Sun 11am-5pm); a very smart deli though one that's fairly priced – and the cheese and wholegrain mustard scones for only 95p are a steal!

Having passed the Robin Hood Inn (note that on a Monday this is the last place serving food before you reach Chollerford), tiptoe through the free-range chickens in the next field and soon after go round the Wallhouses diversion. The trail now travels alongside miles of farmland before eventually arriving at a row of pretty cottages lining the busy road, known as **Halton Shields** (Map 12). Turning left off the road at the end of the hamlet, you come to the next major

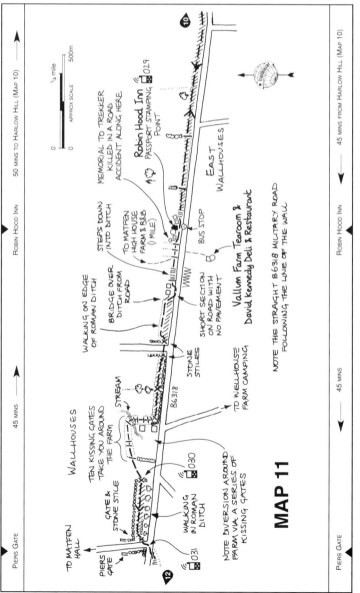

PIERS GATE ◀ 45 MINS ━━▶ ROBIN HOOD INN ◀ 50 MINS TO HARLOW HILL (Map 10) ━━▶

50 MINS TO HARLOW HILL (Map 10)

¼ mile
0 ━━━ 500m
0 APPROX SCALE

MEMORIAL TO TREKKER KILLED IN A ROAD ACCIDENT ALONG HERE

Robin Hood Inn 🏠🍴 029
PASSPORT STAMPING POINT

EAST WALLHOUSES

STEPS DOWN INTO DITCH

TO MATFEN HIGH HOUSE FARM & B&B (¼ MILE)

WALKING ON EDGE OF ROMAN DITCH

BRIDGE OVER DITCH FROM ROAD

BUS STOP

Vallum Farm Tearoom & David Kennedy Deli & Restaurant

SHORT SECTION ON ROAD WITH NO PAVEMENT

WALLHOUSES

TEN KISSING GATES TAKE YOU AROUND THE FARM

STREAM

STONE STILES

B6318

TO WELLHOUSE FARM CAMPING

NOTE THE STRAIGHT B6318 MILITARY ROAD FOLLOWING THE LINE OF THE WALL

GATE & STONE STILE

TO MATFEN HALL

PIERS GATE

031

030

WALKING IN ROMAN DITCH

NOTE DIVERSION AROUND FARM VIA A SERIES OF KISSING GATES

MAP 11

PIERS GATE ◀ 45 MINS ━━▶ ROBIN HOOD INN ◀ 45 MINS FROM HARLOW HILL (Map 10) ━━▶

ROUTE GUIDE AND MAPS

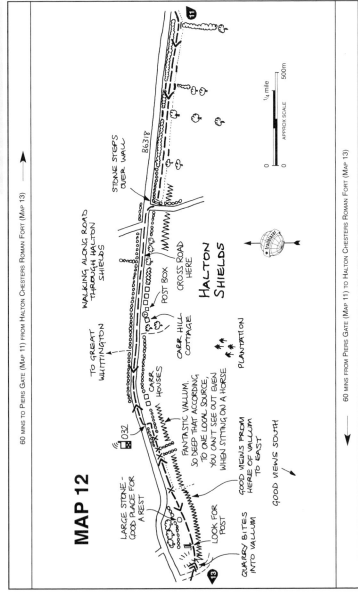

MAP 12

60 MINS TO PIERS GATE (MAP 11) FROM HALTON CHESTERS ROMAN FORT (MAP 13)

60 MINS FROM PIERS GATE (MAP 11) TO HALTON CHESTERS ROMAN FORT (MAP 13)

LARGE STONE – GOOD PLACE FOR A REST

LOOK FOR POST

QUARRY BITES INTO VALLUM

GOOD VIEWS SOUTH

GOOD VIEWS FROM HERE OF VALLUM TO EAST

FANTASTIC VALLUM, SO DEEP THAT ACCORDING TO ONE LOCAL SOURCE, YOU CAN'T SEE OUT EVEN WHEN SITTING ON A HORSE

CARR HOUSES

032

TO GREAT WHITTINGTON

WALKING ALONG ROAD THROUGH HALTON SHIELDS

STONE STEPS OVER WALL

B6318

PLANTATION

CARR HILL COTTAGE

POST BOX

CROSS ROAD HERE

HALTON SHIELDS

1/4 mile
500m
APPROX SCALE
0
0

ROUTE GUIDE AND MAPS

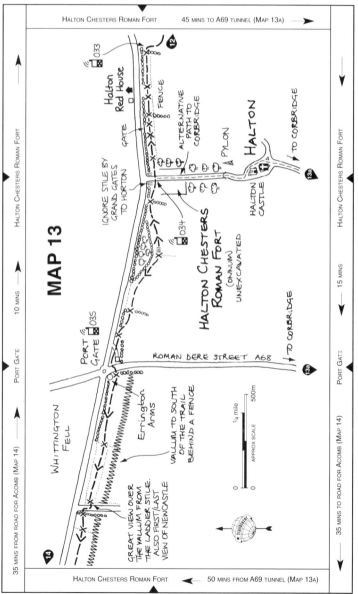

MAP 13

HALTON CHESTERS ROMAN FORT   45 MINS TO A69 TUNNEL (MAP 13A) →

12

🏠 033

Halton Red House

FENCE

GATE

IGNORE STILE BY GRAND GATES TO HORTON

ALTERNATIVE PATH TO CORBRIDGE

A PYLON

HALTON

TO CORBRIDGE

13B

HALTON CASTLE

🏠 034

HALTON CHESTERS ROMAN FORT (ONNUM) UNEXCAVATED

TO CORBRIDGE

PORT GATE

🏠 035

ROMAN DERE STREET A68

13B

WHITTINGTON FELL

Errington Arms

VALLUM TO SOUTH OF THE TRAIL BEHIND A FENCE

GREAT VIEW OVER THE VALLUM FROM THE LADDER STILE. ALSO FIRST/LAST VIEW OF NEWCASTLE

14

¼ mile   500m
APPROX SCALE
0   0

trailblazer

HALTON CHESTERS ROMAN FORT   ← 50 MINS FROM A69 TUNNEL (MAP 13A)

35 MINS FROM ROAD FOR ACOMB (MAP 14) →   PORT GATE   ← 10 MINS →   HALTON CHESTERS ROMAN FORT

HALTON CHESTERS ROMAN FORT   15 MINS   PORT GATE   35 MINS TO ROAD FOR ACOMB (MAP 14)

Roman remain on your walk: the large, soft, curvaceous undulations of the **Vallum** as it burrows its way through the fields south of the trail. The Vallum quickly disappears again, lost beneath the corrugations caused by medieval ploughing and the depredations of an old quarry. The Wall makes an appearance, however, in the fabric of *Halton Red House* (Map 13; ☎ 01434 672209, 🖥 www.haltonredhousefarm.com; 1D/1T, en suite; 🍷; WI-FI), constructed at least in part from Wall stones (£70-75 per room, £50 sgl occ). A little further on, more incongruous grassy bumps beckon by the monumental gates of Halton Castle. These mounds in the field are the remains of **Halton Chesters** (also known as Onnum; Map 13), the second unexcavated Roman fort on this stage. As with Vindobala, there's little to get too excited about with everything covered by a layer of turf and the undulations, other than the outline of the fort itself, difficult to distinguish from other, later, bumps.

Those wishing to take the Corbridge–Hexham–Acomb diversion (see pp131-43) or who are staying in Corbridge overnight should head south from here.

Continuing west, it's not long before the road and trail join forces for the final push up to **Port Gate** (Map 13, see p123; also spelt Portgate). A modern traffic roundabout at the junction of the A68 and the Military Road, this may not seem the most auspicious place to find evidence of Roman occupation. But the A68 to Corbridge was once the old Roman **Dere Street** that ran between the fort (and indeed further on down to York) all the way north to Scotland; and as such, the Port Gate was one of the few gateways the Romans built into the Wall. When the roundabout was built in the '60s it was deliberately moved a little way to the north so as not to disturb the unexcavated archaeological remains around here.

Reaching the roundabout, a pause at the *Errington Arms* (Map 13; ☎ 01434-672250, 🖥 www.erringtonarms.co.uk; pub closed Sun eves and all-day Mon except bank hols; **food** served Tue-Sat noon-2.30pm & 6.30-9pm, Sun noon-4pm; WI-FI), named after an important local family, is scribbled into the itineraries of most trekkers and with good reason; the food here is great, with an extensive menu of dishes including plenty of sandwich options (from £3.95). For evenings, try their delicious moussaka (£9.50). Note the pub's opening hours are often reduced significantly in the winter.

Fully refreshed, head off from behind the Errington Arms through the field, with the **Vallum** a constant and clearly defined companion to your left, before another bout of **Roman ditch** walking follows as you cross the road by the outline of **Milecastle 24** (Map 14).

Through fields and woods the trail continues to **St Oswald's Hill Head** (Map 15), with its lovely little church (see box p126) set in a meadow to the north of the trail and a delightful little **tearoom**, *St Oswald's* (☎ 01434-689010; May-Oct Tue-Sun & bank hols 10am-4.30pm, Mar-April & Nov Fri, Sat & Sun only) just before **Heavenfield**.

Those staying in Acomb or Hexham may wish to turn left south off the trail by the large cross in the corner of Heavenfield to join the route of the Corbridge–Hexham–Acomb diversion (see pp131-43); this is also where those who took the diversion rejoin the path.

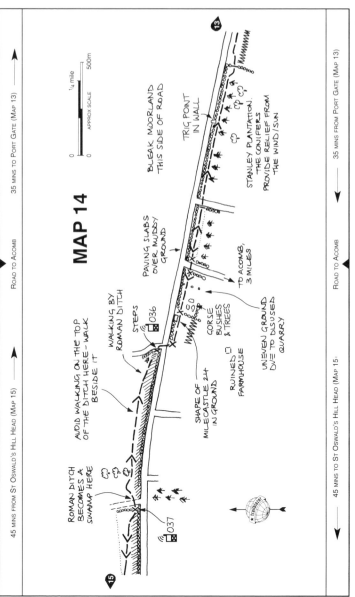

MAP 14

45 MINS FROM ST OSWALD'S HILL HEAD (MAP 15)

ROAD TO ACOMB

35 MINS TO PORT GATE (MAP 13)

ROMAN DITCH BECOMES A SWAMP HERE

AVOID WALKING ON THE TOP OF THE DITCH HERE – WALK BESIDE IT

WALKING BY ROMAN DITCH

STEPS

036

SHAPE OF MILECASTLE 24 IN GROUND

RUINED FARMHOUSE

037

PAVING SLABS OVER MUDDY GROUND

BLEAK MOORLAND THIS SIDE OF ROAD

TRIG POINT IN WALL

STANLEY PLANTATION. THE CONIFERS PROVIDE RELIEF FROM THE WIND/SUN

TO ACOMB, 3 MILES

GORSE BUSHES & TREES

UNEVEN GROUND DUE TO DISUSED QUARRY

0   ¼ mile

0   500m

APPROX SCALE

15

13

❏ **St Oswald's church**
This was built to commemorate the victory of the eponymous saint over his rivals
Cadwallon and Penda at the **Battle of Heavenfield**, the field in which you're now
standing. In the 7th century St Oswald, who was merely a king at this stage, was the
leader of the Angles following the death of Edwin (after whom Edinburgh is named)
in AD633. His defeat of the combined forces of Gwynedd and Mercia, though not
quite the victory of Christianity over paganism that the Venerable Bede portrays in
his *History*, was nevertheless a significant victory for the Anglo-Saxons over the
Celts and, as such, an important moment in English history. Incidentally, at the back
of the church by the font there's a large **Roman altar**.

The church is also the official end (or start) of **St Oswald's Way** (💻
www.stoswaldsway.com) which covers 97 miles of beautiful Northumberland countryside and coastline between here and Lindisfarne, linking some of the places associated with St Oswald.

The rest of you should continue through the fields and across the road down
to **Planetrees**, the first proper bit of Wall on this entire stage. Its existence is
largely due to the efforts of William Hutton, who came across some workmen
taking stones from the Wall to be used as raw materials for a new farmhouse.
Hutton's entreaties to the local landowner responsible for the desecration,
Henry Tulip, ensured that this small fragment survived; though 224 yards
(204m) of the Wall did not, having already been pulled down by Tulip's men
before Hutton arrived. However, the portion that has survived is interesting:
notice how, near the culvert built into the Wall to prevent water from collecting
and weakening the foundations, the Wall changes from being a *broad* Wall on
broad foundations, as we saw at Heddon, to a *narrow* Wall on broad foundations. A similar pattern can be seen at Brunton Turret (see below), just a little
further on, and suggests that it was around here that the Romans gave up building an all-broad Wall and opted instead for a narrower version that nevertheless
still made use of the original broad foundations. But before we get to Brunton
Turret there's a rather dull stretch of road-walking that veers towards, and then
away from, the village of Wall.

WALL   **[Map 16, p129]**
Quite a large place, it's typical of the rather
perverse nature of this trail in that Wall village doesn't actually lie on the Wall. The
village is perhaps of most interest to
trekkers because of a decision by the local
parish council to allow a night's **camping**
on the village green free of charge as long
as you don't stay for more than 24 hours
and leave the place exactly as you found it.
There are toilets nearby but no other facilities, nor indeed is there a shop in town. But
there is a very good pub-cum-B&B at the
southern end of town, about ten minutes

from the trail: *The Hadrian Hotel* (☎
01434-681232, 💻 www.hadrianhotel.co.uk;
2D/2T both en suite/2T shared bathroom;
🍺; 🐾; WI-FI) is an 18th-century coaching
inn that offers **food** (summer daily noon-
8.30pm, winter noon-3pm & 6-8.30pm) and
has some very comfortable **rooms**, including
a few with a four-poster bed. B&B costs
£50-60 for single occupancy, £78-85 per
double.

Tyne Valley's No 880 **bus** service
stops here; see pp46-8.

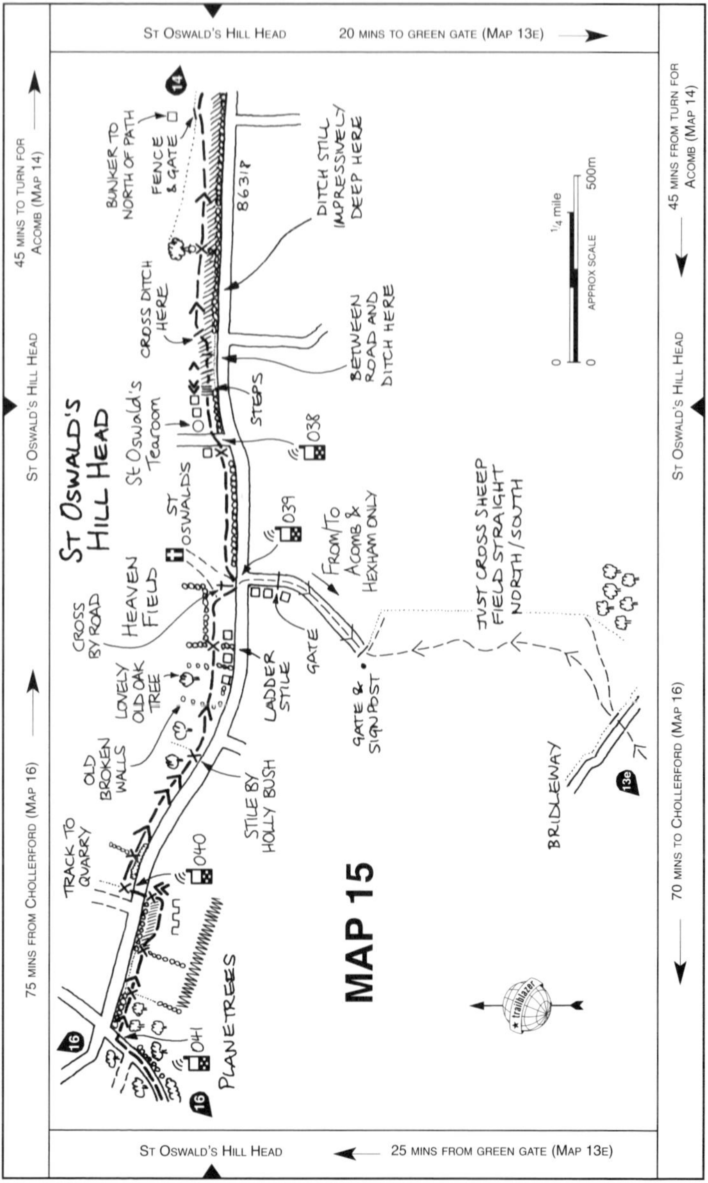

St Oswald's Hill Head   20 mins to green gate (Map 13e) →

45 mins to turn for Acomb (Map 14) →

45 mins from turn for Acomb (Map 14)

St Oswald's Hill Head

14

Bunker to north of path

Fence & Gate

863.1?

Ditch still impressively deep here

Cross ditch here

St Oswald's Tearoom

Steps

Between road and ditch here

St Oswald's Hill Head

038

039

St Oswald's Hill Head

St Oswald's

From/To Acomb & Hexham only

Cross by road

Heaven Field

Lonely Old Oak Tree

Old Broken Walls

Gate

Ladder Stile

Just cross sheep field straight north/south

Gate & Signpost

Stile by Holly Bush

Track to Quarry

040

MAP 15

16

OH

Planetrees

16

Bridleway

13e

75 mins from Chollerford (Map 16)

70 mins to Chollerford (Map 16)

¼ mile

APPROX SCALE

0   0   500m

trailblazer

St Oswald's Hill Head   ← 25 mins from green gate (Map 13e)

ROUTE GUIDE AND MAPS

> ❏ **Important note – walking times**
> Unless otherwise specified, **all times in this book refer only to the time spent walking**. You will need to add 20-30% to allow for rests, photography, checking the map, drinking water etc. When planning the day's hike count on 5-7 hours' actual walking.

Instead of turning left at the junction to Wall, if you keep on the path ie turn right you'll soon come upon **Brunton Turret** (officially Turret 26B), sitting in a field to the right of the road. Said to be the finest turret extant on the Wall – up to eleven courses high in places – it was excavated, surprise surprise, by John Clayton in 1876. Note how the Wall is of different widths here, going into the turret at one width and coming out the other side at a narrower gauge. As we've already seen at Planetrees, this kind of chopping and changing with the width of the Wall continues for several miles, though nobody's really sure why. Possibly it was for economic reasons, or maybe it was because the limestone core they used west of here was stronger than the puddled clay used in the eastern section of the Wall, and thus the Romans decided a thinner Wall would suffice.

Continuing along the road, before visiting the fort or collapsing in your temporary abode at Chollerford, those with the necessary curiosity and gumption may want to check out the remains of the Roman bridge abutment on the southern side of the river facing Chesters Fort. It's just over half a mile (1km)

off the trail but it's a pleasant walk and you'll be rewarded with a big fat **phallus** at the end of it that would make your auntie blush; I'm no expert in these matters but in my opinion, given the quality of the carving, the detail and the sheer size, it's the most impressive example of this Roman symbol of prosperity on the entire trail. The symbol is carved into one of the stones on the abutment's eastern side, just above ground level. Two other piers in the water were also discovered but are visible now only when the water is low. Incidentally, this was the third Roman bridge over the Tyne, the first, of course, being Pons Aelius in Newcastle and the second at Corbridge.

CHOLLERFORD (& HUMSHAUGH)
[Map 16]

There's nothing wrong with Chollerford, though to most trekkers it's a bit of a non-event: having crossed the sturdy 18th-century five-arch bridge, the trail turns immediately left and continues along the road to Chesters, all but bypassing Chollerford and its neighbour, Humshaugh.

Note that there are no cash machines here but there are a few services of interest to trekkers. The petrol station, just over the bridge, has a small **shop** (summer Mon-Fri

8am-6pm, Sat & Sun 8am-5pm winter from 9am) selling essentials and next door is the *Riverside Tearooms* (☎ 01434-681325; Apr-Sep Mon-Fri 9am-4pm, Sat & Sun 10am-4pm).

The owners also run the *Riverside Campsite* (contact details as for the tearoom; Easter-Oct) in the field behind, where camping (for walkers only) costs £6pp (including use of the shower/toilet block).

Across the other side of the round-about is *The George* (☎ 01434-681611, 🖳

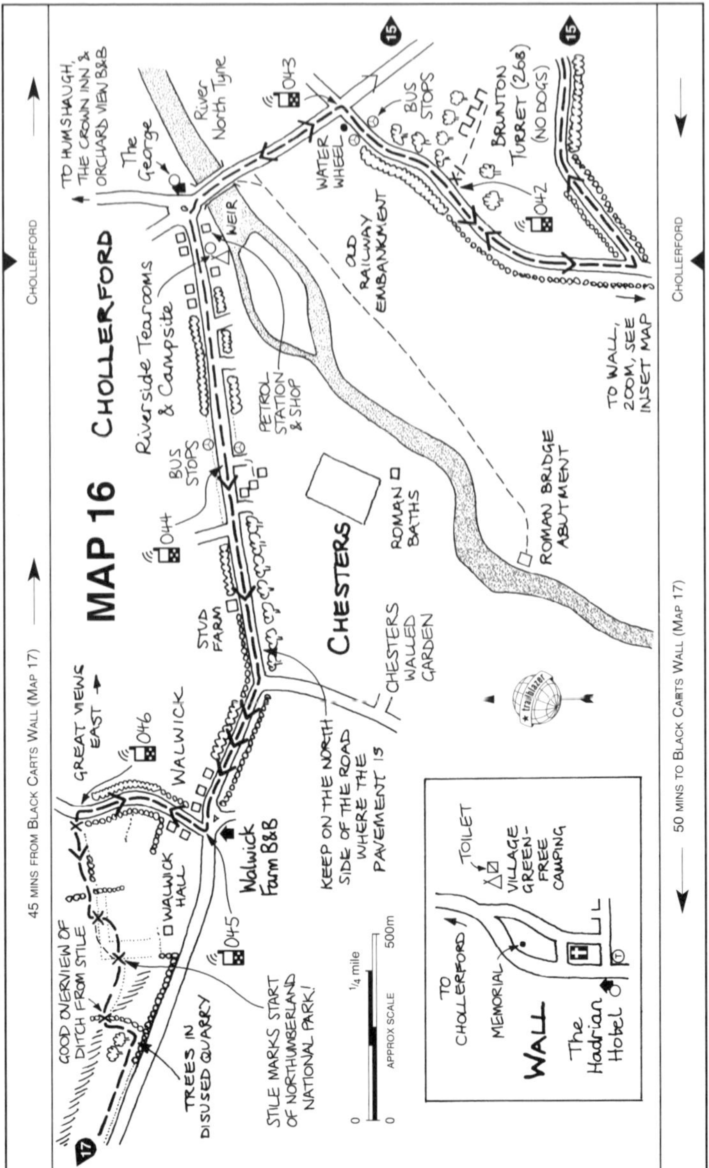

MAP 16 CHOLLERFORD

TO HUMSHAUGH, THE CROWN INN & ORCHARD VIEW B&B

River North Tyne

The George

WEIR

WATER WHEEL

BUS STOPS

BRUNTON TURRET (2.68) (NO DOGS)

□●3

Riverside Tearooms & Campsite

BUS STOPS

OLD RAILWAY EMBANKMENT

□●4

PETROL STATION & SHOP

ROMAN BATHS

ROMAN BRIDGE ABUTMENT

TO WALL, 2.0M, SEE INSET MAP

CHOLLERFORD

CHESTERS

CHESTERS WALLED GARDEN

STUD FARM

KEEP ON THE NORTH SIDE OF THE ROAD WHERE THE PAVEMENT IS

GREAT VIEWS EAST

□●6

WALWICK

WALWICK HALL

Walwick Farm B&B

□●5

GOOD OVERVIEW OF DITCH FROM STILE

STILE MARKS START OF NORTHUMBERLAND NATIONAL PARK!

TREES IN DISUSED QUARRY

45 MINS FROM BLACK CARTS WALL (MAP 17)

50 MINS TO BLACK CARTS WALL (MAP 17)

0   1/4 mile
0   500m
APPROX SCALE

TO CHOLLERFORD

WALL

MEMORIAL

The Hadrian Hotel

VILLAGE GREEN - FREE CAMPING

TOILET

ROUTE GUIDE AND MAPS

www.coastandcountryhotels.com; 2S/9T/ 37D/2F, all en suite, 🍸; 🐾 £10; WI-FI), set in its own landscaped gardens by the North Tyne and boasting its own pool and gym. Rates vary throughout the year but are about £80 for B&B (£119 DB&B) for two sharing; however, contact the hotel for details of special offers and rates for single occupancy. Light snacks are served noon-5pm, with the restaurant open 6.30-8.15pm.

However, several trekkers have got in touch to say that better-value food is available about a mile to the north at the neighbouring village of **Humshaugh** where, past the church, *The Crown Inn* (☎

01434-681231; bar daily noon-11pm, food served Wed-Sat noon-2pm & 6-8pm, Sun and bank holidays lunch only; WI-FI) serves food. Close by is the **Village Shop** (Mon-Fri 7.30am-1pm, Thur 6-7pm, Sat 7.30am-noon, Sun 9am-noon). There's a **B&B** here too, *Orchard View* (☎ 01434-681658, 🖥 www.northumberlandbedandbreakfast.biz; 2D or T en suite; 🍸; WI-FI; ; Ⓛ), a pleasant place which serves evening meals (by prior arrangement) on the nights when the pub doesn't.

Transport-wise, the AD122 **bus** stops outside Chesters Roman fort. See pp46-8 for further information.

CHESTERS   [Map 16, p129]
☎ *01434-681379; Apr-Sep daily 10am-6pm; Oct-Mar 10am-4pm (winter days/hours subject to change, check in advance); £5.40/4.90/3.20 adults/concessions/children; English Heritage members free.*
'Jack Bob and self went to Chesters to view the remains of the Roman Fort and Bridge.' Found in the **diary of a militia officer** and dated June 1761, proving that Wall tourism is not a new phenomenon.

In its day, Chesters, or **Cilurnum** (meaning, curiously, 'Cauldron Pool') as it would have been known then, was *the* fort in which to be stationed out of all of those on the Wall. Set in a beautiful situation amongst mature trees on a bend in the river, the fort was built to guard the nearby bridge over the North Tyne, covered 5¾ acres, and was inhabited by 500 members of the Roman cavalry – who were better paid than their infantry counterparts and seemed to have enjoyed slightly preferential treatment too. The Asturian cavalry from Spain is the auxiliary force most associated with Chesters.

The fort itself was built c AD130 on land previously occupied by Turret 27A. It was excavated by that one-man preservation society, John Clayton, in the 19th century. Indeed, Chesters became the home of this Newcastle town clerk turned archaeologist and conservationist. Having inherited the estate in 1832, he continued working on this and other Wall fortifications until his death in 1890.

Today's visitors will not only be able to **stamp their passports** (see box p38) at reception (or on the wall by the entrance when it's closed) but will also be able to enjoy the beautiful, traditional-style **museum** that Clayton established – full of dusty glass cases filled with some fascinating finds – as well as the ruins themselves. Top billing goes to the fort's **baths**, the highest of all the Roman ruins on the entire trail and located, as is usual, outside the fort itself, in this instance down the hill near the river.

These ruins give a really good idea of how the baths would have looked in their heyday, and how the water was channelled around and heated. Incidentally, during an early excavation of the baths in the 19th century, no less than 33 bodies, together with the remains of two horses and a dog, were discovered interred in the bathhouse. Curiously, their whereabouts are something of a mystery today, though at the time it was speculated that they dated back to the Saxon period. From the scattered remains by the baths you can also make out how the Wall itself would have travelled across the bridge, up to the fort (some Wall remains abutting the fort can be seen), right through the spot where the large country house (Clayton's old home) now stands, and beyond into the hills.

THE CORBRIDGE–HEXHAM–ACOMB ALTERNATIVE [Maps: 13 p123; 13a p132; 13b p133; 13c p138; 13d p139; 13e p143 & 15 p127]

This alternative trail (**4¹/₂-4³/₄hrs**; Halton Chesters Roman Fort to St Oswald's Hill Head via Corbridge, Hexham and Acomb) has a bit of everything. From the point of view of the scenery, the route includes magnificent stretches of woodland, a riparian stroll along the banks of the Tyne and even a few hills – thus far, for those coming from Newcastle at any rate, a rare 'treat'.

The market town of Hexham, with its ancient abbey overlooking the market place, is an unqualified delight, as is the compact town of Corbridge, home to a 17th-century bridge, a pele tower by the church that's made of Roman Wall stones and more pubs than you can shake a Roman spear at. And I haven't even mentioned the object of this diversion yet: the important Roman site (see pp136-7) just 15 minutes west of Corbridge near the banks of the Tyne.

From the Hadrian's Wall Path to Corbridge
There are any number of places where you can leave the Wall trail and head down to Corbridge, perhaps the most appropriate being the Roman Dere Street that once ran from the Firth of Forth through the Port Gate (see p124) to Corbridge and on to York. This, after all, was the main thoroughfare running north–south in Roman times. But for aesthetic reasons – not to mention the fact that it's a rather dangerous, pavement-less road in places – I suggest beginning a little way to the east of here, turning off at the grand, inviting tree-lined driveway leading to Halton Castle. This turn-off is also where the Roman Wall fort of Halton Chesters (Onnum) was once situated.

The path leads left past the castle grounds, where chickens, ducks, horses and a number of over-excitable dogs roam free, and on down the hill along country lanes. Look out for lapwings, buzzards and the ubiquitous rabbits as you go.

Eventually you pass under the A69 where a bridleway leads off right. Follow the directions on the map on p132 and, all being well, 50 minutes after leaving the main trail you arrive in front of Corbridge's old church and pretty market square.

CORBRIDGE   [see map p135]
In many ways Corbridge is a typical little English market town, smart, quaint, with a largely medieval centre and plenty of teashops and pubs to keep the floods of visitors that come every summer refreshed. At one time portrayed in the English press as Britain's snobbiest town – because of locals' objections to a fast-food van setting up in the market square – I'm sure you'll find it as friendly and approachable as everywhere else in this part of the world; and if the locals are more 'snobby' than their neighbours, well at least they've got a lot to feel superior about. And while some may find the place a bit twee – every

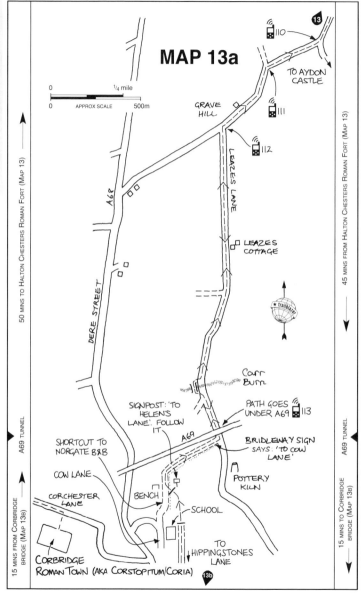

MAP 13a

0   ¼ mile
0   APPROX SCALE   500m

110

TO AYDON CASTLE

GRAVE HILL

111

112

LEAZES LANE

LEAZES COTTAGE

★ trailblazer

A69

DERE STREET

CARR BURN

PATH GOES UNDER A69 113

SIGNPOST: 'TO HELEN'S LANE'. FOLLOW IT

BRIDLEWAY SIGN SAYS: 'TO COW LANE'

SHORTCUT TO NORGATE B&B

A69

COW LANE

POTTERY KILN

CORCHESTER LANE

BENCH

SCHOOL

TO HIPPINGSTONES LANE

CORBRIDGE ROMAN TOWN (AKA CORSTOPITUM/CORIA)

13b

50 MINS TO HALTON CHESTERS ROMAN FORT (MAP 13)

45 MINS FROM HALTON CHESTERS ROMAN FORT (MAP 13)

A69 TUNNEL

15 MINS FROM CORBRIDGE BRIDGE (MAP 13B)

A69 TUNNEL

15 MINS TO CORBRIDGE BRIDGE (MAP 13B)

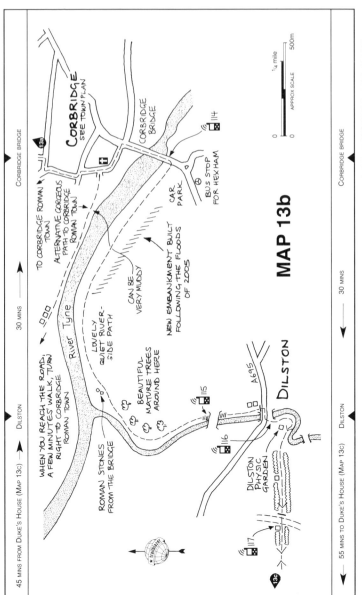

MAP 13b

ROUTE GUIDE AND MAPS

CORBRIDGE
SEE TOWN PLAN

TO CORBRIDGE ROMAN TOWN

ALTERNATIVE GORGEOUS PATH TO CORBRIDGE ROMAN TOWN

CORBRIDGE BRIDGE

CAR PARK

BUS STOP FOR HEXHAM

River Tyne

NEW EMBANKMENT BUILT FOLLOWING THE FLOODS OF 2005

CAN BE VERY MUDDY

LOVELY QUIET RIVER-SIDE PATH

BEAUTIFUL MATURE TREES AROUND HERE

WHEN YOU REACH THE ROAD, A FEW MINUTES' WALK, TURN RIGHT TO CORBRIDGE ROMAN TOWN

ROMAN STONES FROM THE BRIDGE

DILSTON

A695

DILSTON PHYSIC GARDEN

¼ mile

APPROX SCALE   500m

0   0

45 MINS FROM DUKE'S HOUSE (MAP 13c) ───► DILSTON ───► 30 MINS ───► CORBRIDGE BRIDGE

55 MINS TO DUKE'S HOUSE (MAP 13c) ◄─── DILSTON ◄─── 30 MINS ◄─── CORBRIDGE BRIDGE

ROUTE GUIDE AND MAPS

second shop seems to describe itself using the adjectives 'artisan' or 'designer' and there are shops called 'Skrumshus' and 'Kute' – you can't deny that it's pretty and has just about everything a trekker could want.

In addition to the wonderful Roman Town (see pp136-7), in the centre of Corbridge is Northumberland's finest Anglo-Saxon church, **St Andrew's**, built c AD786. In the churchyard there's a **pele tower** built using Roman stones, while a Roman gateway, which presumably originally stood at Corbridge Roman site, separates the baptistry from the rest of the church. Outside the church on the pavement is the site of the **King's Oven**, the main oven of the village in the 14th century.

Services
The centre of Corbridge is compact and in the main square you'll find the **post office** and **tourist information centre** (☎ 01434-632815, 🖳 corbridge.tic @northumberland.gov.uk; Apr-Oct Mon-Sat 10am-1pm & 1.30-4.30pm; Nov-Mar Wed, Fri & Sat 11am-4pm). A website worth looking at is 🖳 www.thisiscorbridge.co.uk.

You'll also find a **Co-op** and one of the town's busiest pubs, the Golden Lion. There's a **cashpoint** (ATM) at Barclays by the steps down to the riverside path to Corbridge Roman Town.

Transport
[See pp46-8] Arriva's/Stagecoach's No 685/85, Go North East's Nos 10 and X84/X85, and Wright's No 888 all stop here. **Train**-wise, there are plenty of services to Hexham – with some continuing on to Carlisle – and to Newcastle. The railway station is about three-quarters of a mile south of the river.

Where to stay
Near the Market Place, the *Wheatsheaf* (☎ 01434-632020, 🖳 www.wheatsheafhotelcorbridge.co.uk; 1S/4D/1T, all en suite, 🐾; WI-FI) looks smart; B&B in the single costs £57 and it's £99 for two sharing. In a similar style, and perhaps the most down-to-earth place in the village, the *Golden Lion* (☎ 01434-632216, 🖳 www.goldenlion-corbridge.co.uk; 5D/1T; 🐾; 🐕; WI-FI) is a surprisingly vast place with a warm welcome and some fair value rooms at £49.95 for a single, £69.95 for a double.

Across the other side of Corbridge, *The Angel* (☎ 01434-632119, 🖳 www.angelofcorbridge.co.uk; 5D/2F sleep 4, all en suite, 🐾; WI-FI) is the smartest place in town, a former coaching inn dating back to 1726. Striking the right balance between stylish and cosy, it charges £95 for the double rooms, £115 for the family rooms (£75 sgl occ) for B&B. Across the road and now under the same ownership, *The Angel Radcliffe* (contact The Angel for bookings; 1S/6D/1T, all en suite; 🐕; WI-FI) has a single room for £45, otherwise the rates are the same as at The Angel. Breakfast is served in The Angel (see Where to eat).

Heading about 500m east up the hill lie two more options: *2 The Crofts* (☎ 01434-633046, 🖳 www.2thecrofts.co.uk; 2D/1T, all en suite; 🐾; WI-FI) charges £75-80 for two sharing (£50-55 sgl occ). A further option lies virtually opposite: *The Hayes* (☎ 01434-632010; 🖳 www.hayes-corbridge.co.uk; 1S/1D, T or F shared bathroom, 2D, T or F, en suite; 🐾; WI-FI), Newcastle Rd, a huge place set in seven acres charging £36 for the single, £37.50-39pp for two sharing.

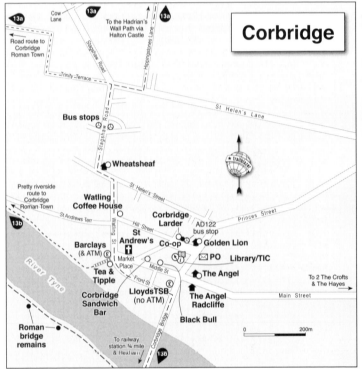

Where to eat and drink

Watling Coffee House (☎ 01434-634820; Mon-Sat 8am-5pm, Sun 9am-5pm; 🐕) is one of the smartest of the many coffee shops in Corbridge and the only one I could find that allowed dogs. A little way south, *Tea and Tipple* (Mon-Sat 9am-5pm, Sun 10.30am-3pm) claim to serve the 'biggest and bestest cheese scone' for just £1.70, with lashings of butter and homemade jam to boot. Up on the main square, the *Corbridge Larder* (☎ 01434-632948; 💻 www.corbridgelarder.co.uk; shop Mon-Fri 9.30am-5pm, Sat 9am-5.30pm, café Mon-Fri 10am-4pm, Sat to 4.30pm) has lots of local produce. Food is also served at *The Angel* (see Where to stay; Mon-Thur noon-9pm, Fri & Sat to 9.30pm, Sun noon-5pm only).

Cheaper and better value is *Corbridge Sandwich Bar* (Mon-Fri 9am-3pm, Sat 10am-3pm), by the square, with a range of tasty snacks and freshly made paninis, many of which cost less than £3, and jacket potatoes from £2.50.

For something more substantial try one of the pubs, such as the Sunday carvery (£7.95 for one course, £8.95 for two) at the *Golden Lion* (see Where to stay; Mon-Fri noon-3pm, 6-9pm, Sat to 8pm, Sun to 5pm) or some decent portions at the **Wheatsheaf** (see Where to stay; food served Mon-Sat noon-3pm & 5-9pm, Sun noon-3pm only) or another Corbridge pub that's gone a little upmarket, the **Black Bull** (☎ 01434-632261; food: Mon-Sat noon-9pm).

CORBRIDGE ROMAN TOWN [Map 13a, p132]

☎ *01434-632349; Apr-Sep daily 10am-5.30pm; Oct daily 10am-4pm; Nov-Mar Sat & Sun 10am-4pm (winter days/hours subject to change, check in advance); £5.40/4.90/3.20 adults/concessions/children, English Heritage members free*

It is, perhaps, a measure of how much we still have to learn about the Romans in Britain that when the first edition of this book was published this site was known as 'Corstopitum' after what everybody believed was the Roman name for the fortress that originally stood here. However, doubt has recently been cast as to whether this was true, with many experts now believing that the fortress, built to guard what was, at ten piers wide, Britain's largest stone bridge in Roman times, was actually called 'Coria' by the Romans. Proponents of this latter theory point to the Vindolanda postcards (see p161) to back up their assertions. On one of the tablets, commanding officer Julius Verecundus reports that there were 337 soldiers at 'Coris', and this is just one of nine definite references to Coria/Coris on the Vindolanda tablets. But while it is generally accepted now that Coria was the most likely name for this site, it is not universally so, with a dwindling band of archaeologists still preferring the name Corstopitum (even though there is only one contemporary occurrence of this name, in a document known as the *Antonine Itinerary*). As such, and until the correct name can be ascertained, this site has now been 'rebranded' as Corbridge Roman Town.

Regardless of what the original name was, the new name that it's been given is actually more informative. For whilst its origins were undoubtedly as a Roman fortress – indeed it was, for many years, the nerve centre of Roman operations in northern England – the site was rebuilt time and again over the years, each time with modifications to suit its changing function. As such it is one of the most important sites near the Wall for archaeologists have been able to peel back each of these different stages, like layers on an onion, to discover the history of the fort; and bits of each of those layers are visible to the visitor today.

That history is a long and complex one. The first fort, built around AD85 under the governor Agricola, was situated about half a mile west of here and lasted only about 20 years before it was burnt down, to be replaced by a second, made of turf and built on this site, the following year. This, too, lasted fewer than 20 years before being abandoned, as Hadrian began to build his Wall and troops were moved north to the new fortresses such as Halton Chesters (Onnum; see p124) that lay along its length. Corbridge was revived again, however, c AD140 under the Emperor Antoninus, when it became a supply base for the soldiers fighting his Scottish campaign. Soon after this, c AD180, its function seemed to change again and in place of its strictly military role the fort began to take on the appearance of a town. By the 3rd century it was home to a largely civilian population, though still with a military core, and remained like this until the Romans departed in the 5th century. Thus, while this site probably once had the typical 'playing-card' layout so familiar from the fortresses along the Wall – and, indeed, in many parts still does – there are also ruins from its days as a largely civilian settlement. And it is these that make this place unique.

ROUTE GUIDE AND MAPS

The proof of the importance of this fortress to the Romans can be seen merely by looking at a Roman road atlas. Running from the fortress to the north is **Dere Street**, the road the Romans built and would eventually use to launch their campaigns north into what is now Scotland; to the south, across the bridge, the same road continued to York; while running away to the west from here all the way to Carlisle was the **Stanegate**. As such, Corbridge was the transport hub of the region and a major supply town for forts along the Wall.

The Stanegate is still the main thoroughfare through the fort, though now it's at a higher level than the rest of the site thanks to all the resurfacing that went on during its lifetime. A stroll along here will take you past the **granaries** with their underfloor channels, built around AD180 when this site was metamorphosing from a regular fort into a supply base for troops on the Wall; the **fountain** next door which would once have been the centrepiece of the entire site; and the remains of various civilian buildings to the south of the Stanegate. I can't remember seeing such buildings *within* the boundaries of the Wall forts before – usually they were built outside the fort walls – which gives a good indication of just how much this Roman fort changed over time.

Incidentally, if you're wondering about the original fortress that lay half a mile (1km) west of here (the one that was built under the reign of Agricola and burnt down), that was discovered only in 1974 during the construction of the Corbridge bypass. You can see some of the things the archaeologists dug up there, as well as the best of their excavations here, in the museum adjacent to reception. Most famously of all, the so-called **Corbridge Hoard** – the contents of an iron-bound leather-covered wooden chest found on-site in 1964 – are now on display; dating from around 138AD, it comprises armour, tools, weaponry, wax writing tablets and papyrus – the essential possessions, one assumes, of your average Roman soldier. You can also see a replica of the famous **Corbridge Lanx** (the original is in the British Museum, London), a silver salver discovered in the 1730s near the riverbank by a young girl out walking.

From the fort, the quickest way back into town is to turn right and head east along pavement-less Corchester Lane. A far more pleasant route, however, is to turn left and, after a short distance, left again. This leads alongside a tributary down to the North Tyne, from where it's a pleasant stroll to the impressive bridge that gave the town its name. Built in 1674, this bridge replaced an Anglo-Saxon one on the same spot that became derelict in the 17th century.

❏ The world's first archaeological dig?

The history of the Roman site at Corbridge didn't abruptly come to an end when the Romans retreated to the Mediterranean. A few Saxon relics have been found to suggest that there was life here after the 5th century. Perhaps the most intriguing part of the fort's history, however, occurred in 1201 when King John undertook an excavation of the ruins in search of treasure. Though he found nothing except 'stones marked with bronze and iron and lead', his hunch was a good one: in 1911, more than 700 years later, 160 coins were found in a bronze jug, the largest hoard of Roman coins ever found in Britain. The find now resides in the British Museum. It may have been a fruitless search for John, but it earned him a prize of sorts: his excavation is seen by some as the first recorded archaeological dig in British history.

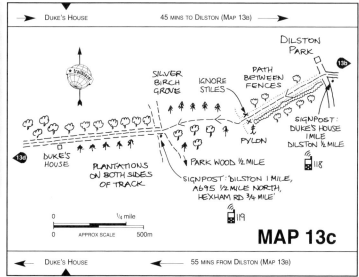

DUKE'S HOUSE · 45 MINS TO DILSTON (MAP 13B)

DILSTON PARK

13b

SILVER BIRCH GROVE · IGNORE STILES · PATH BETWEEN FENCES

SIGNPOST: DUKE'S HOUSE 1 MILE DILSTON ½ MILE

PYLON

DUKE'S HOUSE · 13d

PLANTATIONS ON BOTH SIDES OF TRACK

PARK WOOD ½ MILE

SIGNPOST: 'DILSTON 1 MILE, A695 ½ MILE NORTH, HEXHAM RD ¾ MILE'

118

119

0 ¼ mile

0 APPROX SCALE 500m

MAP 13c

DUKE'S HOUSE · 55 MINS FROM DILSTON (MAP 13B)

Corbridge to Hexham

The walk to Hexham is fine as long as the weather holds – and you find your way OK. Beginning with a crossing of the bridge followed by a gentle waterside stroll, the route winds its way up through **Dilston**, home to **Dilston Physic Garden** (Map 13b; ⌨ www.dilstonphysicgarden.com; mid-Apr to mid-Oct; Wed & Sat 11am-4pm; £4/3 adults/concs), established by a neuroscientist at Newcastle University and containing over 800 plant species that can be used for health and healing. The path continues on up the hill, with glorious views to the north across the valley towards the stately home of Beaufront (owned by the Errington family, after whom the pub at the Port Gate is named; see p124). These views are snatched away from you as you enter into pine plantations, the path leading from there to the riot of chimneys and turrets known as Duke's House (Map 13c), surrounded on all four sides by some beautiful woodland that plays host to deer, badgers and red squirrels. Plenty of paths lead down from here to Hexham which you'll reach about two hours – plus breaks – after leaving Corbridge.

HEXHAM [See map p141]

The main market town for the district is a quaint and compact little place, the modern façades of shops and cafés concealing but not obliterating the medieval character of the town centre.

Pride of place in the heart of town goes to the glorious **Hexham Abbey** (⌨ www.hexhamabbey.org.uk; daily 9.30am-5pm, services permitting; recommended donation £3). The first abbey was built here in AD672, though much of today's construction dates from the 12th century when it was refounded as an

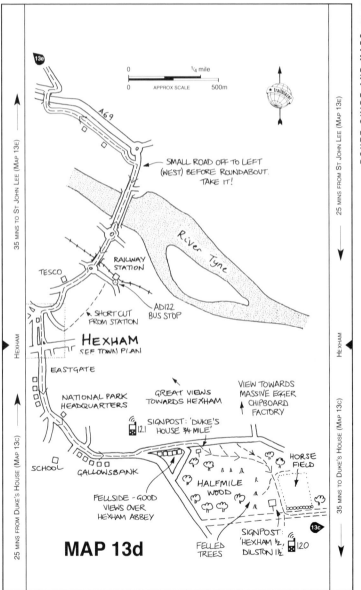

MAP 13d

Augustinian priory. Following the Dissolution of the Monasteries in 1537 it became the Parish Church of St Andrew, which it still is today. Take your time to explore the Abbey's impressive interior and look out for the large memorial to a 25-year-old Roman standard bearer from the 1st century AD – a stone of which you'll see several casts in various museums, including Chesters and Newcastle's Great North Museum: Hancock.

Across the square from the Abbey, the **Old Gaol** (💻 www.experience woodhorn.com/hexham-old-gaol; Apr-Sept & last week of Oct Tue-Sat 11am-4.30pm, plus Bank/school summer holiday Mons; Oct-Nov & Feb-Mar 11am-4.30pm Tue & Sat; £3.95/2.10 adults/children) is England's oldest purpose-built prison, having been built around 1330.

Services

The **tourist information centre** (☎ 01434-652220, 💻 hexham.tic@northum berland.gov.uk; Apr-Oct Mon-Sat 9.30am-5pm, Sun 11am-4pm, Nov-Mar Mon-Sat 9.30am-4.30pm), Hallgate, sits by the car park down the hill from the Old Gaol. For **wi-fi**, there's Mucho Gusto (see Where to Eat) and Wetherspoons in the centre under the Forum Cinema.

There are plenty of **banks/ATMs** in town, a **post office** in Beale's department store, a Boots the **chemist**, a branch of the **trekking shop** Mountain Warehouse as well as a Tesco (see Map 13d) **supermarket** just outside town.

Transport

[See pp46-8] There are plenty of **buses** to and from Hexham. The AD122 bus departs from the bus station and then goes via the railway station before heading towards Walltown. Arriva's/Stagecoach's No 685/85 & Go North East's X84, X85, 10 & 74, Tyne Valley's No 880 and Wright's No 888 also serve here.

From the nearby **railway station** (see Map 13d, p139) there is a frequent service to both Carlisle (approx 60 mins) and to Newcastle (35-40 mins).

Where to stay

Hexham's **B&Bs** lie a little way from the centre. ***West Close House*** (☎ 01434-603307; 2S shared bathroom/1D with toilet and basin; ▼), on Hextol Terrace, is a 1920s detached house with an award-winning garden and, wait for it ... a revolving Victorian-design summerhouse! Needless to say, I think it's the pick of the B&Bs and good value at just £35pp with a wholefood continental breakfast. On Leazes Park, to the north-west of town, ***High Reins*** (☎ 01434-603590; 4S/1T/2D, all en suite; ▼; WI-FI) charges from £37pp, singles £45.

Best Western Beaumont Hotel (☎ 01434-602331, 💻 www.bw-beaumont hotel.co.uk; 2S/12T/19D/1F, all en suite; ▼) is in a great location on Beaumont St opposite the Abbey Gardens. B&B costs from £80 for a single, £110 for two sharing. They also offer a dinner, bed and breakfast rate of £90/130 sgl/dbl or twin.

Where to eat and drink

There are more **cafés** and **tearooms** in Hexham than you can shake a cinnamon stick at. These include the popular ***Mucho Gusto*** (☎ 01434-606200, 💻 www.muchogustohexham.co.uk; Mon-Sat 9am-4.30pm; WI-FI), with views towards the Market Square; the vegetarian ***Hexham Tans*** (☎ 01434-656284; Tue-Sat 9am-4pm), on St Mary's Chare, serving a variety of tasty snacks including jacket potatoes for £4.50 and main meals (11.30am-2.30pm) for a very reasonable £5.50, including a delicious vegetarian chilli; ***Little Angel***

Café (☎ 01434-608765, 🖥 www.thelittleangelcafe.com; Mon-Wed 8am-5pm, Thur-Sat 8am-9pm, Sun & bank hol Mon 8am-3pm) serving 'thin and crusty pizzas' as well as desserts and pastries with an Italian vibe in the **Queen's Hall Arts Centre**; and, nearby, *Mrs Miggins' Coffee Shop* (☎ 01434-605808; Mon 9.30am-4pm, Tue-Sat to 5pm), a more traditional tearoom; fans of *Blackadder* may be interested to know that Rowan Atkinson grew up not too far from here and it has been suggested this tearoom was the inspiration for the pie shop of the same name that featured in the second and third series. However, some people say it was the other way round and that the shop took the name from the series. Opposite the Abbey, *Deli at Number 4* (☎ 01434 608091, 🖥 www.deliatnumber4.co.uk; Mon-Sat 9am-5pm, Sun 11am-5pm) has some lovely food – much of it locally sourced – and a small café off to one side.

For something more substantial, my favourite spot, *Danielle's Bistro* (☎ 01434-601122, 🖥 www.danielles-bistro.co.uk; Tue-Fri noon-2pm, Mon-Sat 6-10pm), is on the way into town from Corbridge; it serves mainly hearty English dishes and charges £14.50 for two courses in the evening, £17.95 for three. There's also an Indian restaurant, *The Valley* (☎ 01434-601234, 🖥 www.valleyrestaurants.co.uk; Tue-Thur & Sat noon-2pm, Tue-Sun 6-11.30pm), right

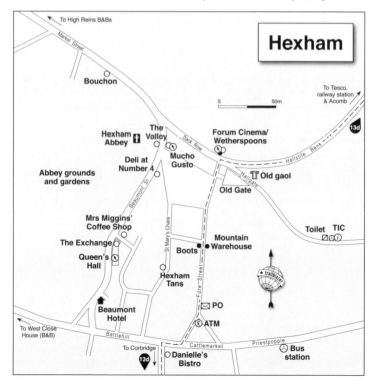

next to the abbey. Finally, there's *Bouchon* (☎ 01434-609943, 💻 www.bou chonbistrot.co.uk; Mon-Sat noon-2pm & 6-9.30pm), 4-6 Gilesgate, voted 'Best Local French Restaurant in the UK' on Gordon Ramsay's *The F Word* TV series in 2011. It's still pretty reasonable, however, with starters from £4.95 and mains, such as fricassée of Parisian gnocchi (tomatoes and courgettes), from £11.95.

Hexham to Acomb

The thrills of walking on this diversion from the Wall don't end at Hexham, though you'd be forgiven for thinking otherwise as you walk on a tarmac bridleway alongside, and then across, the noisy A69. But a minute later you're back in rural splendour, with the venerable **St John Lee Church** (Map 13e) a diverting distraction, followed by a tramp through sheep fields and across a stream (where a woodpecker was busy hammering away when I last came by) and on up to the pant (fountain) at Acomb.

ACOMB   [MAP 13e]

With the sad demise of the YHA hostel, Acomb has seen a sharp decline in the number of trekkers arriving at the end of a long day, panting at the pant (fountain) at the top of the village's Main St. That's a pity as Acomb is a friendly, attractive place, a string of stone terrace cottages inhabited by unassuming locals whose vowels are as flat as the caps the older generation wear on their heads.

There's little to delay those who aren't staying here, save for a small **post office** (Mon, Tue, Thur & Fri 9.30am-12.30pm & 1.30-5.30pm, Wed 9am-1pm, Sat 9am-12.30pm) and no less than three pubs, two of which offer **accommodation**. The first is *The Sun Inn* (☎ 01434-602934, 💻 www.the-suninn-acomb.co.uk; 1T/1D shared facilities, 1T/1D en suite; 🍽; 🐾; WI-FI). Rates are £70 (add a fiver for en suite; £45 sgl occ). Down the hill, *The Queen's Arms* (☎ 01434-607857; 💻 queensarmsacomb.co.uk; 2S/3D/1F, en-suite; 🍽; 🐾; WI-FI) also does accommodation (£45/65/95 for single/double/family rooms) and has takeaway pizzas (daily, 6-9pm) as well as Sunday lunch (noon-3pm).

Back at the top of the hill by the pant, the *The Miner's Arms* (☎ 01434-603909; 💻 www.theminersacomb.com; Mon-Fri 5pm-midnight, Sat & Sun noon-midnight) is a quintessential Northumbrian pub where great local beers are served every night. **Food** (Tue-Fri 5-8pm, Sat noon-8pm, Sun noon-3pm) is available here too, including Cumberland sausage casserole and mash for £7.25. The only other alternative for food is the **chippy** (Fri 11.30am-1.30pm & 4.30-8.30pm, Sat to 8pm), tucked away behind the Queen's Arms at the bottom of the hill, though it is only open two days a week.

The AD122 **bus** stops here as does Tyne Valley's No 880; see pp46-8.

Acomb to the Hadrian's Wall Path

From Acomb the path leads north from just above The Sun Inn, round the back of the houses at the top of the village. It continues via a stream and alongside fields of grain and a farmhouse guarded by Highland cattle to the road. At the road, turn right up the hill before taking a right through a green gate. Continuing on the path through a sheep field, the path dips at the end to reunite with the B6318 (the Military Road) and the main trail, which you rejoin by the wooden cross in the south-western corner of Heavenfield (see p124 and Map 15 p127).

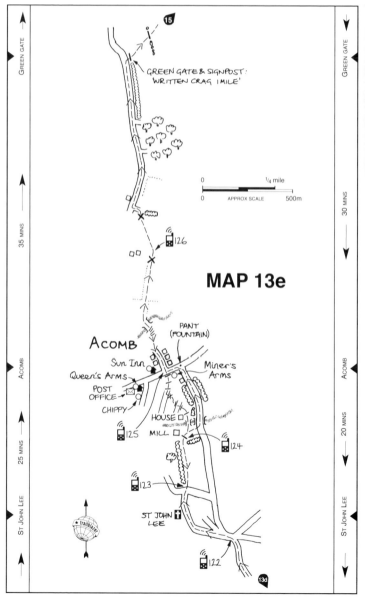

ROUTE GUIDE AND MAPS

15

GREEN GATE & SIGNPOST:
'WRITTEN CRAG 1 MILE'

0 ········· 1/4 mile
0 ········· 500m
APPROX SCALE

126

MAP 13e

PANT
(FOUNTAIN)

ACOMB

Sun Inn

Queen's Arms

Miner's
Arms

POST
OFFICE

CHIPPY

HOUSE

125

MILL

124

123

ST JOHN
LEE

trailblazer

122

13d

CHOLLERFORD TO STEEL RIGG (FOR ONCE BREWED)
[MAP 16 p129 & MAPS 17-23]

Introduction

Perhaps the most thrilling day of the entire walk, this is a **13-mile (21km; 5¼-5½hrs)** stage to be savoured. Encompassing the best-preserved fort on the Wall, the finest views, the most complete sections of the Wall, the northernmost point of the trail and some great if slightly exhausting walking, this is a day for superlatives. So bring plenty of food and water with you (there's nowhere to stock up between Chesters and Housesteads bar perhaps the café van at Brocolitia car park), plenty of memory cards for your camera, bucketloads of stamina – and enjoy!

The route

Despite the thrills to come, the day begins in a rather mundane fashion, with a bit of road walking along the by now all-too-familiar B6318 – the Military Road. Climbing up the hill, the path takes an unexpected turn away from the road opposite **Walwick Farm House** (Map 16; ☎ 01434-681823, 🖳 www.walwickfarm house.co.uk; 1S/3T/2D/2F; 🐾; WI-FI) with rooms (and great views across the valley) for £40 per person, £50 in the single; dinners are also available (£12 for mains) and they're licensed and have an open fire in the lounge – perfect for a chilly day. If you're not stopping here, you'll find yourself heading around the back of a farm, then following the line of General Wade's highway.

Soon after crossing the first possible turn-off for Green Carts Farm (see below) you come to the day's first treat: a cracking bit of Wall known as **Black Carts** that slopes ahead up the hill, has its own **turret** (No 29A) and is even joined, along its length, by the distinctive 'V' of the **Wall ditch**. (Incidentally, to the north the grand house you can see is Chipchase Castle, a medieval tower house with Jacobean and later additions.)

Green Carts Farm (Map 17; ☎ 01434-681320, 🖳 www.greencarts.co.uk; 3T/1D, all en suite; 🍽; 🐾; WI-FI; Ⓛ) is about half a mile from the trail. They offer: **B&B** (£60-70 per room or £50 sgl occ), a well-equipped **bunkhouse** (2 rooms each with 4 beds; £22pp including a continental breakfast; 🐾), a **camping barn** (sleeps 12, £12pp) with some cooking facilities, and a **campsite** (£5pp inc use of shower/toilet facilities, coin-operated laundry facilities, electric hook up) with 30 pitches. If requested in advance breakfast (£7 for a cooked takeaway breakfast), packed lunches (£6) and evening meals (from £12) are available. If staying here it's best to take the first road to the right after passing turret 29A.

Eventually the Wall disappears but that's not the end of the Roman masonry on this part. At **Limestone Corner**, where the Wall and trail take a turn to the south-west, you'll find some large boulders lying in the Wall ditch that clearly display evidence of having been worked on by workmen – and specifically Roman workmen. The rock here is whinstone, a super-hard basalt stone, and it appears the Romans soon realised that trying to hack through this rock was pointless; so they left the blocks where they were and moved on. This is one theory, anyway, and it's interesting that the ditch does stop here (though it's

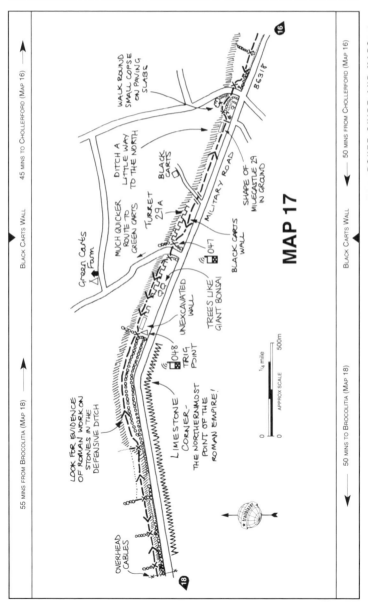

MAP 17

WALK ROUND SMALL COPSE ON PAVING SLABS

DITCH A LITTLE WAY TO THE NORTH

Green Carts Farm

MUCH QUICKER ROUTE TO GREEN CARTS

BLACK CARTS

TURRET 29A

047

BLACK CARTS WALL

SHAPE OF MILECASTLE 29 IN GROUND

MILITARY ROAD

B6318

UNEXCAVATED WALL

TREES LIKE GIANT BONSAI

048 TRIG POINT

LIMESTONE CORNER – THE NORTHERNMOST POINT OF THE ROMAN EMPIRE!

LOOK FOR EVIDENCE OF ROMAN WORK ON THE STONES IN THE DEFENSIVE DITCH

OVERHEAD CABLES

¼ mile
APPROX SCALE
500m
0

trailblazer

worth noting that the Vallum continues unbroken on the other side of the road). Perhaps of more interest, Limestone Corner is the northernmost point of the trail – thus the Wall here would have been the northernmost point of the entire Roman Empire. Continue along the trail and, just before crossing the road you come to a turn-off for ***Hallbarns*** (off Map 18, around a mile from the trail – look for the signpost on the trail pointing north; ☎ 01434-681419; 💻 www.hallbarns-simonburn.co.uk; 2T/1F; ☕; 🐕 sleep in stable; WI-FI; Ⓛ), a pleasant **B&B** with drying facilities that charges £75 (£55 sgl occ) and can provide an evening meal if booked in advance.

The next piece of Roman architecture lies across the road from the turn off to Hallbarns. The **Brocolitia** fort (aka Carrawburgh, pronounced 'Carrawbruff'; Map 18) remains unexcavated. It is, however, an unusual fort, clearly built some time after the Wall, for Brocolitia actually lies over the infilled Vallum. It was around this site in 1876 that John Clayton opened up **Coventina's Well** and discovered 13,487 coins (4 gold, 184 silver and the rest bronze) which would have been tossed into the water for good luck – just as we throw money into wishing wells today. Three hundred of these coins commemorated the pacification of northern Britain following disturbances in AD155; Britannia, who may be found on the back of some 50p coins looking regal and serene, appears slumped and forlorn on these Roman coins.

In addition to the money, Clayton also found carved stones, altars, jars, pearls, brooches and incense burners – the religious stuff having been deliberately placed here for safekeeping following the Theodosian Edict banning pagan temples in AD391 (see box pp148-9). Much of this can be seen at Chesters Museum (see pp130-1). Coventina, by the way, was a local goddess associated with water; as you may have already seen at the temple to Antenociticus in Newcastle (see box p96), the Roman Empire was largely tolerant of other religions and beliefs and even assimilated certain local gods into their pantheon, in much the same way that Hinduism has done with both Christianity and Buddhism.

Though Brocolitia is once more underground, the nearby **Mithras Temple** (see box p148-9) is open to both the skies and the public, though the altars are mere copies of the originals now housed in Newcastle's Great North Museum: Hancock. The temple was discovered by John Gillam in 1949 when a particularly dry summer 'shrank' the surrounding peat to reveal the stones. Incidentally, Mithraism was one of the more popular religions on the Wall and two other Mithraeums, at Carrawburgh and Rudchester, have been unearthed.

If you want to know more about the entire site, including the location of Coventina's Well (to the west of the main site and still producing water), as well as enjoy a lovely cup of coffee, pay a visit to Ant, the man with the tiny little **refreshments van** who *usually* operates out of the car park serving hot drinks to weary trekkers. I have probably received more emails and letters recommending

❑ **Walk side by side and on healthy grass** Don't walk in single file or on worn areas. Protect our heritage!

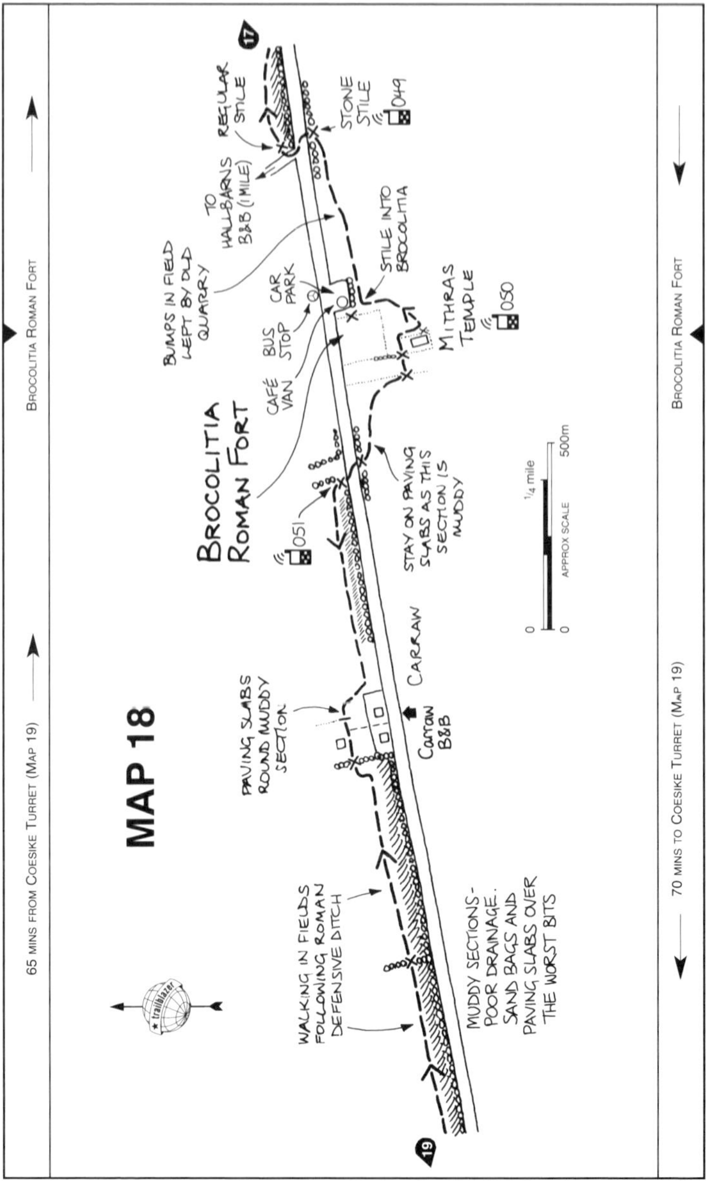
MAP 18
65 mins from Coesike Turret (Map 19)
Brocolitia Roman Fort
70 mins to Coesike Turret (Map 19)
Brocolitia Roman Fort
trailblazer
19
Walking in fields following Roman defensive ditch
Muddy sections - poor drainage. Sand bags and paving slabs over the worst bits
Paving slabs round muddy section
Carraw
Carraw B&B
Brocolitia Roman Fort
051
Stay on paving slabs as this section is muddy
Café van
Bus stop
Car park
Bumps in field left by old quarry
Mithras Temple
050
Stile into Brocolitia
To Hallbarns B&B (1 mile)
Regular stile
Stone stile
049
17
Approx scale
0
1/4 mile
0
500m

this man and his beverages over the past twelve months than I have about any B&B, restaurant etc on the route. His drinks are lovely, his knowledge of Brocolitia profound – and his presence at this site is a very welcome one. Unfortunately, the last time I visited (admittedly towards the end of the season

❏ MITHRAISM

Considering the distant era in which Mithraism enjoyed its greatest popularity, the secrecy with which it was practised and the attempts that various people made down the centuries to suppress it, it's amazing that, on the surface at least, we seem to know so much about this clandestine religion.

This becomes even more remarkable considering that much of the written information we do have for the faith comes not from its adherents – the secrecy surrounding the faith was both strict and all-encompassing – but from its detractors, such as the early Church fathers; people whom, it must be said, are probably not the most reliable of sources. But thankfully, though the followers themselves were silent about their faith, their iconography, by comparison, speaks volumes; and this iconography can be found in every temple throughout the Roman Empire, including those discovered at Hadrian's Wall.

The origins of the faith are uncertain, with one school of thought believing it to be Persian, dating back as far as 1400BC, while another suggests it was a near-contemporary of Christianity. Plutarch mentions it in 67BC, while the earliest physical remains date from the 1st century AD. Whatever its genesis, we do know that the Mithraic faith quickly gathered a huge following. One of the reasons for this popularity is undoubtedly its adoption as the unofficial faith of Roman soldiers. Though originally appealing to slaves and freedmen, the Mithraic emphasis on truth, honour, bravery and discipline would have appealed to the Roman army who would undoubtedly have proselytised the faith wherever they were stationed.

Mithraism enjoyed its heyday in the 2nd century AD; by the 5th century it had all but disappeared. The first blow came with the *sole* accession of Theodosius to the imperial throne in AD392 (prior to this he had ruled with two other 'emperors'). The last emperor of a united Roman Empire (following his demise the split between the empire's western and eastern halves, which first appeared at the beginning of the 4th century AD, became permanent), Theodosius was also the first emperor to make Christianity the official religion and went out of his way to promote his chosen faith, issuing edicts and encouraging Christian subjects to attack pagan buildings. One edict in particular, issued in AD391 before he became sole ruler, banned the worship of pagan gods, and many Mithraic temples were destroyed at this time.

The Mithraic organisation

The faith was a complicated one. Its followers were organised into a strict **hierarchy** of seven grades, or levels. An initiate new to the faith would have been known as a *Corax*, or 'Raven', the first and lowest level in the Mithraic hierarchy. At the other end of the spectrum was the rank of '*Pater*', or 'Father', the seventh and highest level. Their clothes, such as the colour of their tunic or the mask they wore at Mithraic rituals, indicated to which rank they belonged.

Rising through the ranks was no easy matter. Near to many Mithraic temples, including Carrawburgh, an 'ordeal' pit has been found, with a bench very close to what would have been a large fire. It is assumed that followers would have undergone some sort of physical trial by fire, cold or fasting in order to climb to the next level.

on an overcast day in September) the van wasn't there, but subsequent research online has found an application for permission for 'one mobile refreshment van' to be allowed in the car park – so it's hoped he (or someone like him) will be there again next season.

ROUTE GUIDE AND MAPS

The Mithraic beliefs: one theory

As a reward for rising through the ranks, the faithful were given revelations into the secrets and mysteries of the faith. According to their beliefs, the god Mithras was born either from the living rock or from a tree. An early life filled with pain and hardship culminated in the **defeat and slaughter of the primeval bull**. This killing allowed the life force of the bull to be released for the benefit of humanity: plants and herbs came from the bull's body, while wine came from the bull's blood and all livestock came from the slayed bull's semen. This victory over the primeval bull, known as the **tauroctony**, would have been depicted in every Mithraeum, or Mithraic temple, and each time the same few characters appear in the picture, namely a dog, scorpion, snake and raven, as well as Mithras's torchbearers, Cautes and Cautopates.

As for the Mithraeum itself, this would originally have been quite a dark and gloomy place. Indeed, the temple was usually constructed underground in order to simulate the cave in which Mithras was supposed to have killed the primeval bull. Entering via a door in the south-west corner, a worshipper would have first found himself in a small antechamber with a bench and what would have been a large fire, originally the ordeal pit. Beyond a wickerwork screen at the end lay the nave, with benches arranged along the side to allow the faithful to recline when partaking of ritual meals. Four small altars lay at the end of these benches. It is estimated that the average temple would have been able to hold between 30 and 50 men.

Mithraic beliefs: an alternative theory

For 70 years or so, this interpretation of Mithraism was held to be the definitive one. There was, however, one small problem. The whole reason it was believed that Mithraism came from the east is because the name 'Mithras' is the Latin form of the Iranian god Mithra; that, and the fact that the Roman authors themselves believed it to have come from Persia. But if Mithraism did have its origins in Persia and the Indian subcontinent, why have there never been any discoveries of Mithraism in Iran or any parallels in the folklore and mythologies of that region?

Thus, recently, a new interpretation has been suggested. This postulates that the depiction of Mithras slaying the bull, with the dog, raven, snake and scorpion as onlookers, and the torchbearers, Cautes and Cautopates, in attendance, is in fact a symbolic depiction of the cosmos, with the *dramatis personae* symbols of the zodiac. For example, the dog is in fact a representation of the constellation Canis Minor, and Cautes and Cautopates are the sun and moon respectively.

In this theory, therefore, the reason these temples were 'built' underground is because this subterranean chamber represents the night sky. This new theory may sound far-fetched at first but gathers credence when we look at the remains of Mithraea on the Wall. In particular, at Housesteads, there is one depiction of Mithras emerging from what has been called a Cosmic Egg – a depiction of the cosmos in an oval frame. Could it be that this singular sculpture, found in a remote fort in a far-flung corner of Rome's conquered territories, holds the key to our understanding of this empire-wide faith?

Returning to the **Roman ditch** on the northern side of the road, the trail continues into **Northumberland National Park**. *Carraw B&B* (☎ 01434-689857, 🖳 www.carraw.co.uk; 1D/2D or T/1D, T or F, all en suite; ☛; WI-FI; Ⓛ) is a great little B&B just a minute's walk off the trail on the main road. Rates are £85-98 (£65-85 sgl occ). While not serving dinner as such they do offer a 'Carraw supper', namely a bowl of homemade soup and a ploughman's platter (£12.50). One advantage is that they are licensed to sell alcohol. And they even, unusually, have a charge point for electric cars!

Continuing on the trail alongside the ditch, where the B6318 drifts to the left, there's a ladder stile in the wall. Though tempting, those staying in **Grindon** should continue on the trail past Milecastle 33 (Map 19) and then climb onto the road at the next ladder stile, where there's a brief reunion with the Military Road. Turn right and, on the junction with the road down to Grindon you'll come to the wonderful **B&B** that is the four-star *Old Repeater Station* (Map 19; ☎ 01434-688668, 🖳 www.hadrians-wall-bedandbreakfast .co.uk; 2D/1T en suite, 1 bunk-bed room sleeps 2, 1 bunk-bed room sleeps 4; 🐾 by prior arrangement). A wonderful converted stone-and-slate building that makes extensive use of eco-technology (including boreholes, biowaste systems, solar panels and the like), this one-man operation is run by the affable, laconic Les, a man who in my experience is never less than generous with his teapot. Rates, including breakfast, are as follows: for one person in the twin bunk it's £37.50; for two people it's £27.50pp; while in the four-bunk room it's £25pp for three people, £23.75pp for four people. The twin and doubles are £65-70 per room. Special deals are possible for those staying for more than two nights. Call in advance if you want an evening meal (they are licensed; dinner £7.95-13.95 for a main course) or accommodation out of the main season. **Internet access** (charity donation welcome; note it's not wi-fi) is available all day (including to non-residents); he's also the person to ask about **camping** possibilities in the area. (A repeater station, by the way, was a building located roughly halfway between telephone exchanges and was where the signals on telephone cables were amplified to compensate for the loss of electricity which made speech fainter and led to a loss of clarity.) The Old Repeater Station here is great.

Just over a mile (1.6km) further on, down on North Rd, *Hadrian Lodge Hotel* (off Map 19; ☎ 01434-684867, 🖳 www.hadrianlodge.co.uk; 5D/3T/2D, T or F, all en suite; ☛; 🐾 by prior arrangement; WI-FI; Ⓛ) is a comfy and rather smart place that offers free lifts to and from the Wall. Prices start at £74 for two people, with each extra person in the family room charged at £16. They also have a **bunkroom** (4 beds; shower & toilet) which costs £30pp including a continental breakfast. Meals are available by arrangement.

Those not staying in Grindon should continue along the line of the Wall where you will find that the trail leaves the road for good to aim for the comprehensive remains of **Turret 33B**, known as the **Coesike Turret**. It then heads up towards the small copse surrounded by a wall that marks the site of **Milecastle 34 (Grindon Milecastle)**. The next turret, **Grindon Turret** or, more prosaically, Turret 34A, hides behind the next wall. Both it and Coesike Turret – indeed, maybe all the turrets on the Wall – were probably abandoned less than a

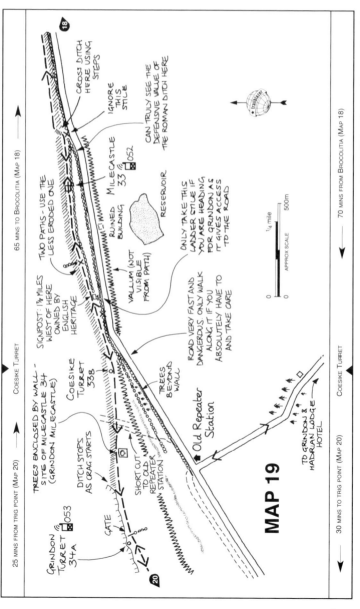

25 MINS FROM TRIG POINT (MAP 20) →

← COESIKE TURRET →

← 65 MINS TO BROCOLITIA (MAP 18) →

GRINDON TURRET 34A 053

GATE

DITCH STOPS AS CRAG STARTS

TREES ENCLOSED BY WALL – SITE OF MILECASTLE 34 (GRINDON MILECASTLE)

SHORT CUT TO OLD REPEATER STATION

COESIKE TURRET 53B

SIGNPOST: 1¾ MILES WEST OF HERE OWNED BY ENGLISH HERITAGE

TWO PATHS – USE THE LESS ERODED ONE

CROSS DITCH HERE USING STEPS

IGNORE THIS STILE

RUINED BUILDING

MILECASTLE 33 052

CAN TRULY SEE THE DEFENSIVE VALUE OF THE ROMAN DITCH HERE

VALLUM (NOT VISIBLE FROM PATH)

RESERVOIR

ONLY TAKE THIS LADDER STILE IF YOU ARE HEADING FOR GRINDON AS IT GIVES ACCESS TO THE ROAD

TREES BEYOND WALL

Old Repeater Station

ROAD VERY FAST AND DANGEROUS. ONLY WALK ALONG IT IF YOU ABSOLUTELY HAVE TO AND TAKE CARE

APPROX SCALE

0   ¼ mile

0   500m

MAP 19

TO GRINDON & HADRIAN LODGE HOTEL

← COESIKE TURRET →

30 MINS TO TRIG POINT (MAP 20) →

70 MINS FROM BROCOLITIA (MAP 18) →

century after they were built, before the end of the 2nd century AD as the Wall forts were established. But unlike the others, after the Romans had gone both these turrets had *shielings* (herdsmen's huts) built into their remains, from which we get the name Sewingshields. Incidentally, notice how the ditch abruptly ends shortly after the Grindon Milecastle. Never an army to leave jobs unfinished, the reason for the ditch's abrupt termination is pretty obvious once you take a look at the area's topography, for it is here that the crags start; crags that form a natural barrier, thus make the digging of a defensive ditch entirely unnecessary.

More Roman delights await beyond Sewing Shields Farm (Map 20) at the crest of the hill. This is a fine **stretch of Wall** and begins at the end of the woods that shelter the farm. To the south of the trail the land slopes away gently down to the Military Road but to the north a 200ft drop awaits those who cross the Wall. These are the **Sewingshields Crags**, a wild and rugged land that, perhaps unsurprisingly, has become the setting of a number of myths and legends, many concerning those stalwarts of British folktales, King Arthur and his knights. Sewingshields Castle, which used to stand at the foot of the crags, was also used by Walter Scott as the setting for his story *Harold the Dauntless*.

Whatever the truth or otherwise of the stories surrounding Sewingshields, there's no doubt that the Romans clearly saw no need to construct a defensive ditch to the north of the Wall here. Coming to **Milecastle 35**, you see that, with such a large drop to the north, there's no northern gate here either, presumably for the same reason. Note, too, that the Vallum is now quite a way south of the Wall, where the ground is less stony.

❑ Northumberland National Park and the Dark Sky Park

Walking along the trail from the east, when you cross the stile around the back of Walwick Hall, you are actually also crossing a boundary into Britain's most northerly national park. Covering 1048sq km (404.6 sq miles), or about a quarter of the entire county after which it is named, Northumberland National park stretches from Hadrian's Wall all the way up to the Scottish border; indeed, if you were to continue from the stile by Walwick Hall along the Hadrian's Wall Path, you'll find you won't actually leave the park until near Thirlwall Castle, almost 20 miles (32km) later.

The park is famous not only for what it has – including several rare species such as black grouse, pipistrelle bats, water voles and bog orchids – but also, beautifully, for what it doesn't. For the lack of any significant light pollution means that visitors to the park are able to witness some of the clearest views of the night sky anywhere in the country. Indeed, such is the area's reputation in this field that in 2013 the International Dark-Sky Association (the leading international organisation combating light pollution worldwide) awarded Dark Sky Park status on the entire area of Northumberland National Park and the adjacent Kielder Water and Forest Park, thus making it the largest protected Dark Sky Park in the whole of Europe. In giving the award the Association described the park as 'a wild and remote place that demonstrates an ability to conserve the dark skies above and a commitment to providing opportunities for the public to enjoy them'

The award was not only deserved but necessary, conferring as it does 'protection' on the clarity of the night sky, with controls in place to prevent light pollution from nearby sources.

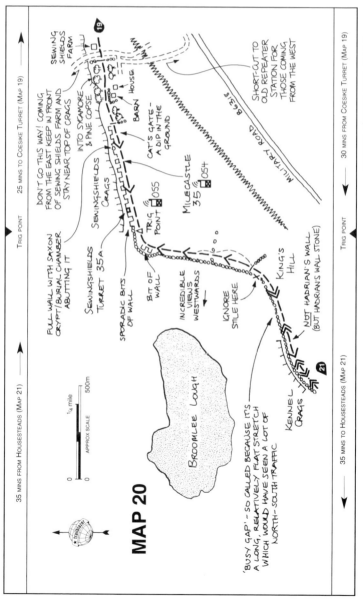

SEWING SHIELDS FARM

DON'T GO THIS WAY! COMING FROM THE EAST KEEP IN FRONT OF SEWING SHIELDS FARM AND STAY NEAR TOP OF CRAGS

INTO SYCAMORE & PINE COPSE

BARN HOUSE

CAT'S GATE – A DIP IN THE GROUND

FULL WALL WITH SAXON CRYPT/BURIAL CHAMBER ABUTTING IT

SEWINGSHIELDS CRAGS

SEWINGSHIELDS TURRET 35a

SPORADIC BITS OF WALL

TRIG POINT 1055

MILECASTLE 35 05+

BIT OF WALL

INCREDIBLE VIEWS WESTWARDS

IGNORE STILE HERE

KING'S HILL

NOT HADRIAN'S WALL (BUT HADRIAN'S WALL STONE)

MILITARY ROAD B6318

SHORT-CUT TO OLD REPEATER STATION FOR THOSE COMING FROM THE WEST

KENNEL CRAGS

BROOMLEE LOUGH

MAP 20

¼ mile

0 .... 500m

APPROX SCALE

'BUSY GAP' – SO CALLED BECAUSE IT'S A LONG, RELATIVELY FLAT STRETCH WHICH WOULD HAVE SEEN A LOT OF NORTH–SOUTH TRAFFIC

N trailblazer

For many people, this is the start of the most splendid part of the trail, with great views, wonderful walking and a really fine, extensive piece of Wall. Though the Wall proper stops at the top of the hill, just past the **trig point**, it is replaced by something more modern and only slightly less attractive which leads all the way to Housesteads Fort, the Wall's finest.

Those not wishing to visit Housesteads should enter the grounds then turn right through **Knag Burn Gate** (Map 21). This was another Roman gateway through the Wall, similar in that respect to the Port Gate which many of you will have passed on yesterday's stage. This gate, however, was introduced into the Wall only in the 4th century AD, presumably to allow the considerable number of locals who lived around the fort to move between the northern and southern sides of the Wall with greater ease. The trail continues north of the Wall, until the far side of Housesteads is reached.

Those who *do* wish to visit the fort, however, should continue to the south of the Wall to the ticket office, near the fort's south-west corner. Note that this office is a **passport stamping station**. They also sell hot drinks, snacks and sandwiches but have no seating (save for a couple of plastic chairs in the museum that the kindly staff will allow you to make use of). Those desiring a more 'café' experience (ie a seating area and proper toilets as opposed to the temporary chemical toilet at the ticket office) will have to saunter down to the car park, down the hill.

The AD122 **bus** calls in at the car park here; see pp46-8 for further information.

HOUSESTEADS   [Map 21]
☎ *01434-344363; Easter-Sep daily 10am-6pm; Oct 10am-5pm; Nov-Easter 10am-4pm (winter days/hours subject to change, check in advance); £6.20/5.60/3.70 adults/concs/children, free for English Heritage and National Trust members*
'*The grandest station in the whole line – in some stations the antiquary feeds upon shells, but here upon kernels*'   **William Hutton**, 1802 (see p60)
This quote pretty much sums up Housesteads. For if you visit only one fort on the Wall, make it this one. In my opinion, Housesteads is the one place where you can really get a feel for how a Roman fort would have looked. Where the ruins of most other sites are rather fragmentary and barely break the surface of the earth, here the walls in places run to six courses or more – up to ten feet (almost 3m) high – with only the roof apparently missing to complete the structure. For this, as usual, considerable thanks must go to John Clayton, who bought the site in 1838 to protect and excavate it.

By positioning yourself up near the Wall at the top of the hill near the North Gate, you get a great overview of the fort as well as some incomparable views north and south, which is presumably why the Romans built it here in the first place. Known to them as **Vercovicium**, Housesteads was constructed around AD122, making it one of the first to be built along the Wall, and housed around 800 men on its five acres. The First Cohort of Tungrians from Belgium is the auxiliary unit most associated with Housesteads, having been based here in the 3rd and 4th centuries AD.

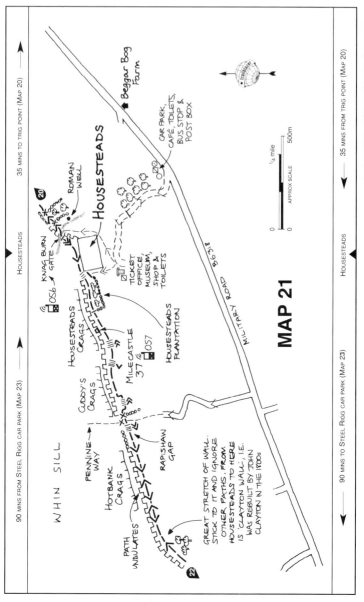

While the fort has the usual playing-card shape, its layout is not entirely typical. For one thing, you'll notice as you approach the fort from the trail that the *whole* of Housesteads lies south of the Wall, unlike Chesters, Segedunum and other sites which protrude north beyond the line of the Wall. Furthermore, Housesteads is elongated west–east (with the **Military Way** forming its central axis), where the longest axis of other forts runs north–south. The central core of the fort is familiar, with the **headquarters** at the centre and the Commander's House or **praetorium** next door. However, on this occasion, the latter lies to the south of the HQ, not to the east as is more typical, probably because the whole fort lies on a ridge and slope. As is usual, the **granaries** and the **hospital** lie nearby, with the near-complete ruins of the **latrines** in the south-eastern corner of the fort. To the south, in the extensive civilian settlement outside the fort walls stands the **Murder House**, so-called because the skeleton of a man with a knife stuck between his ribs was discovered during excavations.

West of here lies the revamped **museum**, where, via the medium of scale models, film, Roman finds and CGI recreations of Roman buildings, you get a good idea of what the place may have looked like 2000 years ago.

Incidentally, for those who have had enough for the day *Beggar Bog Farm B&B* (Map 21; ☎ 01434-344652, 🖳 www.beggarbog.co.uk; 1D/1T, en suite; 🐾 allowed in a separate building; Ⓛ) lies a few hundred yards east of the turn-off to the fort on the Military Road. A traditional stone-built farmhouse with accommodation in a separate self-contained annexe, Beggar Bog is a smart and friendly place with great breakfasts surpassed only by the view from its elevated position up towards Housesteads and along the Military Road. B&B costs £75. Evening meals (£20) are available if requested in advance.

The final section of this stage is no less breathtaking. Indeed, this is the finest section of Wall, known as the 'Clayton Wall' after the archaeologist John Clayton who bought and rebuilt this section. You can tell a bit of Clayton Wall as opposed to regular, unreconstructed Roman Wall because Clayton's method of rebuilding differed from the original Roman style, with no mortar and a turf top. This includes the section of Wall immediately after Housesteads that leads through the wooded Housesteads Plantation. The National Trust owns the Wall for three miles west of Housesteads; it owns the fort too, though the day-to-day maintenance of it remains in the hands of English Heritage. I strongly recommend that you occasionally walk up to the Wall to savour the views stretching away to the north. This is Northumberland's version of the Lake District, with **Bromlee Lough** (Map 20) immediately to the north, **Greenlee Lough** to its west and **Crag Lough** (Map 22) further along the trail.

Continuing your climb, you pass **Milecastle 37**, one of the best preserved and perhaps the most important on the Wall. It was excavated by Clayton in 1853. Note the start of an archway over the north gate, from which the experts were able to extrapolate the height of the arch and from this the height of the milecastle. (Why a north gate was deemed necessary here but not at Milecastle 35 – see p152 – is unclear, for they both have steep drops to the north.) You can also see holes in the floor by the southern entrance – postholes for the wooden door.

This whole ridge that you are walking across is called the **Whin Sill**, while the section you are on now is known locally as **Cuddy's Crags**, after St Cuthbert.

Continuing along the top of the crags, eventually the path drops down to **Hotbank Farm** (Map 22), owned by the National Trust and built by the site of **Milecastle 38.** (The trail currently circumvents this milecastle to avoid further

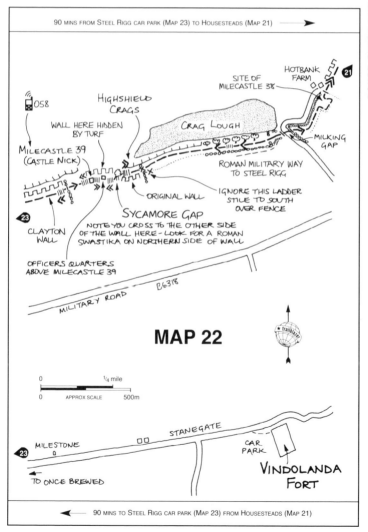

90 MINS FROM STEEL RIGG CAR PARK (MAP 23) TO HOUSESTEADS (MAP 21) ⟶

HOTBANK FARM

SITE OF MILECASTLE 38

058

HIGHSHIELD CRAGS

WALL HERE HIDDEN BY TURF

CRAG LOUGH

MILECASTLE 39 (CASTLE NICK)

MILKING GAP

ROMAN MILITARY WAY TO STEEL RIGG

ORIGINAL WALL

IGNORE THIS LADDER STILE TO SOUTH OVER FENCE

SYCAMORE GAP

CLAYTON WALL

NOTE YOU CROSS TO THE OTHER SIDE OF THE WALL HERE - LOOK FOR A ROMAN SWASTIKA ON NORTHERN SIDE OF WALL

OFFICERS QUARTERS ABOVE MILECASTLE 39

MILITARY ROAD   B6318

MAP 22

trailblazer

0   ¼ mile
0   APPROX SCALE   500m

STANEGATE

MILESTONE

CAR PARK

TO ONCE BREWED

VINDOLANDA FORT

⟵ 90 MINS TO STEEL RIGG CAR PARK (MAP 23) FROM HOUSESTEADS (MAP 21)

damage to the site; it was this stretch of Wall that suffered so much from the group of bankers who walked on it, see p63). It was near here that part of an inscribed stone was found that stated the second legion built this milecastle under the governorship of Aulus Platorius Nepos. As Aulus was governor during Hadrian's time, it provided archaeologists with almost irrefutable proof that this was Hadrian's Wall and not, as had previously been believed, Severus's (see box p51).

Beyond the farm the trail now dodges through a gate to head along the north side of the line of the Wall, then goes through a pleasant wood with Crag Lough glittering in the sunlight below. The path now follows a familiar pattern, rising and falling with the undulations of the land. This includes a drop to **Sycamore Gap**, named after the solitary tree growing in the dip.

The sycamore is something of a local celebrity, having appeared in the film *Robin Hood* alongside Kevin Costner (where, despite the distinct disadvantage of being a tree, it still managed to appear less wooden than its co-star). I've been told there's a Roman carving of a swastika, another symbol of prosperity and good fortune, near the tree on the Wall's northern face, though I have to confess I've never found it.

Following the gap, there's a climb up past the remains of some **officers' quarters**, unique on the Wall, and **Milecastle 39** to **Peel Crags**, before the path falls again to Peel Gap and the very steep **Cat Stairs** via the remains of a turret. Curiously, this is an extra turret, ie a third turret in the mile between milecastles 39 and 40 where normally there would only be two. Presumably it was built to watch over Peel Gap, which is all but invisible from the two turrets on either side. The first road for almost six miles (9.6km) runs through the gap and the award-winning **Steel Rigg car park** lies hidden away behind trees at the top of the hill; indeed, follow the Hadrian's Wall Path and you'll barely notice it's there.

If you haven't already joined the road down to Once Brewed (there's a short-cut onto the road round the back of Peel Bothy – see Map 23), you can do so from here.

ONCE BREWED   [Map 23]

There's not much to Once Brewed other than a decent pub, one of the YHA's oldest hostels, a campsite, an excellent visitor centre, a curious name and a legend. The last two are linked: according to the story, General Wade, he of Military Road fame and bane of Bonnie Prince Charlie, once stayed at an inn here and, unhappy with the quality of the beer, ordered it to be brewed again. Hence the name – or at least that's how one story has it.

The Northumberland National Park **visitor centre** (☎ 01434-344396; Apr-Oct daily 9.30am-5pm, Nov-Mar Sat/Sun only 10am-3pm) is a very helpful little place as well as being a tourist information centre.

They also have toilets, some refreshments, some picnic tables – and even wi-fi. Incidentally, it was announced in 2013 that plans for a brand new £10 million visitor centre and youth hostel at Once Brewed have been given the go-ahead, so expect the information given here to change over 2014-15.

Until those changes take effect, however, *Once Brewed YHA Hostel* (☎ 0845-371 9753, ☐ oncebrewed@yha.org.uk; daily Feb-Nov, group bookings only in winter; 79 beds) remains for the time being the first building you come to when dropping down from Steel Rigg. Opened in 1934, it's a popular stop with Pennine Way

VINDOLANDA [Map 22, p157]

☎ *01434-344277; ⊑ www.vindolanda.com; daily Apr-Sep 10am-6pm, mid-Feb to Mar & Oct to mid-Nov 10am-5pm; subject to change in bad weather so check in advance. Entry to Vindolanda costs £6.50/5.50/4/19 adults/concs/child/family; a joint-saver ticket with entrance to Carvoran Roman Museum costs £10/£8.50/£5.50/£29; the Roman Army Museum (see p169) costs £5.25/£4.50/£3/£15. There is a 10% discount for English Heritage members.*

According to a panel of experts at the British Museum, the artefacts found at the fort at Vindolanda are collectively the single most important historic site on these shores, beating such treasures as the Anglo-Saxon hoard at the Sutton Hoo burial, the Roman Mildenhall Treasure and the Lewis Chessmen.

Upon first arriving at Vindolanda, you may well wonder what all the fuss is about. Sure the 1½-mile (2km) walk or bus ride (see p156) from Once Brewed is nice enough, with a Roman milepost along the road and some decent views of Sycamore Gap. But once through the gates there's none of the spectacular, near-complete ruins found at Housesteads.

Here at Vindolanda the remains rise only just above foundation level. What's more, the only impressive structures on the site are the modern mock-ups of Hadrian's Wall, one in timber and turf and one in stone, that overlook the ongoing archaeological work from the south. (And isn't it ironic that the best reconstructions of the Wall lie at one of the few existing forts that never even lay on the Wall!)

Nevertheless, as those experts at the British Museum tell us, this is *the* most important site along the whole of the Wall. Indeed, it's *the* most important site in Roman Britain, and when the excavation is finally finished – a job that, according to some estimates, could take at least another hundred years – it could even turn out to be the most important Roman site in *the entire world*. And the reason why can be seen in the **museum** at the rear of the site. For thanks to a fortunate combination of silt and water in the soil at Vindolanda, an incredible array of artefacts has been uncovered here, preserved in the earth, providing us with a hitherto unrivalled glimpse into the everyday life of the Roman Empire. Most famously, this is where, in 1973, Robin Birley (having bought the Vindolanda site back in 1929, his old home now houses the museum) discovered the so-called **Roman postcards** (aka Vindolanda postcards) – paper-thin, postcard-sized wooden writing tablets used by the Romans for everything from official reports to birthday invitations, school homework to love letters. Many of the 1900 or so tablets that have so far been discovered are now in the care of the British Museum, though the museum in Vindolanda has some of them on loan and examples of some of the best, too, including a letter from a concerned mother promising to send her son more underwear to protect him from the bitter British winter and the icy northern wind that blows up the toga at certain times of the year. Then we have a misquote from Virgil's *Aeneid* written in a schoolchild's hand, after which somebody else – presumably the teacher – has written 'seg', short for *segnis* or 'sloppy work'. There's also the tablet with the famous reference to the 'Brituculli', or 'wretched Britons'. Humdrum, mundane and everyday, these tablets nevertheless add so much colour to our understanding of life in the Roman Empire. Incidentally, in 2012 Professor Birley's son Andrew discovered more of the aqueduct and piping system – used to supply the site with fresh water during Roman times – that was first discovered by his father 80 years ago. They also found the original spring which would have fed the whole system.

Plenty of other objects amaze as well. Take the beautifully intricate leather sandals, for example, discarded casually by the inhabitants into a ditch when broken but immaculately preserved to this day. There are also keys, cutlery, pottery, weapons and, my personal favourite, a fragment of glass with a gladiatorial scene painted upon it, in colours that are still as vibrant today as they must have been nearly 2000 years ago. Magically, after I said in the first edition of this guide how wonderful it would be to find more of that vase, in May 2007 archaeologists did just that while digging in a ditch some 60m away from where the original piece was found! This second piece, larger than the original fragment and interlocking perfectly with it, shows two more gladiators, a third figure who could be a referee, and a fourth who seems to be awarding a prize.

Overall, the museum at Vindolanda is a fascinating, absorbing, mind-boggling collection that will ruin your planned schedule for the day. But it also, in my opinion, brings home just what life on the Wall during the Roman era was like more than any other attraction on the walk. Don't miss it, or it will haunt you for the rest of your walk.

The **AD122 bus** calls here once a day (at 9.25am) travelling west and twice a day (12.28pm & 4.58pm) travelling east; see pp46-8 for further information.

STEEL RIGG TO BANKS [MAPS 23-30]

Introduction

While this **12¹⁄₂-mile (20km; 6-6¹⁄₄hrs)** stage may not be as spectacular as the previous one, it is perhaps the most interesting. It's also something of a red-letter day, for it is on this stage that we climb to the highest point of the entire trail. It is on this day, too, that we cross from Northumberland into Cumbria and the scenery changes from the windswept moors and crags that provided yesterday's backdrop to the more gentle, rolling, cultivated landscape of England's far north-west. We also cross the watershed on this day, so that by the end of it any river we encounter from now on flows west to the Irish Sea, not east to the North Sea as has previously been the case.

The limestone runs out on this stage, too, at Banks where the Red Rock Fault splits the country. Moreover, to the west of Gilsland, at Willowford Bridge, the Wall was originally made of turf (possibly because of the lack of limestone) and rebuilt in stone only later. Also at Willowford, the broad foundations that have held up the Wall so far are reduced; from now on it is narrow wall on *narrow* foundations. Finally, and also at the River Irthing, the remains of the third Roman bridge on our walk can be seen, which would once have carried both the Wall and the Military Way. Quite a stage indeed! Nor have we even mentioned all the turrets, forts and milecastles – and even, uniquely, a Roman watchtower – that are encountered along the way.

One word of warning, however, before you set off: though this stage ends in Banks, there is just one B&B-cum-campsite there. As such, be prepared to stay before Banks – for example at Greenhead (which has a hotel and a hostel with a B&B nearby and right on the trail; see p172), Gilsland (B&Bs; see pp173-4) or to attempt a longer walk and march on to Walton (two B&Bs and a camping barn and campsite; p184). Off the trail there are some more B&Bs at Haltwhistle which provide further options and are described on pp166-7.

The route

The day's first treat lies just a 10-minute walk from the Steel Rigg car park. This is **Green Slack** (Map 23) on the Winshields Crags, at 345m the highest point on the trail, with a decent section of Roman Wall leading up to it. Whilst the rest of the stage is only slightly less exhausting than the relentless up-and-down rollercoaster ride of yesterday, it is at least some comfort that, for the rest of the trip, there'll be more downhill than uphill!

By the way, if you feel like taking a breather while you're up here, according to scientists there's no better place in England to take it: the lichen that grows on the Winshields Crags requires extremely pure air and, apart from

ROUTE GUIDE AND MAPS

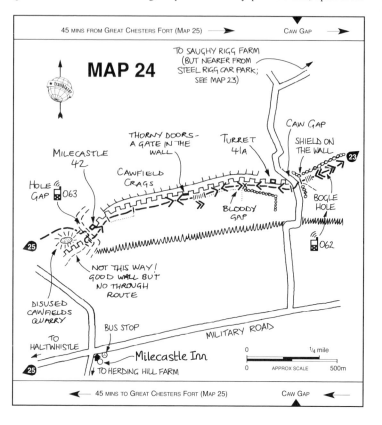

45 MINS FROM GREAT CHESTERS FORT (MAP 25) ⟶   CAW GAP ⟶

MAP 24

★ trailblazer

TO SAUGHY RIGG FARM
(BUT NEARER FROM
STEEL RIGG CAR PARK;
SEE MAP 23)

CAW GAP

THORNY DOORS –
A GATE IN THE
WALL

TURRET
41A

SHIELD ON
THE WALL

23

MILECASTLE
42

CAWFIELD
CRAGS

HOLE
GAP   063

BLOODY
GAP

BOGLE
HOLE

25

062

NOT THIS WAY!
GOOD WALL BUT
NO THROUGH
ROUTE

DISUSED
CAWFIELDS
QUARRY

BUS STOP

TO
HALTWHISTLE

25

MILITARY ROAD

Milecastle Inn

TO HERDING HILL FARM

0   ¼ mile

0   APPROX SCALE   500m

45 MINS TO GREAT CHESTERS FORT (MAP 25) ⟵   CAW GAP ⟵

Dartmoor, this is the only place in the entire country where the air is clean enough for this lichen to thrive.

The trail varies little for the next two miles (3km) or so as you ride the crest of the crags, following the undulations through wild territory uninhabited since Roman times. The names printed on the maps – Bogle Hole, Caw Gap, Bloody Gap, Thorny Doors – only serve to add to the sense that you're in a land of folk-lore and myth.

After **Caw Gap** (Map 24) the Wall continues unbroken for over half a mile (1km). Look out for the swastika etched by the Romans into one of the Wall stones – another symbol of prosperity – on the way to **Milecastle 42**, which originally had an entrance in the north Wall until the builders saw the steep drop beneath, realised such a door was unnecessary and it was blocked up. The trail then rounds the flooded, disused quarry at **Cawfields**. Next to the quarry is a car park (Map 25) and accompanying toilet block. There are a few picnic tables here but no other reason to loiter.

Those heading to Haltwhistle should not cross over the bridge but instead head on the path to the south of the Burn. Alternatively, you can wait until you hit Great Chesters fort, just a short walk further on, and take the path down to Haltwhistle from there.

For either path, see Map 25 and the route below.

Walking to and from Haltwhistle (1 hr)   [Map 25]

The path down to Haltwhistle, particularly if taking the trail that shadows the Haltwhistle Burn, is both easy and lovely. Furthermore, you actually hike in woods under the shade of trees for much of the path – a stark contrast to the more exposed, wind-blasted walking along much of the Wall.

To get to the Burn trail, leave the Hadrian's Wall Path at the road bridge by Cawfields Quarry, taking the path that runs south of the Burn. The path heads towards a small bridge in the middle of a field *but doesn't take it*! Instead, you bend leftwards and continue to follow, roughly, the course of the Burn until it hits the B6318.

If in need of a hot meal turn left when you meet the road to the *Milecastle Inn* (Map 24; ☎ 01434-321372; 🖳 www.milecastle-inn.co.uk; **food** served Good Friday to end Oct Mon-Sat noon-8.45pm, Sun to 8.30pm; noon-2.30pm & 6-8.30pm the rest of the year) with a menu of standard pub fare augmented by some really good 'rural' dishes such as pheasant slow cooked in cider and bacon. Note, however, that dogs are not allowed. Continue for ten minutes or so along Shield Hill (the road running south from Milecastle Inn) and you come to *Herding Hill Farm* (off Map 24; ☎ 01434-320175, 🖳 www.herd inghillfarm.co.uk; 🐾 by prior arrangement and not in bunkhouse; WI-FI) a very well equipped **campsite** with tipis (sleep 4; with woodburning stove; from £55), wooden wigwams (sleep 2-5; minimum 2-night stay; from £48; hot tub £30) and a **bunkhouse** (£17pp) and pitches for tents (£10) as well as a sim-ple shop. **Food** is also served (Easter-Oct Mon-Sat 9-10.30am & 6-7pm only) offering no-nonsense fare such as a bacon roll for £2.75.

The AD122 **bus** service calls both here and at Milecastle Inn: see pp46-8.

If you just want to head straight down to Haltwhistle and rejoin the trail, stride a little way west along the road, and take a left to follow the footpath

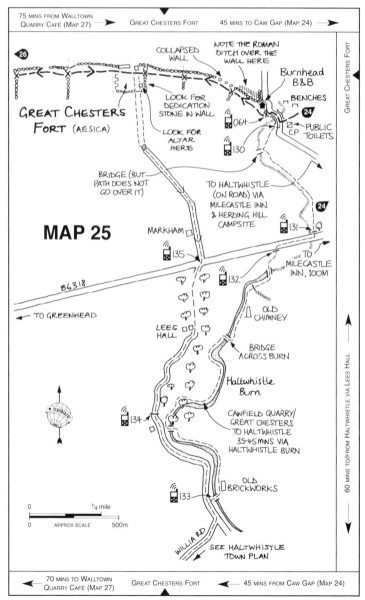

75 MINS FROM WALLTOWN QUARRY CAFÉ (MAP 27) →

GREAT CHESTERS FORT

45 MINS TO CAW GAP (MAP 24) →

GREAT CHESTERS FORT

26

COLLAPSED WALL

NOTE THE ROMAN DITCH OVER THE WALL HERE

Burnhead B&B

BENCHES

24

GREAT CHESTERS FORT (AESICA)

LOOK FOR DEDICATION STONE IN WALL

064

PUBLIC CP TOILETS

LOOK FOR ALTAR HERE

130

BRIDGE (BUT PATH DOES NOT GO OVER IT)

TO HALTWHISTLE (ON ROAD) VIA MILECASTLE INN & HERDING HILL CAMPSITE

24

MAP 25

MARKHAM

131

135

TO MILECASTLE INN, 100M

B6318

132

← TO GREENHEAD

OLD CHIMNEY

LEES HALL

BRIDGE ACROSS BURN

Haltwhistle Burn

134

CANFIELD QUARRY/ GREAT CHESTERS TO HALTWHISTLE 35-45 MINS VIA HALTWHISTLE BURN

60 MINS TO/FROM HALTWHISTLE VIA LEES HALL

trailblazer

OLD BRICKWORKS

133

0   ¼ mile

0   APPROX SCALE   500m

WILLIA RD

SEE HALTWHISTLE TOWN PLAN

which passes a weir, heads through a gate in a stone wall then follows the path as it meanders into the woods that shroud the Burn. The trail continues sedately down before finally ending up at the Old Brickworks on the outskirts of Haltwhistle.

For the return journey, rather than taking the same path back you can follow Willia Rd all the way to its termination at a gate, which you should go through and head towards Lees Hall. Crossing the B6318 once more, you go north down the slope past Markham House, then up towards Great Chesters Fort, which you arrive at behind the old Roman altar.

HALTWHISTLE

Though not on the trail itself, Haltwhistle is an important place for trekkers. Good bus and train connections (Haltwhistle is on the Newcastle–Carlisle line), a variety of accommodation, plenty of shops, restaurants and tearooms and a location almost exactly halfway along the Wall (one of the hotels on the main street is even called The Centre of Britain) ensures that many a Wall walker calls in for the night.

It's also a particularly historic town, with bastle (see p215) houses lined up along Main St and an even earlier Pele Tower now forming part of the Centre of Britain Hotel. These buildings were, of course, built as defensive fortifications during the long-running skirmishes between the English and the Scots, a time when much of the border region was considered bandit country. Such was the fear and enmity between both sides that a plaque in the market square recounts the sad tale of a young local girl who had attempted to run away and marry a Scot. Her reward for this act of 'treason' was to be the last person executed in the Market Sq – along with her beau – in 1597.

Today Haltwhistle is a genteel sort of place with a pretty main street and a plethora of tearooms and eateries, many of which display notices saying that 'Walkers are welcome here' – a nice touch.

Services

The **tourist information centre** (☎ 01434-322002; Easter to Oct Mon-Sat 10am-1pm & 1.30-4.30pm) is in the library and perhaps the office most dedicated to the Hadrian's Wall Path. However, they do not open in the winter months.

There is a Barclays bank with **cashpoint (ATM)** on Main St and another at the

post office (Mon-Fri 9am-5.30pm, Sat 9am-12.30pm), while a little further up there stands, almost uniquely on this walk, a self-service **launderette** (daily 8am-6.30pm; £4 for a load plus £1 for 20 minutes in the dryer). A little further down from the post office, on the opposite side, there's a Boots the **chemist** (Mon-Fri 9am-6pm, Sat to 1pm).

For **provisions**, there's a Co-op (daily 7am-10pm) on the main street and a Sainsbury's (Mon-Fri 8am-10pm, Sat 7.30am-10pm, Sun 10am-4pm) just to the north of Main St behind the shops; Sainsbury's has an ATM and there is a path to it between Lucky Palace and Oceans Fish & Chips.

Transport

[See pp46-8] The AD122 **bus** for Hexham stops in Market Place having called in at the railway station three minutes earlier; buses for Carlisle stop first at the Market Place and then at the station. Arriva's/Stagecoach's No 685 calls here as does Telford's Coaches' No 185.

There are **trains** approximately every hour to Newcastle (journey time 50-60 mins) and Carlisle (just over 30 mins).

Where to stay

Ashcroft (☎ 01434-320213, 🖳 www.ash croftguesthouse.co.uk; 1S/2T/2D/ 1F suite, apartment sleeps 6, all en suite; 🛏; WI-FI), a former vicarage on Lanty's Lonnen, just off the Westgate, is a lovely place with some award-winning terraced gardens. The rooms are full of features and cost from £42.50pp for two sharing (add £5 for a room with four-poster bed), £55-90 for the single/single occupancy.

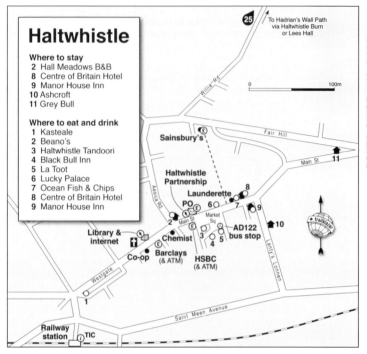

Haltwhistle

Where to stay
2 Hall Meadows B&B
8 Centre of Britain Hotel
9 Manor House Inn
10 Ashcroft
11 Grey Bull

Where to eat and drink
1 Kasteale
2 Beano's
3 Haltwhistle Tandoori
4 Black Bull Inn
5 La Toot
6 Lucky Palace
7 Ocean Fish & Chips
8 Centre of Britain Hotel
9 Manor House Inn

To Hadrian's Wall Path via Haltwhistle Burn or Lees Hall

Willia Rd

Fair Hill

Main St

Sainsbury's

Haltwhistle Partnership

Launderette
PO
Market Sq
AD122 bus stop

Library & internet

Chemist
Barclays (& ATM)
Co-op
HSBC (& ATM)

Adison Rd

Lanty's Lonnen

Westgate

Saint Meen Avenue

Railway station   TIC

Manor House Inn (☎ 01434-322588,
5T/1D, all en suite; 🛏; WI-FI) changed
hands in 2014. A friendly and reasonably
priced place, like most around here, with
B&B from £35 per person).

Just across the road – but a few steps
up in terms of quality – *Centre of Britain
Hotel* (☎ 01434-322422, 🖳 www.centre-
of-britain.org.uk; 5T/7D, all en suite; 🛏;
🐾 £10 by prior arrangement) is the pick of
the hotels on Main St; B&B costs £35-55pp
(£59-79 sgl occ).

Further east on Main St, *Grey Bull* (☎
01434-321991, 🖳 www.greybullhotel.co
.uk; 4D/1T/1D, T or F, all en suite; WI-FI)
charges £70 for B&B (£50 sgl occ).

Finally, *Hall Meadows* (☎ 01434-
321021, 🖳 www.accommodationinhalt
whistle.co.uk; 1T/1D en suite, 1D private
bathroom; 🛏; WI-FI) is a very attractive
late 19th-century building covered with

creepers that looks slightly out of place on
Main St. Prices start at £32.50pp (£50 sgl
occ). Packed lunches provided if arranged
in advance.

Where to eat and drink
One of the main reasons for dropping down
off the path to visit Haltwhistle is the quality (and quantity) of eateries here. Two at
least stand out: *Kasteale* (☎ 01434-394121,
🖳 www.kasteale.co.uk; Wed-Sat 10am-
4pm, Sun noon-4pm; 🐾; WI-FI) is a new
and lovely place at the western end of the
main street, run by enthusiastic baker Jill
whose lovely little traditional tearoom
serves mainly home-baked goods using
organic and locally produced ingredients as
well as a decent cuppa. Just smashing! The
second option is *La Toot* (☎ 07721-697157,
🖳 www.latoot.com; Mon-Sat 10am-4pm;
🐾) which stands on the Market Square

and offers a similar menu to *Kasteale* of soups, sandwiches, breakfasts, pies and quiches.

Other choices include *Beano's* (☎ 01434-321321; Mon-Sat 8.30am-2.30pm, last orders 2pm) a very good-value take-away sandwich shop where a basic bacon butty is only £2.20, jacket spuds are £2.55-3.25 and paninis £2.50-3.10).

For an evening meal there are several takeaway-only places: *Ocean Fish & Chips* (Mon-Sat 11.30am-1.30pm & 5-9pm), *Haltwhistle Tandoori* (☎ 01434-321388; daily 6-11pm) and the Chinese *Lucky Palace* (☎ 01434-322330; Tue-Sun

5-11pm). To eat out there is *Manor House Inn* (see Where to stay; food served summer daily noon-2.30pm & 6-9pm; no food Sun eve in winter), *Centre of Britain* (see Where to stay; daily 6.30-9pm, advance booking recommended for non-residents) where two courses in the evening are £19.95; and, best of the lot by far in my opinion, the *Black Bull Inn* (☎ 01434-320463; food served daily noon-2.30pm & 6-9pm; 🐕; WI-FI), a traditional, cosy, dog-friendly timber-and-horse-brass sort of place, a real ale pub where no mains costs more than the £12.95 ribeye steak.

To continue on the Hadrian's Wall path and reach Great Chesters fort, cross the bridge and climb over the nearby farm wall. That farm, incidentally, is *Burnhead B&B* (Map 25; ☎ 01434-320841, 🖳 www.burnheadbedandbreak fast.co.uk; 2T, en suite; WI-FI), built with Roman stones. Rates start at £35pp; packed lunches (£5) are available if requested in advance.

Soon afterwards, round the back of a neighbouring farm, lies the buried remains of **Great Chesters Fort** (not to be confused with Chesters Fort in Chollerford, see p130), known to the Romans as **Aesica**. It is known that the Dalmatae from the Yugoslav mountains were garrisoned here during Hadrian's reign and later the Hamii from Syria, who were famous archers.

There have been some important finds at Great Chesters, for example, one of the few tombstones of a legionary soldier (as opposed to an auxiliary). Archaeologists also found evidence of an aqueduct that once supplied the fort – bringing water from the head of Haltwhistle Burn, some six miles away! What's more, before the fort, which was built to guard Caw Gap, this farmyard was the home of Milecastle 43. This is yet further evidence that the Wall and its accompanying defences were built in two stages, with the decision to move the forts up to the Wall taken only after the Wall itself and its accompanying milecastles and turrets had already been built; see p50 for details. Indeed, where the Haltwhistle Burn crosses the Stanegate the remains of an early Roman fort have been discovered – presumably the one that was abandoned when Aesica was built, its garrison moved to the new premises.

Alas, there's little remaining of small, three-acre (1.2-hectare) Aesica except for some outer walls and an **altar** to the east of its south gate; heavily eroded, it is nevertheless the only original altar remaining in situ on the Wall and still inspires many a trekker to leave a small fiscal donation on its top, presumably for luck. The path to Haltwhistle leaves from near the altar, heading down the slopes.

Back on the trail, leave the wood (Map 26) to the west of the fort, making sure you check out the gatepost on the right as you descend from the stile – large and cylindrical, it was clearly once a **Roman milestone**. The only other sign of

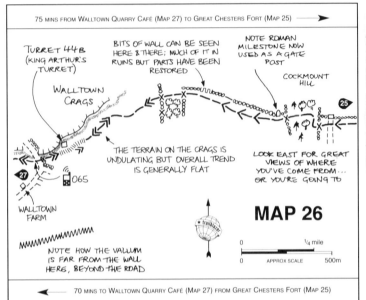

ROUTE GUIDE AND MAPS

TURRET 44B
(KING ARTHUR'S
TURRET)

BITS OF WALL CAN BE SEEN
HERE & THERE; MUCH OF IT IN
RUINS BUT PARTS HAVE BEEN
RESTORED

NOTE ROMAN
MILESTONE NOW
USED AS A GATE
POST

WALLTOWN
CRAGS

COCKMOUNT
HILL

25

THE TERRAIN ON THE CRAGS IS
UNDULATING BUT OVERALL TREND
IS GENERALLY FLAT

LOOK EAST FOR GREAT
VIEWS OF WHERE
YOU'VE COME FROM...
OR YOU'RE GOING TO

27

065

WALLTOWN
FARM

MAP 26

trailblazer

0   ¼ mile
0   APPROX SCALE   500m

NOTE HOW THE VALLUM
IS FAR FROM THE WALL
HERE, BEYOND THE ROAD

Roman construction is the defensive ditch which appears intermittently along this section; the Wall itself disappears from the top of the ridge, while the Vallum lies some way to the south.

Dropping steeply down past **Turret 44B** (King Arthur's Turret), the trail continues along the **Walltown Crags** to the excellently preserved **Turret 45A** (Map 27) and the start of an impressive section of Wall, ended abruptly by a regular farm wall that leads south down to **Walltown Quarry**. It is believed to be one of the few remaining parts of the Wall that hasn't undergone any 19th-century restoration. Once a working quarry, the land around here is now a country park and already plays host to a variety of ducks and other birdlife.

On bright sunny days the benches outside the small café here, *Walltown Refreshments* (Easter to end Oct, daily 10am-5pm), are pleasant places to hang out and soak up the sun, though if the weather's less than perfect but you still want to rest there are *tearooms* at the **Roman Army Museum** (☎ 016977-47485, 🖳 www.vindolanda.com; daily Apr-Sep 10am-6pm, mid Feb-Mar & Oct 10am-5pm, Nov-mid Feb open weekends 10am-4pm only; £5.25 adult, £4.50 senior/student, £3 child, £15 family, see also p161 for details of combined entry tickets), just a few metres down the road. Features include a 3D film of a visualisation of the top of the wall from here to Vindolanda and additional exhibits about life in the Roman army. The museum is situated by the site of the Roman fort, Magna ('Rocks') at **Carvoran**.

❑ **The Elizabethan wall that never was**
Much of the millennium and a half between the departure of the Romans and the ordination of the Wall as a UNESCO World Heritage Site was characterised by the practice of border reiving, where gangs would attack their rivals and neighbours to raid, rustle and rape.

While these days this 'hidden history' of the Wall receives scant attention, there is no doubt that at the time the problem was a serious one, serious enough for a protection racket to be established and a new word, 'blackmail', to be coined (see box p202). Indeed, the raiding reached such a height in Elizabethan times that in 1587 a proposal was made to revive and rebuild the Wall in order to keep some sort of semblance of order. If that wasn't practical, the proposal declared, a new wall, constructed on similar lines to the Roman version, should be built, with *sconses* (castles) at every mile. Unfortunately, the cost was estimated to be a prohibitive £30,000 and was never taken up.

The fort lay to the south of the Vallum by the Stanegate so, presumably, was not a Wall fort, despite its proximity to the Wall. The museum itself has a reasonable collection, though it comes a distant second compared to its sister museum at Vindolanda (see p161). It does, however, have a wonderful **video** featuring a bird's-eye view of the Wall, including computer-generated reconstructions of how the Wall must have looked almost 2000 years ago.

The Roman Army Museum is the terminus for the AD122 bus from Hexham; see pp46-8 for further information. Telford's No 185 also calls in here on its way between Haltwhistle and Carlisle.

As you continue on the trail, the Vallum, for so long a stranger, once again becomes your companion as you stroll down to the bridge. Before it stands one of the more popular B&Bs on the route: ***Holmhead*** (Map 27; ☎ 016977-47402, 🖳 www.bandbhadrianswall.com; 2S or D/2D or T, all en suite; WI-FI). Right in the shadow of enigmatic Thirlwall Castle, right on the line of the Wall, and actually *built* from Hadrian's Wall stones (which, with delicious irony, were nicked from Thirlwall Castle which had nicked them from the Wall in the first place) this delightful farmhouse, surrounded on two sides by pretty streams, provides accommodation for all budgets. **B&B** is £68-78 (£50 sgl occ). The **camping barn** (£13.50pp plus £3.50 to hire a sleeping bag) sleeps five and has a kitchenette with hob, microwave and toaster. The barn has shower/toilet facilities; reservations are recommended as the barns are often booked by groups. They also have a small area where you can **camp** for £7 for one person, £10 for two (basic toilet/shower facilities are available).

If that's not enough, Holmhead also possesses two Roman inscriptions. The first lies beside the kitchen door and says *Civitas Dumnoni*, commemorating the work of a tribe from Devonshire which was drafted up here for Wall construction and repairs. It's quite a rare inscription, for the Wall was built almost entirely by regular Roman troops and manned by auxiliaries from Spain, Bavaria etc; the British rarely got a look in, so why these troops were asked to undertake work on the Wall here is unknown. A second inscription can be found in the wall of the bunkhouse, and tells how the Roman centurion Julius Ianalis oversaw the

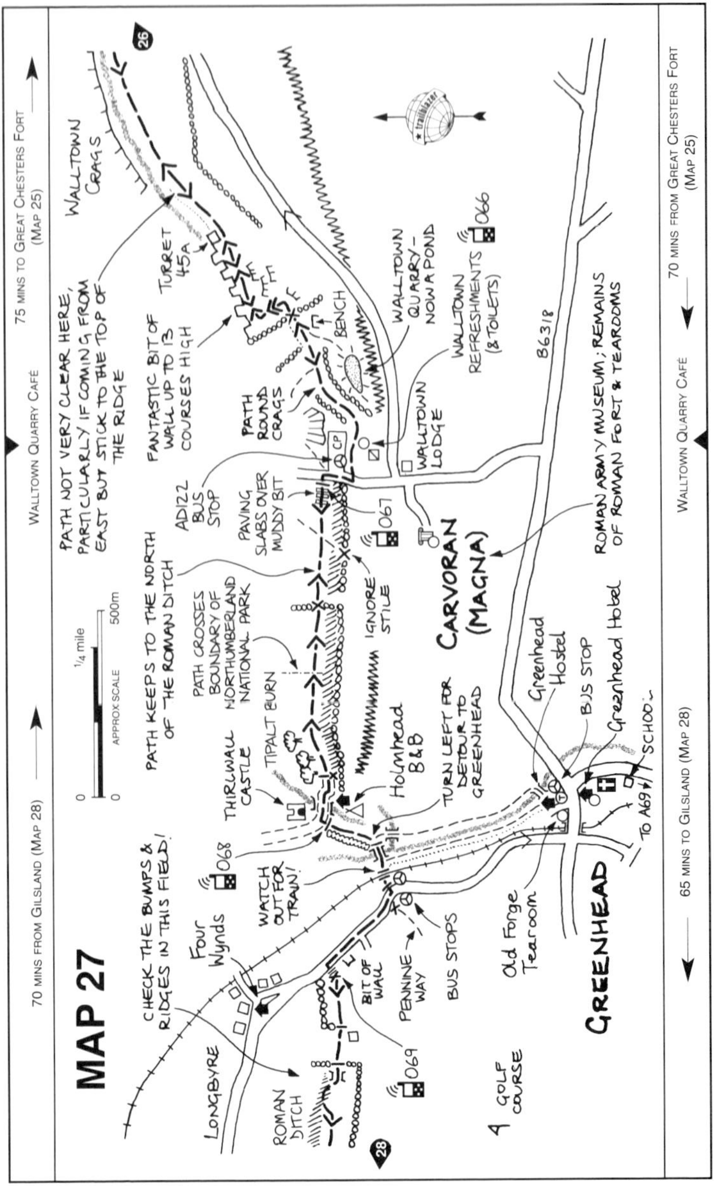
MAP 27
70 MINS FROM GILSLAND (MAP 28)
75 MINS TO GREAT CHESTERS FORT (MAP 25)
WALLTOWN QUARRY CAFÉ
70 MINS FROM GREAT CHESTERS FORT (MAP 25)
WALLTOWN QUARRY CAFÉ
65 MINS TO GILSLAND (MAP 28)
0
1/4 mile
0
APPROX SCALE
500m
26
28
WALLTOWN CRAGS
PATH NOT VERY CLEAR HERE, PARTICULARLY IF COMING FROM EAST BUT STICK TO THE TOP OF THE RIDGE
TURRET 45A
FANTASTIC BIT OF WALL UP TO 13 COURSES HIGH
BENCH
PATH ROUND CRAGS
CP
WALLTOWN QUARRY – NOW A POND
WALLTOWN REFRESHMENTS (& TOILETS)
066
B6318
WALLTOWN LODGE
AD122 BUS STOP
PAVING SLABS OVER MUDDY BIT
067
CARVORAN (MAGNA)
ROMAN ARMY MUSEUM; REMAINS OF ROMAN FORT & TEAROOMS
PATH KEEPS TO THE NORTH OF THE ROMAN DITCH
IGNORE STILE
PATH CROSSES BOUNDARY OF NORTHUMBERLAND NATIONAL PARK
TIPALT BURN
THIRLWALL CASTLE
Holmhead B&B
TURN LEFT FOR DETOUR TO GREENHEAD
Greenhead Hostel
BUS STOP
Greenhead Hotel
SCHOOL
TO A69
GREENHEAD
Old Forge Tearoom
068
WATCH OUT FOR TRAIN!
BUS STOPS
PENNINE WAY
BIT OF WALL
069
Four Wynds
CHECK THE BUMPS & RIDGES IN THIS FIELD!
LONGBYRE
ROMAN DITCH
GOLF COURSE

construction of this section of the Wall. You'll have to ask the owners to point it out to you – it's not easy to locate.

As for the 14th-century **Thirlwall Castle** (Map 27), Thirlwall means 'Gap in the Wall' in the local dialect and the castle was built in a gap in the Wall where it was crossed by the Tipalt Burn. A typically strong, defensible home, Thirlwall was built to protect the owners from the cross-border reiving raids (see box p202) that were rife at this time.

The Thirlwall family (they adopted the name of the local area when they bought the land for the castle) had made their fortune in military campaigns in France. It is one thing to earn a fortune, however, and quite another to keep it, particularly in this part of the world in the 14th century. Hence the extravagant fortifications to their family home, built using whatever material lay close at hand – which, of course, meant the Wall. The castle lasted for 300 years before the family moved to Hexham and the castle was sold to the Earl of Carlisle for £4000. Already in possession of one large country pile, the earl was interested only in Thirlwall's land and allowed the castle to fall into disrepair and, eventually, ruin. There's little to see today except the shell of the keep but it remains an atmospheric and charmingly dilapidated place.

Opposite the castle, a path leads alongside a stream to a railway, where you have a choice. Turn left before the railway, head over the bridge, and you soon arrive at ...

GREENHEAD   [Map 27, p171]

Though well-known to Wall walkers thanks to its proximity to the trail and its facilities, there's little to Greenhead beyond a school, church, the *Old Forge Tearoom* (daily 10am-4pm), which serves homemade dishes, a **pub/hotel** and a **hostel**.

Greenhead Hotel (☎ 016977-47411, 🖳 www.greenheadhotelandhostel.co.uk; 1T/1D/2D, T or F, all en suite; 🢂; 🐾 by prior arrangement, must stay in kennels outside; wi-fi) has a bar and a restaurant and is the focus of the village. Rates start at £80 (around £50 sgl occ). **Food** is served daily noon-8.30pm.

Under the same ownership is *Greenhead Hostel* (see Greenhead Hotel for contact details; open all year; 40 beds; housed in a converted Methodist church. No longer affiliated with the YHA, they charge £15 per person, £75 for the whole room (4 x 6-bed rooms, 2 x 8-bed rooms).

Telford's No 185 **bus** stops by the hotel/village hall and if you walk to the road end (A69), a few minutes away, you can catch Arriva's/Stagecoach's No 685 service. See pp46-8 for further information.

... or continue straight on to the main road where, turning right and then left, you pass a decent chunk of Wall that's been shored up to allow the B6318 to bisect it. For **B&B** stay on the road for *Four Wynds Guest House* (☎ 016977-47972, 🖳 www.four-wynds-guest-house.co.uk; 2T/1D or F, all en suite; 🐾 by prior arrangement; wi-fi); it has rooms for £68 based on two sharing (£48 sgl occ).

The path follows the line of the Wall past the undulations of the Vallum, Military Way and the Wall itself. Continuing to Gap Farm (named after the Tyne Gap which runs nearby and which marks the watershed of Britain), you soon arrive at the friendly town/village of Gilsland.

GILSLAND [Map 28, p175]

The previous edition called Gilsland unpre-possessing. I now feel this was a little harsh. True, most walkers arrive at the village by dropping off the trail and down through the 'back streets', which isn't pretty. Furthermore, the house that the Wall actually runs through is in a parlous state of disrepair; it was never great when I arrived to research the first edition in 2006 and it's been disintegrating ever since, to the point where the roof is now more hole than tile. Nevertheless, I've have grown to really like the place; mainly due, it must be said, to the residents as much as the place itself, though there are pretty corners and the river that runs through it is a delight.

Gilsland is also an important place on the walk. It is here that we find the border between Northumberland and Cumbria; Gilsland is actually still in Northumberland but is the last place that is on this trail. Here, too, we cross the watershed and the Red Rock Fault.

For such a quiet place, Gilsland also seems to be in a constant state of turmoil. No sooner does one pub shut (eg the Station Inn) than another (the Samson Inn) undergoes a radical overhaul and now serves some of the best food on the trail; and while the bus AD122 bus service no longer comes this far west, and the post office and the only shop have also closed and (and in doing so took with it the only cashpoint for miles around), the village can still boast a lovely tearoom and a great bunk/camping barn and a couple of very good B&Bs. Oh, and not forgetting some of the most impressive Roman ruins on the trail too. For it's here that we find **Poltross Burn Milecastle** (No 48), one of the most important on the Wall. In excellent nick, the ruins include a series of steps in their north-east corner; by estimating their direction, archaeologists were able to determine the height of the walkway on the Wall at 12ft (3.66m). It is also, alas, one of the last Roman milecastles we see, providing further evidence that we are leaving the wild, windswept lands of Northumberland behind to enter the more rural, cosy scenery of Cumbria, where the land has been ploughed and cultivated for

centuries, destroying much of the Wall in the process.

Telford's No 185 **bus** leaves from opposite the Bridge Inn/Village Hall. Arriva's/Stagecoach's No 685 also calls in on its way to Newcastle or to Carlisle. See pp46-8 for further details.

Where to stay

There are a couple of **camping barns**, though both are at least a twenty-minute walk from the centre of Gilsland. Perhaps best reached from Birdoswald, which stares it in the eye across the valley, *Slack House Organic Farm* (off Map 29; ☎ 016977-47351, 🖳 www.slackhousefarm.co.uk; 🐾 if no-one else is staying) is a former B&B turned **camping/bunk barn** that's deservedly been receiving great reviews since opening in 2012. Run by the friendly and knowledgeable Diane, a former teacher, and her husband, this independent hostel is immaculate and features a wood burner in the downstairs lounge area, an adjacent kitchen area, a five-bed bunkhouse (£15 per bed) with beds and duvets (sheets required) and a simple camping barn with airbeds (£8.50). There's also a three-bed family room next door on one side (£50 for the room), and the *Scypen* **café** (Thur-Mon 10am-5pm) and fresh food shop on the other where they sell the cheeses that they make on site at the Birdoswald Dairy! All in all, it's just about the best place to stay in this price bracket on (or, rather, just off) the Wall.

Bush Nook (☎ 016977-47194, 🖳 www.bushnook.co.uk; 1S/3D/2T, all en suite; 👄; WI-FI; packed lunch £5.50) is an 18th-century stone-built former farm constructed, at least in part, from Hadrian's Wall stone (though as the genial owner rightly points out, try to find a building that isn't made of Hadrian's Wall stone around here!). Most of the rooms have open-beamed ceilings, there's a delightful conservatory and even a hot tub. They are also licensed and serve **food** (£15-20 per head). **B&B** in the house costs £40-45pp; they also have a self-catering cottage (1D) which can be used on a B&B basis (£45-

50pp) if available, and have just constructed a six-bed **bunkhouse** for groups to use (around £120 for room only). Dogs are welcome but they are not permitted in the bedrooms; however, they have an enclosed area where they can stay. True, it is a walk of at least a mile from the path but if you prefer not to walk this contact them and they will try to arrange transport. To reach Bush Nook, turn left upon hitting the road after the Poltross Burn Milecastle, and another left at the next junction.

The *Samson Inn* (☎ 016977-47880, 🖳 www.thesamson.co.uk; 2S or D/2D or T; 🐾; WI-FI; £50 single, from £75 for a double) also offers **B&B**, in a building next door. Indeed, its new owners began by providing accommodation at the excellent *Willowford Farm* (☎ 016977-47962, 🖳 www.willowford.co.uk; 5D or T, all en suite; ➽; 🐾 by prior arrangement; WI-FI; Mar-Oct; packed lunch £6) which stands at the other end of the village, right on the Wall. The rooms (which, before their conversion, were a milking parlour, cart house, grain store and two pig holes!) are incredibly cosy with underfloor heating, sheep wool insulation and digital radios. With a lovely free-range and (mostly) organic breakfast in the morning and a whacking great bit of Wall right outside, this is a great place. It's also possible – though can't be promised – that they'll give you a lift to the pub if they're free.

A little out of town but very much part of its history, *Gilsland Spa Hotel* (☎ 016977-47203, 🖳 www.gilslandspa.co.uk; 94 rooms inc S, D, T & F, all en suite; ➽; WI-FI) dates back to a time when Gilsland was still a smart town where visitors would flock to take the waters. Set in 140 acres (56 hectares) of park and woodland overlooking the town from the north, it remains an impressive place, as Rabbie Burns and Sir Walter Scott (two previous residents) would surely agree. **B&B** starts at £47.50pp. Their *Galloways Bar* (**food** daily noon-2pm & 6-8pm) is open to anyone.

Not too far away, *Brookside Villa* (☎ 016977-47300, 🖳 www.brooksidevilla .com; 4T, D or F, en suite; ➽; 🐾 by prior arrangement; WI-FI) is an even older institu-

tion, having provided good-quality accommodation to weary travellers since 1888! Recommended by more than one reader, B&B costs from £42pp (£50 sgl occ). They offer a 'trail walkers package' for people staying more than one night; contact them for details. They also serve evening **meals** (from £15.50) and are fully licensed, offering locally brewed ales from Geltsdale Brewery in Brampton, and offer an overnight laundry service too (£7 per load) as well as a drying room that guests can use.

Also worth considering is *The Hill on the Wall* (☎ 016977-47214, 🖳 www.hillon thewall.co.uk; 1D/1T en suite, 1T private bathroom; ➽; WI-FI; Feb-Nov), an award-winning B&B housed in a fortified 16th-century house, or bastle (see p215). It's a beautiful place – perhaps the best-looking accommodation on the entire trail – with wonderful old furniture including a large pine table hewn from the wood of a 17th-century mill. To make you feel right at home, all the rooms are named after Roman celebrities such as Hadrian's Retreat and Caligula's Chamber. Rates start at £37.50-42.50pp (£50-62.50 sgl occ).

Where to eat

For **food** during the day, *House of Meg* (☎ 016977-47777, 🖳 www.house ofmeg.co.uk; Apr/May-Oct Mon-Sat 7.30am-4.30pm, Sun 10am-4pm, Nov-Apr/May Mon-Wed 7.30-11.30am, Thur-Sat 9.30am-4pm, Sun 10am-4pm) is a smart little café that should be able to cater for your nutritional needs by serving huge baguettes and sandwiches which range from the tasty to the absolutely delicious. They also sell a few groceries. The name of the café is derived from a character from Walter Scott's *Waverley*, which was set around here.

For dinner, the *Samson Inn* (see Where to stay; summer daily noon-2.30pm & 6-8.30pm winter eves & weekends only; 🐾) is now more of a restaurant than a pub though it's very relaxed and maintains a good bar. The food is great and we reckon it has amongst the best vegetarian selections on the trail. It's all very reasonably priced with mains around £10-15.

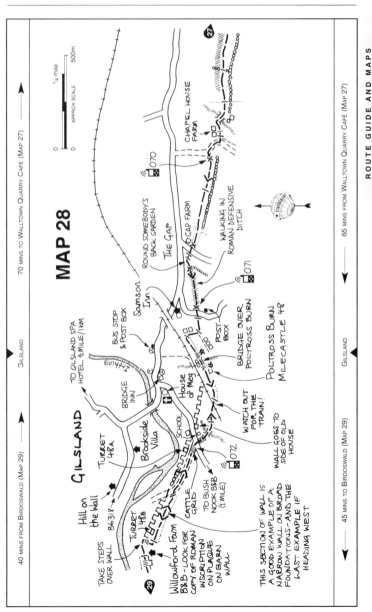

From the Poltross Burn Milecastle, the trail crosses the train tracks to a field where a rather remarkable sight awaits: an extensive and well-preserved piece of Roman Wall clearly going into, and under, the dilapidated (but still occupied) old house. This, I presume, was the Romanway Guest House (aka the Old Vicarage), mentioned by Hunter Davies (see p41) and others, which used to have two Roman altars on its porch. Unfortunately, they don't seem to be accepting guests these days – nor would you want to stay there! - and the Wall is out of bounds.

Across the road you rejoin the Wall, again a decent chunk, this one leading from one farmhouse on the outskirts of Gilsland to another in the middle of a field. This Wall section has its own turrets too, Nos **48A** and **48B**, the latter near Willowford Farm (see p174). Look back from the second turret to the first and, given that the Romans built their turrets at equal intervals between their mile-castles, you get an idea of what one-third of a Roman mile looked like – and thus can imagine roughly what one Roman mile looked like.

Negotiating the various gates and barriers of the second farmhouse (check out the 'Roman-style' plaque stuck to the side of the barn wall), the trail – and Wall – continues down to the Irthing and the **Willowford Bridge** foundations, where the Wall and Military Way crossed the river (Map 29). Note how the river has changed its course down the centuries, for this abutment would once have been on the riverbank. There were a number of bridges at this spot, the first being built around the same time as the Wall in AD122-8. The latest, **Irthing Bridge**, one of the most beautiful on the trail, is made of weathered steel and lies just a few metres away.

The Willowford crossing also holds quite an important place in the history of the Wall. It was here that the stone Wall, which the Romans started to con-struct in Newcastle and extended westwards, finally met up with the turf Wall from Bowness-on-Solway. In other words, this was the last section of Wall to have been built; once they'd done this bit and joined the two sections together, their ambition to build a barrier across Britain had been realised. Any construc-tion done after this – moving the forts up to the Wall, for example, or convert-ing the turf Wall into a stone one – were mere refinements carried out when their infrastructure improved and allowed them to transport limestone this far west. It was also here that the broad Wall foundations ran out. Presumably, by the time the stone wall to the west of the Irthing was being constructed, to replace the original turf and timber one, the Romans had settled on a narrow Wall so built narrow foundations to suit it.

After the bridge, it's a bit of a schlep up to **Milecastle 49**, followed by a lengthy section of Wall leading up to Birdoswald. Don't be in too much of a hurry to get there: there are estimated to be half a dozen or so engravings on this section of the Wall. Two of the best known include a dedication stone, just over halfway between the milecastle and the fort (look for the large brown stone near the top of the Wall) and, best of all, a great phallic symbol near Birdoswald itself. To find the latter, look for where a 'modern' stone wall hits Hadrian's Wall at a 90° angle on its northern side, not long before you enter into

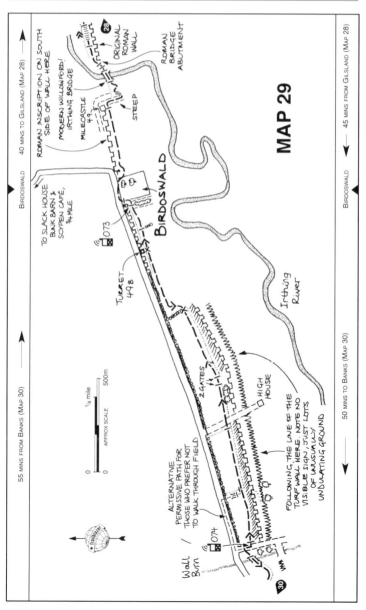

BIRDOSWALD

TO SLACK HOUSE
BUNK BARN &
SOYPEN CAFÉ,
¾ MILE

073

TURRET 49B

ROMAN INSCRIPTION ON SOUTH
SIDE OF WALL HERE

MODERN WILLOWFORD/
IRTHING BRIDGE

MILECASTLE
49

STEEP

ORIGINAL ROMAN WALL

ROMAN BRIDGE ABUTMENT

28

BIRDOSWALD

MAP 29

Irthing River

2 GATES

HIGH HOUSE

FOLLOWING THE LINE OF THE
TURF WALL HERE. NOTE NO
VISIBLE SIGN, JUST LOTS
OF UNUSUALLY
UNDULATING GROUND

ALTERNATIVE
PERMISSIVE PATH FOR
THOSE WHO PREFER NOT
TO WALK THROUGH FIELD

074

Wall Burn

30

½ mile

500m

0

0

APPROX SCALE

ROUTE GUIDE AND MAPS

Birdoswald itself. You'll notice that at this point there is a hole in the foot of the Wall – presumably a culvert to allow the water to drain properly. Facing this hole, look to the left of it and a few metres away you'll see a second, smaller hole in the foot of the Wall. Almost directly above this, at about chest height, is the symbol. Incidentally, it was to the west of Milecastle 49 that the Wall was originally made of turf, and was only converted to stone much later.

If you are not visiting Birdoswald Fort remember to **stamp your passport** before you continue on.

If you want to stay in the area note that the Birdoswald YHA Hostel, which is set within the ruins of the fort, is now for groups only, so your only option is to head 500m north to Slack House Organic Farm (see p173).

BIRDOSWALD   [Map 29, p177]
(☎ 016977-47602; *Apr-Sep daily 10am-5.30pm; Oct 10am-5pm; Nov-mid Feb Sat & Sun 10am-4pm only, £5.40/4.90/3.20 adults/concs/children; English Heritage members free*)

The Roman name for Birdoswald was **Banna**, meaning 'Spur' and the fort does indeed sit on a spur above the River Irthing. It's a lovely position up here, with views in every direction best appreciated, perhaps, from the picnic area set up at the southern end of the fort. Unfortunately, the ruins themselves fail to live up to their setting.

But no matter, for the beauty of Birdoswald lies mainly in the details. There are the carvings on the Wall leading up to Birdoswald, as mentioned on p176; the pleasant **farmhouse** which dominates the site, with Roman stones clearly visible in the fabric of its walls which actually date back to the early 17th century; the remains of a **granary**, the only extensive set of ruins that have thus far been excavated in this fort that once held a thousand soldiers; and the **excavated Roman gates**, one of which, on the east side, is said to be among the best preserved on the Wall, with the *voussoir* (arch stone) and the impost stone (the stone that supported the arch) still extant.

The **museum** is one of the smartest, too, and deals not only with the Roman occupation of the site but with the location's entire history. There is also a *café* here.

Perhaps the most remarkable discoveries, however, were the 19 or so religious altars, all but one dedicated to Jupiter, that were found in the same area to the east of the fort. The theory is that these altars were deliberately buried there as part of some elaborate ritual, possibly on Jupiter's day on January 1 after the annual parade. (The only altar not dedicated to Jupiter was dedicated instead to the Cumbrian war god, Codicus.) We can assume only that, to whomever they were dedicated, they were all put up by the Dacians from Romania who occupied the fort in the 3rd and 4th centuries AD.

After Birdoswald, the Wall continues for a little longer until the trail deserts both it and the road to follow what appears to be either the line of the Vallum or the ditch, a clear topographical feature for the next few miles. But it's a little more complicated than that. Remember, west of the Irthing the Wall was originally built of turf and these clear, steep undulations in the earth are the remnants

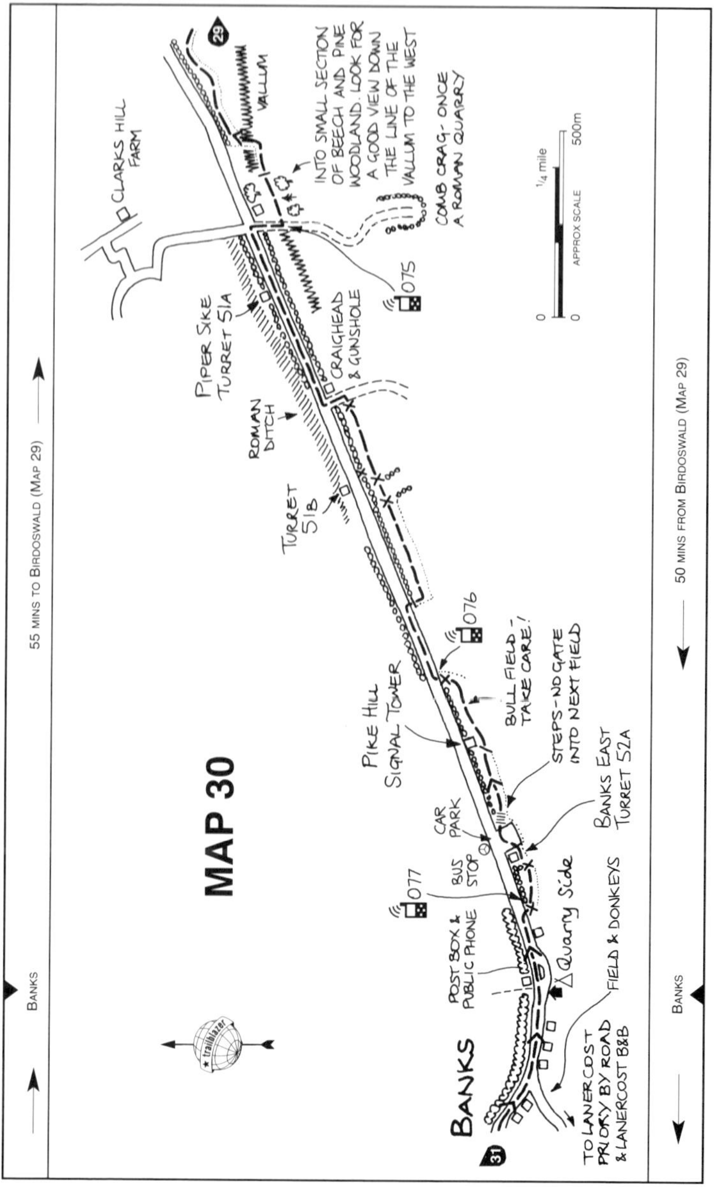
MAP 30
55 MINS TO BIRDOSWALD (MAP 29)
50 MINS FROM BIRDOSWALD (MAP 29)
BANKS
29
31
CLARKS HILL FARM
VALLUM
INTO SMALL SECTION OF BEECH AND PINE WOODLAND. LOOK FOR A GOOD VIEW DOWN THE LINE OF THE VALLUM TO THE WEST
COMB CRAG - ONCE A ROMAN QUARRY
075
076
077
PIPER SIKE TURRET 51A
CRAIGHEAD & GUNSHOLE
ROMAN DITCH
TURRET 51B
PIKE HILL SIGNAL TOWER
BULL FIELD - TAKE CARE!
STEPS - NO GATE INTO NEXT FIELD
BANKS EAST TURRET 52A
CAR PARK
BUS STOP
POST BOX & PUBLIC PHONE
Quarry Side
FIELD & DONKEYS
BANKS
TO LANERCOST PRIORY BY ROAD & LANERCOST B&B
0
1/4 mile
0
500m
APPROX SCALE
trailblazer

of this, the turf Wall (the only obvious turf section left on the entire trail), which would later be replaced by stone.

What you are actually following for the next couple of fields is, immediately to your left, the ditch and the Vallum, with the two separated by the remains of the turf Wall. But note how the turf Wall is *not* on the same line as the later stone Wall you followed from Birdoswald, which is down near the road.

There's one other point of interest about this stretch: neither the stone nor the turf Wall have particularly good views to the north, unlike the Wall of the previous two stages which insisted on following the tops of ridges and crags. Why this is so is unclear, though a popular theory is that the local Brigante tribe in this area were more trouble than the Caledones to the north, so the Romans decided to locate the Wall with good views to the south rather than north.

The turf Wall peters out altogether as you progress down the hill past Turret 50B (which is actually not on the trail). After crossing over the farm track and **Wall Burn** the path has been rerouted away from the Vallum, though it rejoins it briefly for a short stretch through woodland before forsaking it once more to reunite with the stone Wall (Map 30).

Passing **Piper Sike Turret** (No 51A), the trail continues on or near the road to **Pike Hill Signal Tower** – the only signal tower on the Wall. A pre-Hadrian construction, the tower was possibly built for the Roman campaigns in Scotland under Agricola, where other such towers have been found, to give early warning of any movements by the Caledones. As these campaigns came to an end and the Wall was built, the tower was integrated into the Wall defences. Note how the Wall kinks to incorporate the tower – proof, if it were needed, that the tower came first. As you'd imagine, the views from the signal tower are pretty extensive – even though the actual construction rises only a few feet above the ground.

BANKS   [Map 30, p179]

A semi-circular huddle of houses, there's not much to Banks at all, though there is a post box, telephone box, and a **B&B**: *Quarryside* (☎ 01697-72538, 🖳 www .quarryside.co.uk; 1T/1D share bathroom, 1D en suite; 🛥; 🐎 by prior arrangement; WI-FI; packed lunch £5) on the west side of the semi-circle, charges £60-70 (£35-45 sgl occ). Lifts to and from the local pub may be available by prior arrangement. They also have a **campsite** (25 pitches, £5pp) with toilet and washing-up facilities. If there is space, campers can have breakfast (about £6). Incidentally, they also run a holiday cottage for those who want to spend some more time around here.

BANKS TO CARLISLE   [MAPS 30-38]

Introduction

Today we finally say goodbye to the last remnants of the Wall itself. By the time we reach Walton there is pretty much nothing left save for the odd trace of Vallum and ditch. The depredations of man on this side of the Pennines have served to destroy the Wall completely; odd, considering that Newcastle, the largest of all settlements on the route, still manages to muster two or three remaining sections of its own (see pp93-4 and box pp95-6). But though central Carlisle has much olde-worlde charm, there is nothing left of Roman Britain outside the museums, save for some stones, the remnants of an old Roman bridge that were dredged up from the bottom of the River Eden.

Still, no matter, for the walking is no less pleasant on this **14½-mile (23.3km; 6-6¼hrs)** stage and the scenery, in places at least, just as interesting. And occasionally, just occasionally, you do get proof that the trail is still following the line of the Wall and its associated defences.

The route

The various pieces of Wall on this stage occur quite early on. The first is **Hare Hill** (Map 31), just ten minutes or so of road walking from Banks. Once thought to be the highest remaining piece of Wall left on the trail, it is now widely believed to be little more than a 19th-century reconstruction that used original Roman stones. That's not to dismiss it altogether, however, for if you walk around the side of the Wall facing away from the road you should be able to find, at approximately head height, a small Roman inscription indicating that Primus Pilus, a senior centurion of the First Cohort, built it. In fact, this stone was taken from a site called Moneyholes, some distance to the west.

The next feature on the Wall is Haytongate Farm where a '**snack hut**' (daily 7am-11pm) sits by the path. As with all such huts – and you'll find others near Crosby-on-Eden and at Drumburgh – the owners are relying on your honesty to pay for anything you consume; don't betray their trust. The hut even has its own website now – 🖳 www.itrod.co.uk – selling some neat Hadrian's Wall themed T-shirts, though you can also buy them here. About 150m along the driveway there's also a **toilet**.

Having crossed Burtholme Beck, beneath the trees on your right you'll see an original piece of Wall, unaltered and unreconstructed, with the original mortar still *in situ*. It's good to see how the Wall is still marking a boundary, showing a continuity across the ages. To be honest the Wall is in a bit of a parlous state at the moment but is currently undergoing repairs as part of the half-a-million-pound restoration of the Wall (you will already have seen some of this con-

❑ Lanercost Priory [Map 31, p182]

Lanercost Priory (☎ 01697-73030; £3.60/3.20/2.20 adults/conc/children, English Heritage members free; Apr-Sep daily 10am-6pm; check 🖳 www.english-heritage.org.uk for winter opening days/times) was founded in 1166 by Sir Robert de Vaux and built, like so much else, from masonry taken from the Wall which has been combined with the local sandstone. The mortally ill Edward I (see p204) rested here for five months as he headed north to fight the Scots. A wealth of Roman stones and remains are housed within, including one of the 19 altars found at Birdoswald.

There's also a **B&B** in the grounds at Abbey Farm: ***Lanercost*** (☎ 016977-42589, 🖳 www.lanercostbedandbreakfast.co.uk; 4D or T; ☕; 🐕; WI-FI) is an award-winning place with lovely rooms, superior breakfasts, a large open fire and walls that are once again made from pilfered Wall stone. Rates are £90-95 per room (£80-85 sgl occ). Nearby is the ***Lanercost Tearoom*** (☎ 016977-41267, 🖳 www.lanercostexperience.co.uk; daily 10am-5pm) and even a **Hadrian's Wall Visitor Centre** (daily 10am-5pm).

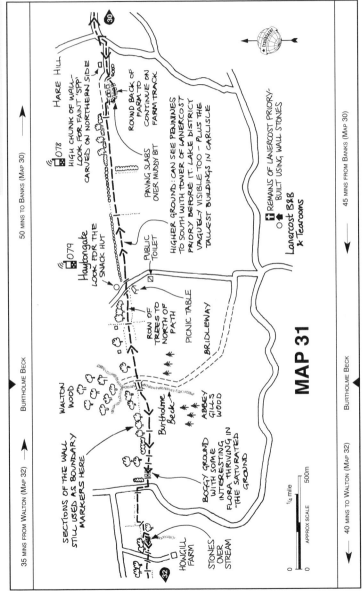

MAP 31

35 MINS FROM WALTON (MAP 32) ◀ | BURTHOLME BECK | 50 MINS TO BANKS (MAP 30) ▲

40 MINS TO WALTON (MAP 32) ▼ | BURTHOLME BECK | 45 MINS FROM BANKS (MAP 30) ◀

SECTIONS OF THE WALL STILL USED AS BOUNDARY MARKERS HERE

WALTON WOOD

Burtholme Beck

ABBEY GILLS WOOD

BOGGY GROUND WITH SOME INTERESTING FLORA THRIVING IN THE SATURATED GROUND

HONGILL FARM

STONES OVER STREAM

¼ mile

APPROX SCALE

0 — 500m

ROW OF TREES TO NORTH OF PATH

PICNIC TABLE

BRIDLEWAY

PUBLIC TOILET

HIGHER GROUND: CAN SEE PENNINES TO SOUTH WITH TOWER OF LANERCOST PRIORY BEFORE IT. LAKE DISTRICT VAGUELY VISIBLE TOO - PLUS THE TALLEST BUILDINGS IN CARLISLE

Haytongate LOOK FOR THE SNACK HUT 079

HIGH CHUNK OF WALL - LOOK FOR FAINT 'SPV' CARVED ON NORTHERN SIDE 078

HARE HILL

PAVING SLABS OVER MUDDY BIT

ROUND BACK OF FARM TO CONTINUE ON TRACK

REMAINS OF LANERCOST PRIORY - BUILT USING WALL STONES

Lanercost B&B & Tearooms

30

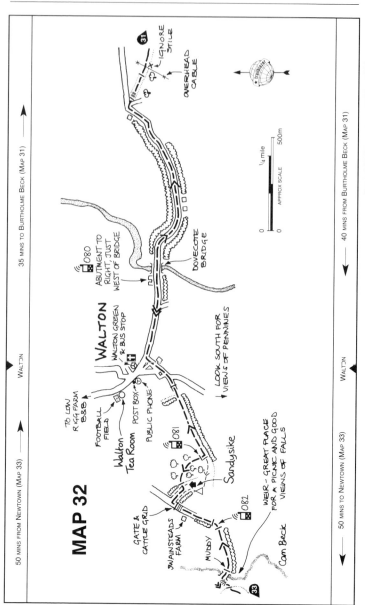

servation work near Great Chesters). The masons tasked with carrying out the work are using coloured stones to make it easy to differentiate between original Wall and their construction. Let's hope they do a good job – for this is the last serious bit of the Wall left on the entire trail for those heading west.

Or perhaps we should say that it's the last section of the Wall that's *visible*, for there is one more major piece of Roman masonry just before the village of Walton, itself reached by a delightfully pleasant stroll through fields, across bridges and along roads. The Roman ruins in this case were once the abutment to a bridge and lie just above where the 'modern' Dovecote Bridge (Map 32) sits today. Unfortunately, being made of sandstone, the abutment and the Wall which once led up to it have since been backfilled to prevent them eroding away completely, though you can find a description of them in Hunter Davies's travelogue *A Walk along the Wall* (see p41).

The path used to follow the line of this Wall to the river (a tributary of the Irthing) but for almost the past decade walkers have been encouraged to take what they say is a 'temporary' diversion along the road. However, it would appear that this has become a permanent path and the prettier, riparian option is now, alas, closed to the public.

WALTON [Map 32, p183]

Walton is not an unattractive little place but there's little of interest for Wall walkers, particularly as the Centurion Inn, once the quintessential Wall pub, remains closed and with little sign of reopening. There's an old church with **phone-** and **post-boxes** opposite. The village's main appeal is the *Walton Tea Room* (☎ 07984-425691; Tue-Sat 10.30am-4pm; closed in winter), housed in the old reading room; run by the enthusiastic and chatty Vicky and Heather, they serve basic food and drinks and, of course, a fine selection of cakes.

Low Rigg Farm (☎ 016977-3233, 🖳 www.lowriggfarm.co.uk; 1T/1D/1F; family room en suite; Apr-Oct; 🍽; 🐾; WI-FI; packed lunch £6), a 125-acre (5-hectare)

working dairy farm, makes its own bread and preserves and uses them as ingredients for breakfast. B&B here is from £35pp. The views across to the Pennines are gorgeous – as, indeed, are the multitude of cats and chickens that roam around the courtyard. The farm can either be reached from the village or by taking a right (rather than a left to Swainsteads) to continue along the road.

Walton has a rather limited **bus** service, with Stagecoach's No 97 leaving from Walton Green on Wednesdays and Fridays and there's a Monday-Friday school bus (that you can catch) to Brampton in the morning, returning mid-afternoon during term-time.

From Walton, one couple wrote in to say that they got slightly lost; follow the signs carefully. The trail drops through more farmyards following, approximately, the line of the Roman ditch. Crossing a small stream, the path climbs through woods to *Sandysike* (Map 32; ☎ 016977-2330, 🖳 sandysike@talk21.com; 1S private bathroom, separate toilet/1T/1D 'more-or-less' en suite; WI-FI), a working farm where B&B in the gorgeous Georgian farmhouse costs £32-40pp, and there's also an equally charming eight-bed **bunkhouse** (£12pp; bedding hire £6pp). They also allow **camping** (£6pp; shower/toilet facilities in the bunkhouse). Dogs are welcome (except in B&B) by prior arrangement;

NEWTOWN   50 MINS TO WALTON (MAP 32)

0   ¼ mile

0   APPROX SCALE   500m

PATH GOES
THROUGH FARM

083

HORSE
FIELD

STONE
STEPS

TO CASTLESTEADS
CAMBOGLANNA
FORT - NO ENTRY!

COMING FROM THE EAST,
AFTER BRIDGE TURN RIGHT
FOR 20M THEN FOLLOW SIGNS
CLOSELY

GATE IN CORNER
OF FIELD

A6071

BACK
GARDEN

HORSE FIELD

BETWEEN TALL CORRUGATED
IRON AND WOODEN PANEL FENCES

Newtown Farm B&B

PUBLIC PHONE

VILLAGE
GREEN

TO
HETHERSGILL

TO BRAMPTON, 2½ MILES
SEE TOWN PLAN

NEWTOWN

KISSING GATE BY THE
LAST HOUSE IN NEWTOWN

084

MAP 33

34

TO IRTHINGTON

NEWTOWN   50 MINS FROM WALTON (MAP 32)

packed lunches and evening meals can be provided. However, debit/credit cards
are not accepted. Overall, a cracking place.

From Sandysike, the path follows the farm track, taking a first left
through the cow field before the farm buildings (there should be a signpost
there), then drops again to a bridge over a second, slightly larger stream with
a series of little waterfalls: this is **Cam Beck**. A 3³/₄-acre (1.5-hectare) Roman
fort, **Castlesteads** (Map 33), lies just a few hundred metres to the south,

❏ **Walk side by side and on healthy grass** Don't walk in single file or on worn
areas. Protect our heritage!

unfortunately it's out of bounds. Unusually, **Camboglanna** (as the Romans knew it; the name means 'Crooked Glen') lay between the Wall and the Vallum and not actually on the Wall. At different times it was garrisoned by troops from Spain, Gaul and Tungria. In his book, *A Walk along the Wall,* Hunter Davies (see p41) mentions visiting the house that now occupies the site and finding Roman altars lying around in the summerhouse.

One more stream and a whole patchwork of fields are crossed as you make your way towards Carlisle, a city whose highest buildings start to appear on the horizon as you progress westwards. It can start to feel, as you cross field after field, that this part of the walk is some sort of treadmill. But there are some things of interest on the way. There are also some small hamlets, such as aptly named **Newtown**, home to *Newtown Farm* (☎ 016977-2768, 🖳 www.new townfarmbedandbreakfast.co.uk; 1T or F/1D, both en suite; 🛆; 🐾; WI-FI; packed lunches & evening meals by arrangement) where B&B costs £35pp (£50 sgl occ).

Turn left onto A6071 Longtown Road to reach **Brampton**, 2¹/₂ miles to the south east.

BRAMPTON

Brampton's a lovely little market town sitting snugly in the Irthing Valley, reasonably convenient for the trail and with virtually every second building either a pub, hotel or tearoom. Granted a Market Charter in 1252, the main market day is Wednesday. The main sight is **St Martin's Church** (🖳 www.stmartinsbrampton .org.uk; usually open during the day), the only church designed by architect Philip Webb, with some wonderful stained-glass windows by his fellow pre-Raphaelite Edward Burne-Jones.

Services

The **tourist information centre** (☎ 016977-3433; Mar-Apr & Sep-Oct Mon-Sat 10am-4pm, May-Aug 10am-5pm, Nov-Feb to 3pm) is in the Moot Hall at the eastern end of Front St, the main street in the town. They will book accommodation (see box p42).

For **wi-fi** you'll find the Howard Arms (see Where to eat) has a fast and reliable internet service. There's a Co-op **supermarket** (daily 7am-10pm) behind Market Place, with a Spar (Mon-Sat 7am-10pm, Sun 8am-10pm) across the road from the TIC.

Just a couple of doors down is the H Jobson **pharmacy** (Mon, Wed, Fri 9am-

6pm, Tue & Thur to 5.30pm, Sat to 3pm) and next door is a **bank** (HSBC) with ATM (with a Barclays a little further down on the opposite side). Next door to that is the **post office** (Mon-Fri 9am-5.30pm, Sat to 12.30pm).

Transport

[See pp46-8] Arriva's/Stagecoach's No 685/85 **bus** calls in here as do Stagecoach's Nos 94 & 97 and Telford's/Wright's No 680.

Note that, while Brampton does boast a **train station**, it's 1¹/₂ miles out of town. The walk takes you through woods and is pleasant – but it's still the most inconvenient station on the walk by some distance.

Where to stay

Oakwood Park (☎ 016977-2436, 🖳 www.oakwoodparkhotel.co.uk; 1S/2T/1D/ 1D or F, all en suite; 🛆; WI-FI; Mar-Nov; packed lunches & evening meals by prior arrangement), Longtown Rd, is a Victorian pile set in ten acres of grounds about a mile north of town on the way to the Wall. B&B starts at £32pp (from £38 sgl occ; £70 for three people in the family room).

In town the Georgian *Oval House* (☎ 016977-2106, 🖳 www.ovalhousebedand

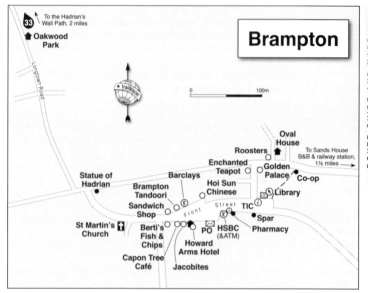

To the Hadrian's
Wall Path, 2 miles

33

Oakwood Park

Longtown Road

trailblazer

0   100m

Brampton

Oval House

Roosters

To Sands House
B&B & railway station,
1½ miles

Enchanted Teapot

Golden Palace

Co-op

Statue of Hadrian

Barclays

Hoi Sun Chinese

Library

Brampton Tandoori

Front Street

TIC

Sandwich Shop

St Martin's Church

Berti's Fish & Chips

PO

HSBC (&ATM)

Spar

Pharmacy

Howard Arms Hotel

Capon Tree Café

Jacobites

breakfast.co.uk; 1T private facilities/1D/2D or F en suite; 🛏; WI-FI) offers B&B for £70 per room (£40-70 sgl occ). *Howard Arms Hotel* (☎ 016977-42758, 🖥 www.the howardarmsbrampton.com; 2S/4T/5D, all en suite; 🛏; 🐾; WI-FI) charges £89 per room for B&B, £59 for a single.

Where to eat and drink
During the day *Capon Tree Café* (☎ 016977-3649; Mon-Sat 9.15am-4.30pm) is good value with their diverse range of scones for just £1.30-1.90 each. Twenty metres away, *Jacobites* (☎ 016977-3535; summer Mon-Thur 8.30am-5pm, Fri & Sat 8.30am-8pm, winter Mon-Sat 8.30am-5pm) is another popular spot with a similar menu, with jacket spuds from £5.65; they serve tapas on Friday and Saturday evenings in the summer. My favourite café, however, is the dog-friendly *Enchanted Teapot* (☎ 016977 41951) with a great selection of scones and cakes, the most popular being their unusual, malty chocolate and Guinness cake (£2.40).

The *Sandwich Shop* (☎ 016977-42888; Mon-Sat 7am-3.30pm) serves breakfasts, sandwiches and baguettes, all at rock-bottom prices (sandwiches £1.50-2.50). *Howard Arms Hotel* (see Where to stay; daily Mon-Thur noon-3pm & 6-9pm; Fri & Sat noon-9pm, Sun noon-6pm) is probably the best place for an evening meal with mains starting at £8.95 for the pasta; they also have wi-fi.

There is the usual abundance of take-aways in Brampton too, including *Brampton Tandoori* (☎ 016977-2600/1; Sun-Fri 6-11pm, Sat 4-11pm); *Hoi Sun* Chinese (☎ 016977-2090; Tue-Thur 5-10.30pm, Fri-Sun 5-11pm); *Berti's Fish & Chips* (☎ 016977-2218; Mon-Sat 5-9.30pm plus Wed-Sat 11.30-1.30pm) on Front St; *Golden Palace* (☎ 016977-2232; Wed-Mon 5-11pm); and *Roosters* (☎ 016977-42471; Mon-Sat 11am-10pm), another chippie (haddock and chips £4.20) that also does pizzas and grills. Incidentally, this place may deliver up to Sandysike (see p184) near Walton.

From Newtown, follow both the Vallum and ditch. A short-cut tree-lined path leads from the grassy track off north to **Laversdale** (off Map 34), home to the pleasant little *Stonewalls Campsite* (☎ 01228-573666), where a pitch costs £5pp; shower (£2) and toilet facilities are available and they have a neat little shed-cum-kitchen where you can make your own breakfast (an honesty box is provided). If you don't want to cook your own food in the evening, just up the road is the **Sportsman Inn** though its future was very uncertain at the time of writing and it has changed hands several times over the past twelve months. Hopefully by the time you visit things will have settled down and they'll be serving food again. If they don't Roosters and Hoi Sun in Brampton (see p187) both deliver this far out but you'll need to pay extra for this service.

Stagecoach's No 97 **bus** service stops in Laversdale; see pp46-8 for details.

The trail eventually meets up with a road at **Oldwall** and the 17th-century Old Wall Cottage as well as a bus stop; if you are planning to stay in Laversdale and missed the short-cut path turn right onto the road here; it's a 15- to 20-minute walk.

After **Bleatarn Farmhouse** you walk past the blea ('blue') tarn itself – with Carlisle Airport hidden away to the south – on a slightly raised, arrow-straight path. This is actually both the Roman Military Way and the base of the Wall that you are walking upon. The minor road that follows also marks out the course of the Wall, though you leave it after half a mile (1km) or so to join a *clarty* (the local word for muddy) bridleway, Sandy Lane (Map 35), down to **Crosby-on-Eden**. Here, again, the Romans intrude on the modern world: the road you join at Crosby is actually part of the Stanegate. Just before the road is a long-established **refreshment stall** with hot and cold drinks and snacks. Don't forget to use the honesty box!

CROSBY-ON-EDEN
[Maps 35, p190 & 36, p191]

A village split into two parts connected by the A689, Crosby-on-Eden lies an hour or two from Carlisle on the trail and thus is a perfect place to take the weight off your feet, get yourself a drink and gird your loins for that final push into the city. As with many of the minor villages encountered in this western half of the walk, Crosby is built around, and consists of little more than, the main road. It's here you'll find the **Church of St John**, on the way into Low Crosby village, erected in 1864 on the site of a much older edifice.

Along the main road in Low Crosby, you'll find *The Stag Inn* (Map 36; ☎ 01228-573210; bar daily 11am-11pm; 🐾), otherwise known by exhausted trekkers as *The Stagger In*. This 17th-century inn-turned-'gastro-pub' serves hot food daily

year-round (noon-3pm & 6-9pm), with sandwiches and salads available 3-6pm.

About half an hour outside Crosby, but only five minutes from the path, newly refurbished Wallfoot Hotel has now been renamed *Park Broom Lodge* (☎ 01228-573696; 🖳 www.parkbroomlodge.co.uk; 2S/1D or T/2D/2D, T or F, all en suite; ☻; 🐾 £5 by prior arrangement; WI-FI). Lying on the busy A689, it is licensed and serves meals (daily noon-9pm) in the restaurant, which is open to non residents as well. B&B is £25-45 per person. If arranged in advance they are happy to pick guests up in Carlisle or take them there free of charge.

Transport-wise, Telford's No 185 **bus** stops by the Stag Inn; Stagecoach's No 94 also stops in Crosby. See pp46-8 for more information.

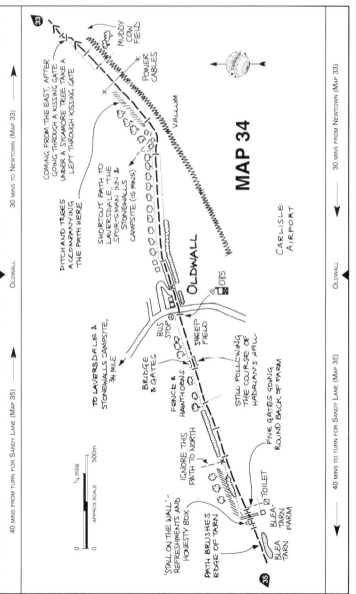

33

COMING FROM THE EAST, AFTER GOING THROUGH A KISSING GATE UNDER A SYCAMORE TREE TAKE A LEFT THROUGH KISSING GATE

MUDDY COW FIELD

POWER CABLES

VALLUM

DITCH AND TREES ACCOMPANYING THE PATH HERE

SHORTCUT PATH TO LAVERSDALE, THE SPORTSMAN INN & STONEWALLS CAMPSITE (15 MINS)

MAP 34

OLDWALL

085

CARLISLE AIRPORT

TO LAVERSDALE & STONEWALLS CAMPSITE, ¾ MILE

BUS STOP

SHEEP FIELD

BRIDGE & GATES

FENCE & HAWTHORNS

STILL FOLLOWING THE COURSE OF HADRIAN'S WALL

FIVE GATES GOING ROUND BACK OF FARM

IGNORE THIS PATH TO NORTH

¼ mile

APPROX SCALE

500m

TOILET

BLEA TARN FARM

'STALL ON THE WALL' — REFRESHMENTS AND HONESTY BOX

PATH BRUSHES EDGE OF TARN

BLEA TARN

35

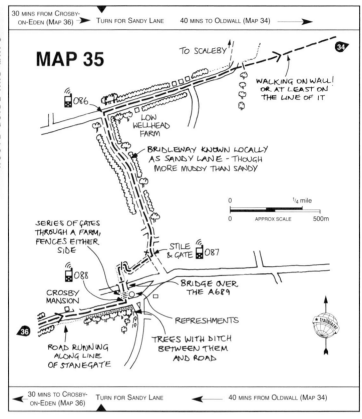

30 MINS FROM CROSBY-ON-EDEN (MAP 36) ► TURN FOR SANDY LANE 40 MINS TO OLDWALL (MAP 34) ⟶

MAP 35

TO SCALEBY

34

WALKING ON WALL!
OR AT LEAST ON
THE LINE OF IT

086

LOW
WELLHEAD
FARM

BRIDLEWAY KNOWN LOCALLY
AS SANDY LANE - THOUGH
MORE MUDDY THAN SANDY

0   1/4 mile

0   APPROX SCALE   500m

SERIES OF GATES
THROUGH A FARM,
FENCES EITHER
SIDE

STILE
& GATE   087

088

CROSBY
MANSION

BRIDGE OVER
THE A689

REFRESHMENTS

36

ROAD RUNNING
ALONG LINE
OF STANEGATE

TREES WITH DITCH
BETWEEN THEM
AND ROAD

★ trailblazer

◄ 30 MINS TO CROSBY-ON-EDEN (MAP 36) TURN FOR SANDY LANE ◄ 40 MINS FROM OLDWALL (MAP 34)

From Crosby-on-Eden, you now forsake the line of the Wall altogether to indulge, as you did on the first stage from Newcastle, in a little bit of riverside strolling. It's a pleasant walk, curtailed by a diversion to Linstock to cross the M6.

The remains of **Linstock Castle** (Map 37), an old fortified house and pele tower now incorporated into a modern farm, lies to the right of the trail as you

> ❏ **Important note – walking times**
> Unless otherwise specified, **all times in this book refer only to the time spent walking**. You will need to add 20-30% to allow for rests, photography, checking the map, drinking water etc. When planning the day's hike count on 5-7 hours' actual walking.

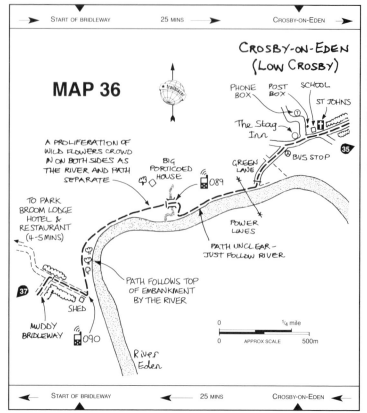

ROUTE GUIDE AND MAPS

CROSBY-ON-EDEN
(LOW CROSBY)

MAP 36

trailblazer

PHONE   POST   SCHOOL
BOX   BOX

ST JOHN'S

The Stag
Inn

A PROLIFERATION OF
WILD FLOWERS CROWD
IN ON BOTH SIDES AS
THE RIVER AND PATH
SEPARATE

BIG
PORTICOED
HOUSE

GREEN
LANE

BUS STOP

35

089

TO PARK
BROOM LODGE
HOTEL &
RESTAURANT
(4-5 MINS)

POWER
LINES

PATH UNCLEAR –
JUST FOLLOW RIVER

37

PATH FOLLOWS TOP
OF EMBANKMENT
BY THE RIVER

SHED

MUDDY
BRIDLEWAY   090

0   ¼ mile

0   APPROX SCALE   500m

River
Eden

enter the village. After the M6 another lengthy piece of road-walking follows before the trail joins a cycle route, separated from the road by a hedge.

This cycle route takes you round the back of **Rickerby** (Map 38), an entire hamlet that, with all its towers and turrets, resembles one enormous Victorian folly. There's even a tower to the north of the trail in a field of rape. This eccentric architecture was the work of a presumably eccentric man with an undoubtedly eccentric name: George Head Head.

Crossing a pleasant park at the end of Rickerby, the trail takes an iron bridge and continues past a school and golf course and then follows the water's edge to the **Sands Sports Centre** which has a *café* (Mon, Tue, Thur & Fri 9am-6pm, Wed 9am-9.45pm, Sat 9am-5pm, Sun 10am-5pm) and a **passport-stamping point** (see box p38). Turn left here to head into Carlisle.

ROUTE GUIDE AND MAPS

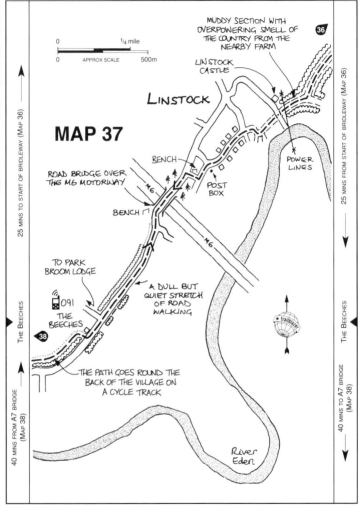

MUDDY SECTION WITH
OVERPOWERING SMELL OF
THE COUNTRY FROM THE
NEARBY FARM

36

LINSTOCK
CASTLE

LINSTOCK

MAP 37

BENCH

POWER
LINES

ROAD BRIDGE OVER
THE M6 MOTORWAY

M6

POST
BOX

BENCH

M6

TO PARK
BROOM LODGE

091
THE
BEECHES

38

A DULL BUT
QUIET STRETCH
OF ROAD
WALKING

trailblazer

THE PATH GOES ROUND THE
BACK OF THE VILLAGE ON
A CYCLE TRACK

River
Eden

0   ¼ mile
0   APPROX SCALE   500m

25 MINS TO START OF BRIDLEWAY (MAP 36)

25 MINS FROM START OF BRIDLEWAY (MAP 36)

THE BEECHES

THE BEECHES

40 MINS FROM A7 BRIDGE
(MAP 38)

40 MINS TO A7 BRIDGE
(MAP 38)

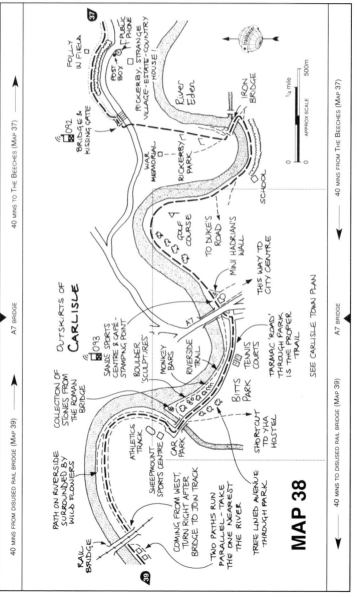

40 MINS TO THE BEECHES (MAP 37)

A7 BRIDGE

40 MINS FROM THE BEECHES (MAP 37)

40 MINS FROM DISUSED RAIL BRIDGE (MAP 39)

A7 BRIDGE

40 MINS TO DISUSED RAIL BRIDGE (MAP 39)

37

FOLLY IN FIELD

PUBLIC PHONE

POST BOX

092 BRIDGE & KISSING GATE

RICKERBY, STRANGE VILLAGE-ESTATE-COUNTRY HOUSE!

WAR MEMORIAL

RICKERBY PARK

River Eden

IRON BRIDGE

SCHOOL

TO DUKE'S ROAD

GOLF COURSE

MINI HADRIAN'S WALL

THIS WAY TO CITY CENTRE

A7

APPROX SCALE
1/4 mile
500m

OUTSKIRTS OF CARLISLE

COLLECTION OF STONES FROM THE ROMAN BRIDGE

093

SANDS SPORTS CENTRE & CAFÉ - STAMPING POINT

BOULDER 'SCULPTURES'

MONKEY BARS

RIVERSIDE TRAIL

TENNIS COURTS

BITTS PARK

TARMAC 'ROAD' THROUGH PARK IS THE PROPER TRAIL

SEE CARLISLE TOWN PLAN

SHORTCUT TO YHA HOSTEL

PATH ON RIVERSIDE SURROUNDED BY WILD FLOWERS

ATHLETICS TRACK

SHEEPMOUNT SPORTS CENTRE

CAR PARK

RAIL BRIDGE

COMING FROM WEST, TURN RIGHT AFTER BRIDGE TO JOIN TRACK

TWO PATHS RUN PARALLEL - TAKE THE ONE NEAREST THE RIVER

TREE LINED AVENUE THROUGH PARK

MAP 38

39

CARLISLE

Though it cannot compare, in scale, fame or importance with that other Wall city, Newcastle, Carlisle is a pleasant place with a fair bit to see and do and a compactness and modest size that, unlike its Geordie rival, is never intimidating. It has also, in the last couple of years, become very keen to celebrate its Roman connections and as you walk along the path you'll see several pillars emblazoned with the word 'Luguvalium' – the name of the original Roman fort at Carlisle – dotted throughout Bitts Park. There's also a model of the entire Wall round the back of the Sands Sport Centre, right on the path.

These modern additions go some way to making up for the fact that there is a distinct lack of any significant Roman ruins within the city boundaries today. Sure, there is a small huddle of ninety or so stones lying to the north of the path in Bitts Park that were dredged up from the Eden and which were, apparently, the remains of an old Roman Bridge. There are also, inevitably, Roman stones in the fabric of Carlisle Castle and a recent archaeological dig at the castle's foot which finished in 2010 discovered over 80,000 Roman artefacts! But there are very few Roman ruins left *in situ*, one of the largest extant being the sunken shrine in the grounds of the **Tullie House Museum** (see p198) – a museum which, in my opinion, is also the only essential port of call in Carlisle for anyone interested in the Romans and their Wall.

The lack of anything Roman is even more remarkable when one considers two salient facts. Firstly, St Cuthbert visited the city in AD685 and was taken to see a 'remarkable' Roman fountain (see box below). Secondly, that 2000 years ago this city was the headquarters for the whole Wall and the home of two forts, one of which was the largest of them all. This was **Uxelodunum**, commonly known as **Stanwix** after the suburb that exists today in this location on the north side of the Eden, measuring 9.3 acres (3.72 hectares) in total and garrisoned by the 1000-strong Ala Petriana cavalry – said to be the largest body of calvary stationed anywhere in the entire empire!

Stanwix was not the first fort in town, however. That was **Luguvalium**, stretching from Botchergate (near the train station) to the Castle – in other words, pretty much the whole of the city centre. This first fort was built around AD72 by governor Cerialis to defend the Stanegate. (There is some evidence that Agricola had a turf fort here around AD80.) Despite the presence of Stanwix, built around 50 years later when the Wall was constructed, Luguvalium (the name is derived from the sun god, Lug) continued to be used until the 4th century or so, although it filled a role that was less military and more civic as time went on.

The local tribe, the Carvetii, saw the presence of such a large garrison not as a threat but an opportunity, and began trading with the Romans and inhabiting the land near the Luguvalium fort. This continued until the Carvetii's settlement became their unofficial capital – and Carlisle was born (though the name, Caerluel, is a post-Roman invention meaning 'Castle of Luel'), rising to provincial capital status by the end of the 4th century.

❏ The Wall's first tourist?

According to the Venerable Bede, in AD685 St Cuthbert came to Carlisle to visit an English queen staying in a nunnery in town. Whilst there, Cuthbert was taken by the citizens of Carlisle to look at the town walls and the 'remarkable fountain, formerly built by the Romans'. Thus, with this brief mention by Bede, Cuthbert becomes the first recorded tourist to visit the Wall. The 'remarkable fountain', incidentally, has never been found, though in the 1930s a building was excavated with a fountain in its central courtyard, which dated back to AD78 and the reign of Vespasian. Could this be the fountain Cuthbert was shown?

ROUTE GUIDE AND MAPS

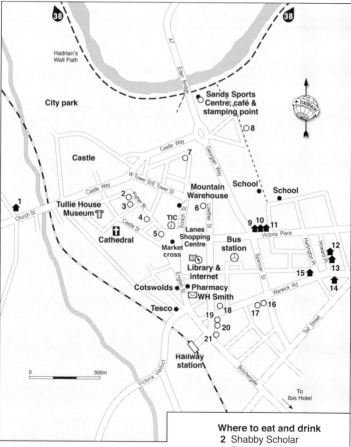

Carlisle

Where to stay
1 Carlisle YHA Hostel
9 Brooklyn House
10 Cartref
11 Ashleigh Guest House
12 Derwentlea
13 Langleigh Guest House
14 Cornerways Guest House
15 Howard Lodge Guest House

Where to eat and drink
2 Shabby Scholar
3 The Lane
4 Sandwich Place
5 Franco's
6 Howard Arms
7 Adriano's
8 Turf Tavern
16 Alexandros
17 Davids
18 Yummy's
19 Pizza Bravo
20 La Mezzaluna
21 Home & Away

But apart from the essential and absorbing Tullie House Museum, and perhaps a visit to the Castle, see p198, there's nothing that demands your time in Carlisle, leaving you free to enjoy the shops, restaurants and cheery atmosphere of this interesting little city.

Services
The focus of the city centre is Market Cross, the cobbled pedestrian-only junction where you'll find the Old Town Hall, now home to the **tourist information centre** (TIC; ☎ 01228-625600, 🖳 www.discovercarlisle.co.uk; Mar-Oct Mon-Sat 9.30am-5pm, Nov-Feb Mon-Sat 10am-4pm, bank holiday Mon 9.30am-4pm; also open Sun in Jul & Aug 10.30am-4pm). They will book accommodation.

The **post office** (Mon-Sat 9am-5.30pm) is in WH Smith at 51-53 English St. For **internet access**, if you have your own laptop or mobile device you'll find most bars and cafés advertise free wi-fi. There's a Boots **pharmacy** on English St. Those looking for some last-minute **trekking gear** have plenty of choices, with Cotswolds on English St and Mountain Warehouse on Scotch St. For a **supermarket**, Tesco Metro is near the station.

Transport
[See pp46-8] Though Wall walkers usually turn off the trail into the city at Eden Bridge, those arriving by public transport will alight either at the **bus station** on Lonsdale St, home to both local and National Express buses, or at the **railway station**, just to the south of the city centre off Botchergate.

Telford's No 185 **bus** leaves from English St and also stops in West Tower St (convenient for Tullie House and the Castle). Telford's No 680 leaves from English St but Wright's No 680 leaves from Warwick Rd. Arriva's/Stagecoach's No 685 is another useful service, leaving from the bus station for Newcastle; Stagecoach's No 94 and 97 stop on The Crescent and depart from English St; while, perhaps of most interest of all is Stagecoach's No 93/71 service from Carlisle Bus Station to Bowness-on-Solway.

Train services run hourly to Newcastle via Brampton, Haltwhistle, Hexham and Corbridge.

If you need a **taxi** try City Taxis (☎ 01228-520000).

Where to stay
Finding somewhere to stay in Carlisle is not as easy as it should be. B&Bs are relatively plentiful but often book up quickly, while the city's only hostel is open only in high summer and, for the moment at least; the nearest campsite is in Beaumont (see p204).

The **hostel** is *Carlisle YHA Hostel* (☎ 0845-371 9510) on Bridge Lane, Caldewgate, housed in the halls of residence of Carlisle's university and thus open only when the students have returned home at the end of the academic year (ie June, July and August). If that doesn't sound too charming, do remember that these halls were converted from a Theakston's brewery, and the conversion has been a sensitive one; indeed, it's won awards. The Old Brewery Residences have 56 beds (seven single rooms in each flat) as well as kitchens (it's self-catering only). If staying here it would be quicker to take the short cut shown on Map 38 than to follow the A7 (main route) into town. Being a student hall of residence, it must be said that it's a little tatty but it does have two distinct advantages: a location across the river from the castle near the heart of the city and, wonderfully, you get your own single room – rare indeed in a YHA hostel. Rates start at £24pp.

For a **B&B**, the first area to look is Victoria Place, just a five-minute walk from Eden Bridge and the trail, where three listed buildings stand next to each other: *Cartref* (☎ 01228-522077; 2S shared facilities/6D or T, all en suite; 🐾; WI-FI; Ⓛ £5), at No 44, is perhaps the smartest of these, a large and attractively furnished place. The owners work really hard to make this place as comfy as possible and they succeed. Rates are £27.50-35pp with their award-winning breakfast included, and while there are no baths, each room comes equipped with a foot spa. Next door, at No 46, *Ashleigh Guest House* (☎ 01228-521631, 🖳 www.ashleighbandand

breakfast.co.uk; 2S/2D/ 2T/3D, T or F, all en suite; WI-FI; (Ⓛ) is one of the more established places in town. B&B starts at £30pp. On the other side of *Cartref*, at No 42, is **Brooklyn House** (☎ 01228-590002, 🖥 www.brooklynhouse.co.uk; 3S/3D or T/2D, T or F, most en suite; ☛; 🐾; WI-FI; (Ⓛ), B&B costs £25-30pp.

At 107 Warwick Rd, *Cornerways Guest House* (☎ 01228-521733, 🖥 www.cornerwaysbandb.co.uk; 3S/1D/1T/ 4D, T or F, most en suite, some shared facilities; WI-FI) is a cosy, friendly place with B&B for £40 in a single, twins £65-75, doubles £70-80 and 3 people in the family room is £85-95. Nearby, at No 90, *Howard Lodge Guest House* (☎ 01228-529842, 🖥 www.howard-lodge.co.uk; 2S/1D/3F, all but two en suite; 🐾 £5; WI-FI) prides itself on its large breakfasts and charges £32.50pp in a double, £35-40 for a single.

A little further on, at 6 Howard Place, *Langleigh Guest House* (☎ 01228-530440, ☎ 0781-045 6650, 🖥 www.langleigh house.co.uk; 3S/1D/3D or F en suite; ☛; WI-FI; (Ⓛ) has huge, immaculate rooms and charges £37.50pp, £40 single. The owners have another place, *Derwentlea* (☎ 01228-409706, 🖥 www.derwentlea.co.uk; 2S/1D/ 2F, en suite; ☛; WI-FI; (Ⓛ), 14 Howard Place, where rooms are the same price and are wonderfully furnished; the owners can also dry damp boots in the Aga. Evening meals (£16 for two courses, £25 for three) are available at both establishments if requested at least 24 hours in advance.

Down in Botchergate, the road running south from near the station, are several larger hotels. They include *Ibis Hotel* (☎ 01228-518000, 🖥 www.ibishotel.com; 102 rooms inc D/T & F, all en suite; 🐾 £5 ; WI-FI), a depressingly ugly place on the outside but comfortable inside; rates start at £34 (room only).

Where to eat and drink

Unlike the accommodation situation, you'll have no trouble finding food in the city.

The first place to look for **takeaway** food is The Crescent, near the station. Here you'll find plenty of places with late opening hours including *Home & Away* (☎ 01228-512615; Sun-Thur 11am-midnight, Fri & Sat 11am-3am), a chippie; *Pizza Bravo* (☎ 01228-558844; daily 5pm to 'late') near the centre of The Crescent, which does kebabs as well as pizzas; and, next-door, *La Mezzaluna* (☎ 01228-534472, 🖥 www.lamezzalunacarlisle.co .uk; Mon & Wed-Sat 10am-10pm, Sun 11am-9pm), an Italian restaurant which also offers a take-out service. Not too far away, *Yummys* (☎ 01228-598800; Sun-Thur 5pm-midnight, Fri & Sat 5pm-2am) provides for those looking for Chinese food to take away.

For lunch, on Fisher St the *Sandwich Place* (☎ 01228-514550; Mon-Fri 9am-3pm, Sat 10am-3pm) is a great spot for takeaway sandwiches and baguettes; it also does a packed lunch offer of £3.20 for baguette, crisps and a drink or chocolate bar. If it's raining, you can pay a visit to nearby *Howard Arms* (☎ 01228 532926; food served noon-2pm), with simple pub food that rarely costs more than £6 – a real bargain.

One of the first eateries you'll see as you walk into town from Eden Bridge is *Turf Tavern* (☎ 01228-515367; food served daily noon-9pm), one of the Hungry Horse chain offering basic but filling and good-value pub fare and with lots of special deals (eg curry and a pint for £4.99 on Wednesdays).

For more upmarket dining there's *Davids* (☎ 01228-523578, 🖥 www.davids restaurant.co.uk; Tue-Sat noon-1.30pm & 6.30-9pm), a cracking little place on Warwick Rd. The menu changes regularly (£18.95 for two courses, £22.55 for three) but if available check out the grilled fillet of lakeland beef on a shallot purée with braised oxtail croquette and a braising liquor jus (supplement £6).

Just a few doors down, *Alexandros* (☎ 01228-592227, 🖥 www.thegreek.co.uk; Mon 5.30-9.30pm, Tue-Thur noon-2pm & 5.30-9.30pm, Fri to 9.45pm, Sat 6-10pm) is a Greek eatery. If you're unsure whether you'll like Greek food, try their mini-meze (available at lunch and 5.30-6.30pm) for just £11.50pp (though don't be fooled by the term 'mini'– you'll still find there's more food on the table than you can possibly manage to eat in one sitting).

The Lane (☎ 01228-318013, 💻 www.thelanecarlisle.co.uk; Wed-Sat noon-late), situated down a little alleyway running off Lowther St, is a bar with a decent kitchen and a lovely courtyard for when the sun shines (which it does, sometimes). Food is mainly sandwiches and salads though they do a decent tapas too, a compliment that can also be levelled at *The Shabby Scholar* (☎ 01228-402813; Tue-Sat 10am-midnight), just round the corner.

There are several good Italian places in town including *Franco's* (☎ 01228-512305, 💻 www.francoscarlisle.com; Mon-Fri 11.30am-2.30pm & 5.30-10pm, Sat 11.30am-10pm, Sun noon-2.30pm & 6-9pm) on Market Square behind the TIC; this is Carlisle's oldest Italian restaurant having been founded here in 1974. They also run *Adriano's* (yes, it is named after Hadrian; ☎ 01228-599007, 💻 http://ristoranteadriano .co.uk; Tue-Sat 11.30am-1.30pm, 5.30-9.30pm, Mon to 9pm, Sun 5.30-9pm) on Rickergate, with pizzas £7.50-9.10. They also have a happy hour (currently 11.30am-1pm and 5.30-6.30pm) when most dishes are around £1.50-2 cheaper.

What to see and do

The only must-see sight is housed in one of Carlisle's most historic buildings, the Jacobean **Tullie House Museum** (☎ 01228-618718, 💻 www.tulliehouse.co.uk; April-Oct Mon-Sat 10am-5pm, Sun 11am-5pm, Nov-Mar Mon-Sat 10am-4pm, Sun noon-4pm; £7/5/free adults/concs/children) on Castle St. As interesting as the 16th-century townhouse that forms part of the museum (and for which it is named) may be, the main reason for calling in is the chance to see their £1.36 million Roman Frontier Gallery. Opened in 2011, it's a wonderful run-through of the Roman story in this area and includes many interactive exhibits and some gorgeous items from belt buckles to brooches, tombstones to trinkets. There's also the absolutely gob-smacking Staffordshire Moorlands Pan on loan from the British Museum, aka the Ilam Pan, named after the place where it was found (Ilam Parish is in Staffordshire) in 2005 by a metal detectorist. Made of bronze and enamel, this late 2nd-century AD

pan has the names of four Wall forts inscribed into the bronze, namely MAIS (Bowness), COGGABATA (Drumburgh), VXELODUNUM (Stanwix, Carlisle) and CAMMOGLANNA (Castlesteads), as well as the mysterious phrase 'RIGORE VALI AELI DRACONIS' (the middle two words mean Hadrian's Wall, and Draco could be the name of the person who ordered the pan to be made, though taken as a whole the meaning of this phrase is uncertain). Presumably, somebody visited or even worked at the Wall and had it made to commemorate their time there. Another display recreates a murder case, the victim, possessing severe injuries to the skull, found covered with rubbish at the bottom of an old well within the city of Carlisle. Younger visitors should enjoy creating their own Roman avatar and dressing up in the Roman costumes the museum provides.

Nor should the rest of the museum be ignored either, with absorbing displays on the reivers (see box p202) and in another Roman section, a fantastic reconstruction of the wood-and-turf version of Hadrian's Wall that really gives you a good idea of how imposing and formidable a barrier it was. They also have a sunken Roman shrine in the grounds of the house – for a long time the only Roman ruins discovered in situ in the city. I have long rated the Tullie Museum as the most educational, relevant and enjoyable museum for Wall walkers with its sections on Romans and reivers. This Roman Frontier Gallery collection means that it's just got even better!

From Tullie House a curious subway – called the Millennium Gallery – leads under the ring road. At the other end of it is Carlisle's other main attraction: its large **castle** (☎ 01228-591922, 💻 www.english-heritage.org.uk; varied opening times but usually daily 10am-4 or 5pm, closed weekdays in winter except for school holidays; £5.70/5.10/3.40 adults/concs/children; free for English Heritage members). Now sandwiched between the park and the noisy ring-road, a castle was originally built on this site by William Rufus in 1092, though this earth-and-timber construction was replaced in 1122 under orders of Henry I. It still looks impressive and imposing.

CARLISLE TO BOWNESS-ON-SOLWAY [MAPS 38-45]

Introduction

This is an unusual end to the walk. There are no ruins, neither of Wall nor fort, and only occasional glimpses of Vallum and ditch. There are no moors either, nor crags, nor even really any gradients worth moaning about.

Nevertheless, there are some delights in store on this **14-mile (22.5km; 4³/4-5hrs)** stage, including a couple of cute villages, some great views over the River Eden to Scotland and a stroll through an Area of Outstanding Natural Beauty; and if the weather holds, the walk is both a peaceful, gentle pleasure and the perfect way to finish and reflect upon the epic journey you've just undertaken.

There are a couple of mysteries surrounding this last stage. The first is why the Wall dodges around so much? In all, it changes direction 34 times over the 14 miles between Carlisle and Bowness (the trail is, as usual, a little longer). By comparison, on the way into Carlisle there were just 19 changes in 17 miles. One theory, and it's the only one we have at the moment, is that 2000 years ago the Eden, which the Wall roughly follows on this last leg, was itself full of kinks and changes in direction. (It is interesting to note, too, that the Vallum strays from the line of the Wall after leaving Carlisle – again nobody is entirely sure why.)

The other mystery, of course, is why there are so few ruins, especially considering that this stage was bookended by the two largest Roman forts on the entire Wall (see box p200) with three more along its route. The trail can't be blamed on this occasion. Unlike at Newcastle – where the trail deliberately deviates from the line of the Wall to provide walkers with a more pleasant experience as they make their way through the city – one look at an archaeological map of the Wall proves that the route continues to follow, as faithfully as the modern landscape and the current laws on rights-of-way allow, the line of Rome's northernmost frontier. And the bridge stones in Carlisle, the various churches along the way that have been built from Roman masonry as well as the odd altar that now finds secondary employment as a lintel decoration or garden ornament are all proof that the trail has not forsaken its duty and continues to adhere, as closely as it can, to the line of the Wall.

❏ **High tide in the Solway Estuary**

For the final section (Carlisle to Bowness-on-Solway) it is vital that you check beforehand to see when the high tides occur in the Solway Estuary!

You can do this in a number of ways: many B&Bs and hostels have a **booklet** of tide times; there are **noticeboards** at Bowness-on-Solway and Dykesfield (where the trail floods; see Map 42) with the times printed on; or you can check on the internet.

Visit the website 🖳 http://easytide.ukho.gov.uk, then click on Predict then Area, choose 1-4 for Europe, then England in Country/regions and then look down the list and choose Silloth. Alternatively check 🖳 www.tidetimes.org.uk/silloth-tide-times.

If walking during British Summer Time (late Mar to late Oct) you will need to **add two hours** to the high-tide times given (one hour in winter) as Silloth, while the nearest port to the trail, is not located on the path. You need to avoid being on this walk an hour either side of the high-tide point, as the trail will still be flooded.

❑ Where has the Wall gone?

One of the most noticeable aspects of the walk from Carlisle to Bowness on Solway is the lack of any concrete evidence (or more accurately, facing-stone-on-rubble-and-puddled-clay-or-limestone-mortar evidence) of the actual Wall on this stretch of the trail. Indeed, one can say that the Wall pretty much vanishes *before* Carlisle too, with the last solid evidence of the Wall if heading west being the bridge abutment before Walton – which of course has now been turfed over for its own protection too, so even here the Wall, while extant, remains hidden. Thus, for a distance of some 26 miles (42km), which equates to almost the entire last third of the route, walkers have to make do without any visible evidence of the main reason why the trail exists in the first place!

This is even more curious considering that this stage was bookended by the two largest Roman forts on the entire Wall (with Carlisle's Stanwix being the largest, Bowness the second) with a third fort at Burgh-by-Sands and a fourth at Drumburgh. Indeed, Carlisle was the headquarters of the entire frontier, with not one but two forts located within the boundaries of the modern city (see p194). Logic would therefore suggest that this would have been the most populated and heavily fortified part of the Wall – which you would have thought would yield the greatest amount of evidence that the Romans were here.

So why then, is there such little evidence of Hadrian's greatest architectural achievement on this westernmost stretch of the trail? Well, part of the answer can be found in the churches passed on this stage. St Mary's at Beaumont, St Michael's at Burgh-by-Sands and St Martin's at Bowness are all clearly built with Roman masonry, the very fabric of the churches made up from bits of the Wall (indeed, at Beaumont the church's exterior wall is said to include a 'building stone' inscribed by the 5th cohort of the 20th legion; the stone is in the left-hand wall as you head up the hill). One can also point to the marshes on the way to Bowness, where no evidence of a Wall has ever been found between Milecastles 73 (at Dykesfield) and 76 (at Drumburgh). That's not to say that the Wall wasn't built on the marshes – as the old archaeological adage goes, absence of evidence is *not* the same as evidence of absence. But there is, possibly, a case to be made that the Wall builders decided that the mud and sand of the Solway would be defence enough and thus never bothered to construct a Wall here – and you won't find any evidence of Wall if the Romans didn't bother building one!

Nevertheless, despite the lack of the Wall itself, there are some charming little Roman 'curios' that provide some sort of proof that they were here. The old Roman sandal, framed and hung on the wall in the Rosemont Café at Burgh-by-Sands, or the two Roman altars (one unattractively painted) at the front of Drumburgh Castle, are just three examples. Some of the best artefacts currently in the new Roman Gallery at Carlisle's Tullie Museum are also from the west of the city, including a tiny figure of Mars found on the site of Aballava Fort in Burgh-by-Sands; a rough sandstone head of the goddess Minerva with her classical Corinthian helmet, found at Kirkandrews-on-Eden; and a small stone altar dedicated to the Goddess Latis, deity of the pool and found in Kirkbampton. There is also said to be a fragment of an altar dedicated to Hercules at Cross Farm in Burgh, which sits above the stable door. All of which, of course, amount to very little – but with archaeologists claiming that only about 5% of the Wall has been properly studied, there's hope that plenty more will emerge from this western end of the trail in due course.

The route

The stage begins where the last one left off, with a stroll by the Eden through the outskirts of Carlisle. Eventually the trail forsakes the river near the village of **Grinsdale** (Map 40) which has little save for a wooden box with drinks and snacks and an honesty box (with CCTV to make sure you remain honest!). Note that although the river is the dominant feature, the trail still follows the line of the Wall where it can, invisible though it is. Proof of this is in the reappearance of the Vallum, the dip in the field to your left as you cross the little **Sourmilk footbridge** (where a sandstone head of Minerva, goddess of wisdom and warfare, was found in the 19th century; it's now in Carlisle's Tullie Museum (p198).

Then there's **Beaumont** and its church, situated at the top of the 'beautiful mountain' that gives the village its name and which is now reached via a diversion following a landslip that swept away part of the path. Unsurprisingly, the church is largely built with stones from the Wall and is in fact the only church on the whole route that lies directly on the line of the Wall. If you take a left at the junction near the church instead of a right you'll end up at *Roman Wall Lodges* (☎ 07784-736423, 🖥 www.romanwall-lodges.co.uk; 🐾; WI-FI).

(cont'd on p204)

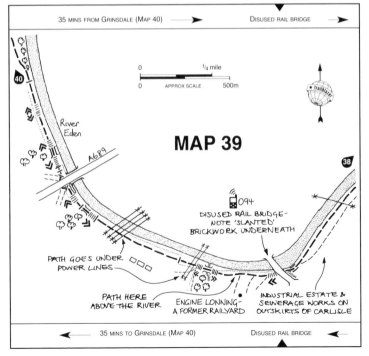

35 MINS FROM GRINSDALE (MAP 40) ➡   DISUSED RAIL BRIDGE ➡

0   ¼ mile
0   APPROX SCALE   500m

trailblazer

River Eden

A689

MAP 39

40

38

📱094

DISUSED RAIL BRIDGE–
NOTE 'SLANTED'
BRICKWORK UNDERNEATH

PATH GOES UNDER
POWER LINES

PATH HERE
ABOVE THE RIVER

ENGINE LONNING–
A FORMER RAILYARD

INDUSTRIAL ESTATE &
SEWERAGE WORKS ON
OUTSKIRTS OF CARLISLE

⬅ 35 MINS TO GRINSDALE (MAP 40)   DISUSED RAIL BRIDGE ⬅

❏ The reivers

The Middle Ages, particularly the 300 years or so between the War of Scottish Independence c1315 and the Union of the Crown in 1603, was a tempestuous and bloody time for the Wall region. The almost constant warring between Scotland and England meant that those poor souls who chose to live in the borderlands between the two were subject to frequent harassment by one side or another. Their crops were regularly destroyed or appropriated by the troops and their livestock slaughtered to feed the army. As a result, many locals chose to engage in sheep and cattle rustling, a practice known as **reiving**, in order to eke out a living and ensure their survival.

Such was the ubiquity of this practice that reiving eventually became a way of life and one that local borderers regarded as a profession rather than a crime. Nor was it merely English families raiding Scottish ones and vice versa, for often they stole from their fellow compatriots. Nor, for that matter, was reiving confined merely to the destitute and desperate – local nobles condoned and occasionally even indulged in the practice themselves, as did the Wardens of the Marches, the very people who were supposed to be upholding the rule of law in the region!

As the reiving continued through the generations, various strange (or so it seems to us now) laws were put in place to try to regulate the situation. For example, a victim of a reive had two courses of action open to him. The first was to file a complaint with the warden who would then be compelled to investigate. Or, and this was by far the more common choice, the victim could raise a raiding party of his own and pursue the reivers himself. It became enshrined in Border Law that anybody encountering this counter-raid was compelled to ride along with them and offer such help as they could, or else stand accused of being complicit in the original raid. If this counter-attack caught the reivers within 24 hours they could fight to retrieve their livestock. If, however, the 24 hours passed without any encounter with the thieves, the reivers could keep their booty. Eventually, to try to combat the worst excesses of reiving, the two countries decided to set up armies, known as Borderers, as a first line of defence against raiding parties from across the border. Heavily armed, the Borderers were recruited from local families and travelled on horseback, using their intimate knowledge of the local area to launch guerrilla attacks on local reiving parties.

The whole phenomenon of reiving effectively ended with the accession of James VI of Scotland to the English throne. His attempts to unify the two countries included appropriating the land of reiver families, the introduction of a ban on weapons and a drive to arrest and execute notorious reivers. There was even talk of rebuilding Hadrian's Wall to limit and control cross-border movement. Whereas before the reivers could raid in one country then cross into another for safety, with the two countries unified no such safe haven existed and the reivers could be pursued relentlessly. The construction of the Military Road in the mid-18th century also helped the authorities police the region more efficiently.

But though the phenomenon of reiving no longer exists, echoes of this troubled period in the region's history can still be heard. The terms 'kidnapping' (a favourite pastime of the reivers), 'blackmail' (originally protection money paid to the reivers, as opposed to legitimate rent paid to a landowner which was called 'greenmail') and 'bereaved' (which originally meant to lose a loved one by the hand of the reivers) are all words that come from this period. Imposing fortifications, now just ruins – for instance bastle (see p214) houses such as Drumburgh Castle in the village of the same name, pele towers (such as the ones at Burgh-by-Sands and Linstock, as well as off the Wall in Corbridge's churchyard) and larger fortifications such as the wonderful Thirlwall Castle – were built by well-to-do families to protect themselves from reivers.

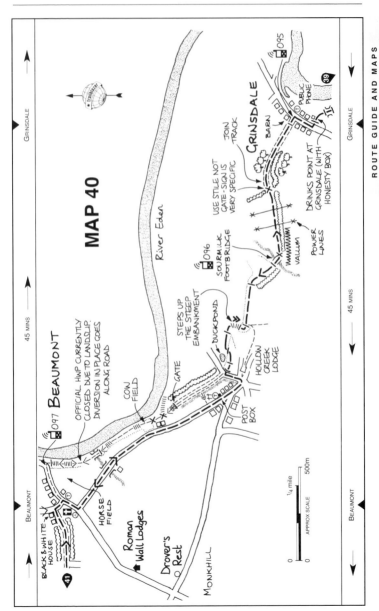

MAP 40

BEAUMONT

GRINSDALE

River Eden

097 BEAUMONT

OFFICIAL HWP CURRENTLY CLOSED DUE TO LANDSLIP. DIVERSION IN PLACE GOES ALONG ROAD

STEPS UP THE STEEP EMBANKMENT

096

SOURMILK FOOTBRIDGE

USE STILE NOT GATE - SIGNS IS VERY SPECIFIC

JOIN TRACK

GRINSDALE

BARN

095

PUBLIC PHONE

39

DRINKS POINT AT GRINSDALE (WITH HONESTY BOX)

POWER LINES

VALLUM

DUCKPOND

HOLLOW CREEK LODGE

POST BOX

GATE

COW FIELD

HORSE FIELD

BLACK & WHITE HOUSE

41

Roman Wall Lodges

Drover's Rest

MONKHILL

45 MINS

BEAUMONT

GRINSDALE

45 MINS

BEAUMONT

1/4 mile

APPROX SCALE

500m

0

0

(cont'd from p201) **Roman Wall Lodges** has a **campsite** (pitches from £10) with a couple of smart wooden 'wigwams' (sleep 4-6, £35) in a small field by the quiet roadside. The owners are amiable and can conjure up a cooked breakfast (£5), packed lunch (£3.50) or just a simple bacon butty (£2.50). For something more substantial, continue along the road and take a left at the end for *The Drover's Rest* (☎ 01228-576141; food served noon-2pm & 5-9pm) at **Monkhill** (Maps 40 & 41) with standard pub grub such as steak pie (£11.95).

Stagecoach's No 93/71 **bus** service calls here; see pp46-8 for further details.

BURGH-BY-SANDS [Map 41]

Burgh-by-Sands (pronounced 'Bruff-by-Sands') is the largest settlement on today's walk, a village that stretches out along the road. The 13th-century **St Michael's Church** is the main focus for Romanophiles here, its walls largely made from Wall stones and its location at the centre of what was once a five-acre (two-hectare) Roman fort. This was **Aballava**, garrisoned for much of its history by auxiliary troops of Moors from North Africa. Comparatively little is known of Aballava, though we do know that the bathhouse (which, as is typical, would have been outside the fort) was located where the vicarage is today, and excavations have revealed a number of Roman artefacts, including glassware and metalwork, and in 1928 a section of Wall foundations was uncovered in the graveyard. Today, some stone slabs line the churchyard path and recount the history of the village for visitors.

There's more evidence of Roman occupation within the church itself, where the face of a pagan god can clearly be discerned on the east wall of the chancel behind the altar, emerging from the blank plaster that covers the rest of the wall. Presumably the builders of the church weren't fussy about which Roman stones they used, hence the pagan face. Isn't it curious how it hasn't been removed, especially as, when the faithful face the altar and bow, they are also bowing to this

pagan god? At the opposite end of the aisle, note how the church tower has no exterior door and only tiny slit windows, presumably because it was once a pele tower used to protect the locals against raiders.

Virtually opposite the church, a road leads up to the **Edward I monument**, marking the spot where the so-called Hammer of the Scots died from dysentery while waiting to cross the Solway Firth on 7 July 1307. The king's body lay in state in the church before being buried in Westminster Abbey. There's an impressive statue by The Greyhound pub in Burgh, which was erected on the 700th anniversary of the same event. A mile to the north of the trail there's also a Victorian monument to the same event, right on the marshes. If you're staying in Burgh and have got some time to kill there are worse things to do than head over there – see Map 41 for where you should turn off the trail.

Other than these sights there's little reason to dally in Burgh, except perhaps to call in at *The Greyhound Inn* (☎ 01228-576579, 🖳 http://thegreyhoundinn-burgh.co.uk; bar Mon-Wed 4-11pm, Thur & Fri noon-2pm & 4-11pm, Sat noon-11pm, Sun noon-10pm; **food** served Thur-Sun noon-2pm & 5-8pm). The other option is *Rosemount* (☎ 01228-576440; 🐾; WI-FI; usually Mon-Fri 10.30am-4pm but check in advance), a former B&B which comes to the rescue of weary trekkers with some reviving cakes

Statue of Edward I

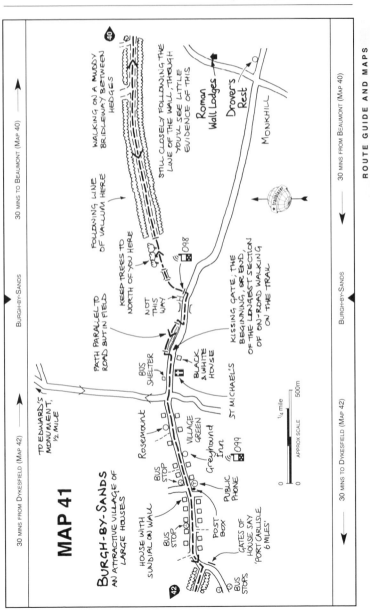

BURGH-BY-SANDS

MAP 41

BURGH-BY-SANDS
AN ATTRACTIVE VILLAGE OF
LARGE HOUSES

TO EDWARD'S
MONUMENT,
½ MILE

WALKING ON A MUDDY
BRIDLEWAY BETWEEN
HEDGES

STILL CLOSELY FOLLOWING THE
LINE OF THE WALL, THROUGH
YOU'LL SEE LITTLE
EVIDENCE OF THIS

FOLLOWING LINE
OF VALLUM HERE

KEEP TREES TO
NORTH OF YOU HERE

PATH PARALLEL TO
ROAD BUT IN FIELD

NOT
THIS
WAY

☎ 098

KISSING GATE, THE
BEGINNING, OR END,
OF THE LONGEST SECTION
OF ON-ROAD WALKING
ON THE TRAIL

Roman
Wall Lodges
Drover's Rest

MONKHILL

BUS
SHELTER

BLACK
& WHITE
HOUSE

ST MICHAEL'S

Rosemount

VILLAGE GREEN

Greyhound
Inn   ☎ 099

BUS
STOP

PUBLIC
PHONE

HOUSE WITH
SUNDIAL ON WALL

BUS STOP

POST
BOX

GATES OF
HOUSE SAY
'PORT CARLISLE
6 MILES'

BUS
STOPS

¼ mile   500m

0   APPROX SCALE   0

BURGH-BY-SANDS

and light lunches. And just to prove that the Wall used to run through here, a Roman shoe sits in a frame on the wall of the café; when Rosemount was having an extension built in 2007 it was discovered by the archaeologist overseeing the work (archaeologists are compulsory when any sort of

building work takes place in the village, such is the wealth of undiscovered artefacts still believed to be lying buried there).

Finally, leaving Burgh, Stagecoach's Nos 93/71 **buses** come through the village on their way to Bowness or Carlisle; see pp46-8 for further information.

After Burgh, the path continues along the road. It also still follows the line of the Vallum, though the only suggestion that this is the case is the name of one of the houses – 'Vallum House' – along the way.

Continuing your tarmac travails, you come next to **Dykesfield** (Map 42) and on, over the cattle grid, to the area of the trail that is liable to flooding at certain times of the year; see box p199. It's also one of the most interminable stretches, a wearying trek over flat terrain with a floodbank blocking your views to the south and the wind whipping off the shore to chill your marrow from the north. But if the weather's fair and the traffic's minimal it can be quite pleasant, with herons swooping above the sunbathing cows. You can vary the walk slightly by walking atop the embankment to the south of the road – one of the last vestiges of the old railway that ran through here to Port Carlisle – where at least you can get a better view of Skiddaw and the Lake District peaks to the south (though watch your step as the embankment is precarious in places). But even this thrill palls after a while, probably even before you reach, on your left, a road leading to the small village of Boustead Hill.

BOUSTEAD HILL   [Map 42]

Most people whizz through this last section from Carlisle to Bowness, hurrying along to make sure they arrive at the end of the trail to catch the last bus back. But those who take their time are rewarded with some very pleasant accommodation, good food and lovely people; and Boustead Hill, at approximately halfway between Carlisle and the end of the walk, is a logical place to stop. True, it's little more than a row of rather grand houses, amongst which are two **B&Bs**. But the accommodation, the people and the views across the marshes to the estuary are reason enough to stop for a night.

Of the B&Bs, *Hillside* (☎ 01228-576398, 🖳 www.hadrianswalkbnb.co.uk; 1T/1D shared facilities; 🛏; 🐾; WI-FI; Apr-Oct) is a welcoming place charging £25-30pp. They also have a **bunk barn** (open all year; sleeps about 12) with its own kitchen (including microwave, crockery, cutlery and gas cooker), shower and toilet; they charge £10pp. The owner is typical of the sort of person you meet at this end of the trail – chatty, friendly, and oh-so-

helpful in a very unfussy way. Breakfasts are also available to guests of the barn if requested in advance, though aren't included in the price. Oh, and the wi-fi is excellent here too, and the showers in the bunkhouse are hotter and more powerful than anyone has a right to expect for £10. All in all, thoroughly recommended.

The other B&B, just down the hill and the first you come to, is *Highfield* (☎ 01228-576060, 07976-170538, 🖳 www .highfield-holidays.co.uk; 1D or T en suite /1D or F with a Jacuzzi; ⓛ £5), a smarter affair where B&B starts at £70 (£65 sgl occ) – great value considering the quality of the accommodation. They even have their own family of barn owls living on their 300 acres of land and a **campsite** (🐾; Mar-Oct) out back charging from £10 per pitch, including use of showers, hot and cold water and kitchen facilities. If arranged in advance breakfast (about £6) is available for campers.

Stagecoach's No 93/71 **bus** service calls here; see pp46-8 for further details.

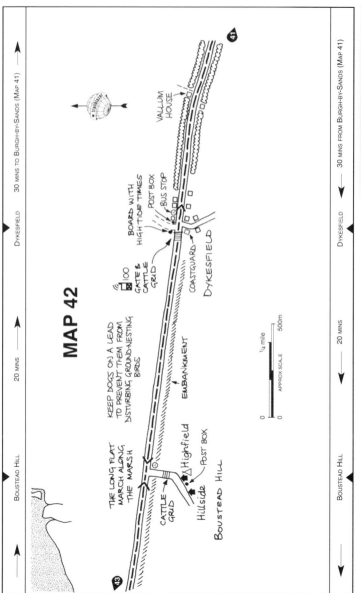

MAP 42

KEEP DOGS ON A LEAD TO PREVENT THEM FROM DISTURBING GROUND-NESTING BIRDS

THE LONG FLAT MARCH ALONG THE MARSH

CATTLE GRID

△ Highfield

Hillside

POST BOX

BOUSTEAD HILL

EMBANKMENT

⌂ 100 GATE & CATTLE GRID

BOARD WITH HIGH TIDE TIMES

POST BOX

BUS STOP

COASTGUARD

DYKESFIELD

VALLUM HOUSE

41

¼ mile

0 · · · · · APPROX SCALE · · · · · 500m

0

BOUSTEAD HILL ← 20 MINS → DYKESFIELD ← 30 MINS TO BURGH-BY-SANDS (MAP 41) →

BOUSTEAD HILL ← 20 MINS → DYKESFIELD ← 30 MINS FROM BURGH-BY-SANDS (MAP 41) →

43

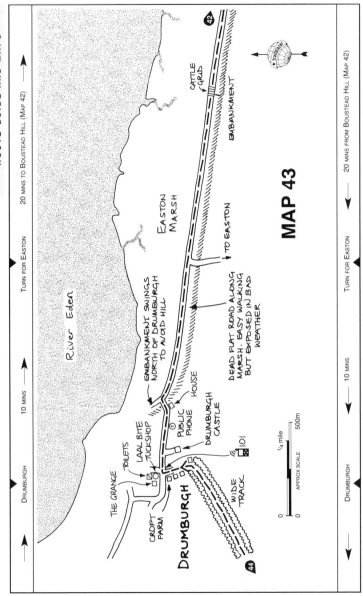

ROUTE GUIDE AND MAPS

MAP 43

20 MINS TO BOUSTEAD HILL (MAP 42) →

TURN FOR EASTON

10 MINS →

DRUMBURGH →

River Eden

EASTON MARSH

EMBANKMENT SWINGS NORTH OF DRUMBURGH TO AVOID HILL

42

CATTLE GRID

EMBANKMENT

TO EASTON

DEAD FLAT ROAD ALONG MARSH. EASY WALKING BUT EXPOSED IN BAD WEATHER

20 MINS FROM BOUSTEAD HILL (MAP 42)

TURN FOR EASTON

10 MINS

DRUMBURGH

THE GRANGE

TOILETS

LAAL BITE TUCKSHOP

CROFT FARM

PUBLIC PHONE

DRUMBURGH CASTLE

101

WIDE TRACK

DRUMBURGH

44

0 ¼ mile
APPROX SCALE
0 500m

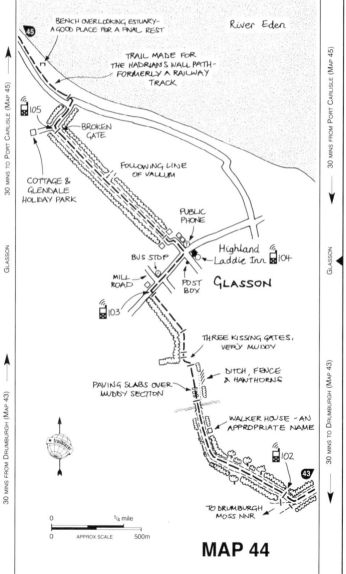

BENCH OVERLOOKING ESTUARY—
A GOOD PLACE FOR A FINAL REST

River Eden

45

TRAIL MADE FOR
THE HADRIAN'S WALL PATH—
FORMERLY A RAILWAY
TRACK

105

BROKEN
GATE

COTTAGE &
GLENDALE
HOLIDAY PARK

FOLLOWING LINE
OF VALLUM

PUBLIC
PHONE

BUS STOP

Highland
Laddie Inn
104

MILL
ROAD

POST
BOX

GLASSON

103

THREE KISSING GATES,
VERY MUDDY

DITCH, FENCE
& HAWTHORNS

PAVING SLABS OVER
MUDDY SECTION

WALKER HOUSE — AN
APPROPRIATE NAME

102

43

TO DRUMBURGH
MOSS NNR

★ trailblazer

0   ¼ mile
0   500m
APPROX SCALE

MAP 44

30 MINS TO PORT CARLISLE (MAP 45)

30 MINS FROM PORT CARLISLE (MAP 45)

GLASSON

30 MINS FROM DRUMBURGH (MAP 43)

30 MINS TO DRUMBURGH (MAP 43)

It's worth mentioning here, as you continue your yomp along the marsh, that there has never been any evidence of the Wall, nor milecastles nor turrets, uncovered on this stretch. Of course, just because we haven't found anything doesn't mean there isn't anything to find; and it's far too big a leap to say that the Romans didn't bother building across the marsh – but does introduce an element of doubt to the claim that the Wall was a continuous, unbroken construction. So Wall worriers will have to wait until the hamlet of **Drumburgh** on the other side -which had both a milecastle, number 76, and a fort, **Congabata** – to find more archaeological nourishment to feed their obsession.

DRUMBURGH   [Map 43, p208]

Drumburgh ('Drumbruff'), an unassuming little farming community, resides where once a small Roman fort stood. This fort was known as Congabata/Concavata, built to watch over the salt flats nearby.

Today the hamlet's highlight is **Drumburgh Castle**, on the left as you enter, a bastle (see p215) house built in 1307 to provide protection against reivers (see box p202). The livestock would be housed on the ground floor, with the family living upstairs. Note the heraldic crest above the door, the griffins perched on the roof and not one but two Roman altars out front.

Drumburgh has little else to interest the trekker except, and this is lovely, a serve-yourself tuckshop called, *Laal Bite* (Easter to Oct, daily 8am-6pm) at The Grange (☎ 01228-576551, ▣ www.the grangecottage.co.uk), opposite where the trail turns left off the road. They sell ice creams and snacks and have drinks machines and a toilet, as well as a picnic table and a bench in the shade of a couple of apple trees outside. They also have a cottage which can be rented on a weekly basis. Laal Bite, incidentally, translates as *Little Stand*, a 'stand' being a position allocated to a fisherman from where he can fish and which are traditionally given names by the locals.

Stagecoach's No 93/71 **bus** service calls here; see pp46-8 for further details.

From Drumburgh the trail takes a deviation away from the road to pass through a few farms, emerging eventually at **Glasson.**

GLASSON   [Map 44, p209]

For trekkers the appeal of Glasson starts and ends with the *Highland Laddie Inn* (☎ 016973-51839; bar daily noon-midnight; **food** served daily noon-2.30pm, to 2pm on Sun, & 6.30-8.45pm). They also have a few **rooms** (1D/2T, one en suite; 🐾; WI-FI;) for £31 single, £50 double; guests also receive 10% off the menu.

Stagecoach Bus No 93/71 calls in at Glasson on its way to Bowness and Carlisle; see pp46-8 for further information.

Opposite the Highland Laddie Inn, a bridleway heads off north-west, following the line of the Vallum (though you'll have trouble spotting any evidence of this), past the Cottage & Glendale Holiday Park with its 'village' **shop** (daily 9.30am-4.30pm) – the first shop since Carlisle and the last shop on the trail too – before dodging back to the shoreline, emerging back onto the road at the end of Port Carlisle.

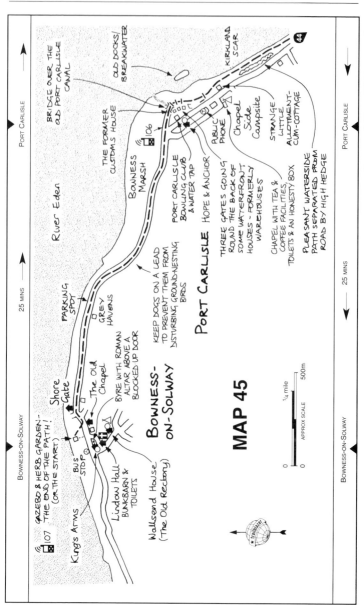

PORT CARLISLE [Map 45, p211]

The path chooses to ignore Port Carlisle, preferring to hug the shore and turn onto the road only at the end of the village, one of the more interesting on this stage. For one thing, at one time there were big plans for Port Carlisle, with both a railway line and a canal terminating here – both of which followed the line of the Wall. Stephenson's *Rocket* actually travelled along the line in 1829, and indeed it was hoped that the village would become a major port for goods to and from Scotland and Ireland. However, factors conspired against Port Carlisle and the railway line shut after 100 years of use, while the canal was abandoned after just 30 years.

Thereafter, Port Carlisle slipped back into the sleepy backwaters of the British Isles. Today, you can see the remains of the lock and port, and you cross the last vestiges of the canal on the walk. Look out across the water too and, just a few metres away, are the remains of the harbour walls.

Today the village is home to the Port Carlisle Bowling Club which has a **water tap** on the wall of its clubhouse that you can use; and the *Hope and Anchor* (☎ 016973 51460, 🖳 www.hopeandanchorinn.com; 1D/1F en suite/2T private bathrooms; 🛏; 🐾; WI-FI) which provides **B&B** for £30 per person. The family room

sleeps four in a double bed and two singles. They also serve **food**, usually from noon–2pm & 6-8pm daily but the new management are very keen on supporting Hadrian's Wall walkers, so if you stagger in outside those hours exhausted and ravenous they will do their best to provide you with something to eat.

Less than a quarter of a mile up the road at Kirkland House Farm, the basic *Chapel Side Campsite* (☎ 016973-51400) has pitches for £5 per person (though there's no hot water, just cold showers). Should the weather be particularly inclement or you just fancy something a little more comfy, they've also converted their milking parlour into a **camping barn**, equipped with a simple bench around the walls on which to sleep, a hot shower, small kitchen with kettle and two-ring stove; rates are £10 per night. Incidentally, there were kitchen facilities at the chapel next door that was, for the 2013 season at least, open to the public. A kettle, microwave, **tea and coffee** were all available – as well as an honesty box, of course.

By the way Hesket House, the last house in the village, was formerly the *Steam Packet Inn* and above the door is a small grey stone **altar**, distinctly Roman, set into the brickwork. It fits in rather well.

From Port Carlisle it's an uneventful 20-minute stroll along the coastal road to Bowness, the trill of the oystercatcher a welcome accompaniment. At Bowness you can get a pint, food, possibly some accommodation or maybe a bus back to Carlisle. As you enter the village the trail takes a sudden and unexpected turn right towards the coast, where a small shelter and pretty garden mark the end of the trail. In the shelter you can find the final **passport stamp**, as well as a seat to rest upon.

And that's it. According to 18th-century bishop, the Wall continued for another quarter of a mile west of here. And if you've got time to kill, you can continue on beyond the King's Arms for a quarter of an hour to ensure you've fully walked the entire length of the Wall – even though there is no actual Wall left, of course. The super-ambitious could, I suppose, carry on along the newly constructed cycleway running to Ravenglass – thereby taking in the site of the Roman fort at Maryport. But if you've had enough, don't worry: the trail is at an end, and the walk is done.

And you're done.

Well done!

BOWNESS-ON-SOLWAY
[Map 45, p211]

Bowness is a lovely, peaceful place to fin-ish the walk. Indeed, it's almost eerily quiet and you get the sense that the outside world has little to do with Bowness – and vice versa.

The name Bowness comes from the bow-shaped corner of the *ness*, or peninsu-la here. As the last place where the Solway is fordable, it is understandable why the Romans decided to finish their Wall here, and a large 7-acre (2.8-hectare) fort was built where the village now stands. This was **Maia**, the second largest fort on the Wall (indeed, 'Maia' can be translated as 'Larger'). Originally, the Wall was sup-posed to continue a little way beyond the fort at Bowness, for the Romans were wary that the Caledones and Irish could sneak by the Wall and land on Cumbria's west coast. However, the Romans soon decided to build a series of towers on that coastline instead, including one at Maryport – now known as the Western Sea Defences.

Today, there's very little evidence of the Romans, though there is an old Roman altar above a blocked-up byre door. (To find it, having emerged onto the main street in Bowness, turn right and, after passing a turn-off to the left there's a low barn or 'byre', followed by a taller one; here you'll see the outline of a blocked-up door with a clear Roman altar above it.) There are also some purloined stones from the Wall in the fabric of the Norman church, which stands on the site of the fort. Yet the destruction of the Wall around here seems to be quite a recent event: in 1801 there were said to be 500 yards of Wall just outside the village.

In the absence of much in the way of Wall or fort remains it's fair to say that Bowness is a little lacking in tourist attrac-tions, though the church has a couple of bells inside at the back behind the font which were nicked from villages across the Solway in the 17th century – yet another manifestation of the antipathy that sim-mered for centuries between neighbours in this part of the world. It is apparently a tra-dition for every new vicar across the water to formally ask the parish for the bells back.

It's also true that some of the locals are a little concerned that this end of the walk is being ignored. It was bad enough that the AD122 bus no longer comes here (in fact for the 2014 season at least, it no longer goes further west than Walltown); but when the helicopter failed to fly anywhere west of Carlisle during the Lighting of the Wall in 2010 some villagers began to get worried that they were slowly, inexorably, being separated from the rest of the walk – with a view to being removed altogether from the official path, perhaps because of the lack of much evidence of the Wall around here. As anyone who is celebrating the end of their walk in the King's Arms on a busy sum-mer's evening will testify, this would be a *big* shame.

Visiting Bowness requires a bit of for-ward planning. There's no ATM for one thing, and only one B&B that takes credit cards so make sure you have the necessary readies on you before you get here. The transport links are few and seldom, too, so make sure you know how you're going to get back to Carlisle and beyond and what time your bus leaves. This is especially important in high summer, for accommoda-tion options are few (though the new bunk barn should help somewhat). Nevertheless, turn up during the summer holidays with nothing booked and your chances of find-ing a place to stay are, like the village itself, rather remote.

Where to stay

The centre of the village is the **King's Arms** (☎ 016973-51426, 🖳 www.kingsarmsbow-ness.co.uk; 3T/1F, one en suite; 🐾; B&B £25) which has become the spiritual, if not the official, end of the trail. As if to cement this position the pub issues Wall certificates (£1) and achievers' badges (£3.95) for those who've finished the trail (to be fair, they were the ones who thought of the certifi-cates first), sells souvenir T-shirts and has a Wall walkers' visitors book that usually contains a few useful recommendations for those about to start their walk – in addition to lots of comments about the weather/hardships suffered/joy they now feel from those who've just finished. On the outside wall they also have a map showing where the original Roman fort would have stood, with the pub lying almost at its heart.

Wallsend House remains the smartest and most established B&B in town (☎ 016973-51055, 💻 www.wallsend.net; 1S/2D/1T/1D, T or F, all en suite; 🐾; 🐴; WI-FI), which charges from £40pp for two sharing (£45 single, £100 family room sleeps 3) and is housed in a lovely building, the Old Rectory, at the western end of the village just below the church. They also have a few '**wigwams**' – luxury en-suite camping cabins (sleep 4; 🐴; WI-FI in building) for which they charge £60.

Providing stiff competition, *Shore Gate* (☎ 016973-51308, 💻 www.shoregate house.co.uk; 3D or T en suite/1D, T or F; WI-FI; ©) is right at the beginning of the village and offers really sumptuous views of the estuary. Add to this some smart – and, unusually, 'modern' rooms, and eager-to-please owners and you have a welcome addition to the B&B scene at this end of the trail. Prices are £70 (£60 sgl occ).

The Old Chapel (☎ 016973-51126, 💻 www.oldchapelbownessonsolway.com; 1S/2T/1F en suite; 🐾; 🐴; WI-FI; ©) is a converted sandstone Wesleyan chapel from 1872 that lies on the route. The family room upstairs sleeps four people. They also, unusually, give guests access to a modern kitchen area complete with cooker, microwave, fridge – and washing machine! Rates are from £30 including a continental breakfast.

There is one more accommodation option opening in summer 2014: *Lindow Hall* (☎ 016973-51788; 💻 bookings@bow nessparishhall.co.uk), just up from the church and the home of the village's public toilets, has received lottery funding to convert the old reading room upstairs into an 18-bed **bunkhouse**. Rates are £12-15 per person and there are kitchen facilities as well as hot showers (on a meter). Breakfast packs are available for an additional charge.

Where to eat
Should you arrive in Bowness hungry and you're too early for the pub to help out,

Wallsend House has now established a **tea-room** (Easter-Sept daily 11am-5pm; will also open outside of these times for groups who book in advance).

The *King's Arms* (see Where to stay) serves massive meals (Mon-Fri 5.30-8.30pm, Sat noon-2pm & 5.30-8.30pm, Sun noon-2pm & 7-8.30pm; bar open daily Easter to Sep 11am-11pm, rest of year 5.30-11pm, longer if walkers are around;) with nothing currently above £11 and most around £6-8. However, they cook on Wednesdays only if people are staying, either here or at local B&Bs so check/book in advance. Note that they do not accept credit/debit cards.

Transport
To get back to Carlisle is tricky. If it's a **Sunday or a Bank Holiday**, the only public transport is a **Taxi Bus** service (£7 per person; Apr-Sept) which leaves Bowness twice a day, at 10.40am and 5pm, travelling to Carlisle railway station via Port Carlisle (10.50am & 5.10pm) and Burgh (11.05am & 5.20pm). You must book a seat on this service at least 90 minutes in advance, by calling the Taxi Bus Enquiries line on ☎ 07592-763503.

From Monday to Saturday there's Stagecoach's **bus** No 93/71 which calls in at the bus stop opposite the King' Arms and departs at 7.30am, 10.20am, 2.10pm & 6.50pm (Mon-Fri) or 7.40am, 10.20am, 2.10pm & 7.20pm (Sat). Two additional buses run on Friday and Saturday only, leaving at 9.50pm and 11.48pm. It takes about 42 minutes to reach Carlisle.

Another option is the **shared taxi** run by Metro Taxis (☎ 07592-763593; £7 per person), leaving Bowness at 10.40am and 3pm (or 9.40am and 2pm from Carlisle Station for those heading in the other direction). Always check the times as they may have changed. See pp46-8 for further information. Alternatively, ask your B&B owner or the landlord of the King's Arms and they may be able to sort you out a lift for around £25; if that fails the only other option is a **private taxi** – though expect to pay about £30 for a trip to Carlisle; try C&P Taxis (☎ 01228-535425) who also run the Sunday Taxi Bus (see above).

APPENDIX A – GLOSSARY

Antonine Wall Turf wall built to the north of Hadrian's construction by his successor, Antoninus Pius

Bastle house A fortified house built during the Middle Ages in the border region to protect the owner and his family from bandits

Brigantes The main tribe whose land was crossed by the Wall

Caledones The collective name for the tribes living north of the Wall

Gask Frontier The first border separating the conquered lands in the south from the 'Barbarians' in the north. Established by Domitian (AD81-96), it was also built to watch over the glens but moved further south when troops were required elsewhere in the empire

Milecastle A series of 'mini-castles' spaced 1000 paces apart (or one Roman mile) along the entire length of the Wall. Built to house troops, each could hold an estimated 32 men

Military Road Now the B6318, the Military Road was an 18th-century thoroughfare built on the orders of General Wade to thwart further attacks from Bonnie Prince Charlie

Military Way A Roman thoroughfare built around AD160 between the Stanegate and the Wall, often along the northern earthwork of the Vallum (which had by then been largely decommissioned)

Pele tower A square defensive tower built by wealthier families in the 16th century in the border counties of England and Scotland to defend themselves against the trepidations of reivers. The layout would typically follow the same design, with a storeroom on the ground floor, from which a staircase would lead upstairs to the living quarters. On the roof the family would light a beacon to summon help during a raid.

Reivers Bandits and cattle rustlers during the Middle Ages

Stanegate The east–west road that ran between the Roman settlements of Carlisle and Corbridge which was one of the major reasons for the construction of the Wall

Turret Stone observation posts, 161 in total, spaced evenly along the Wall to watch for movements to the north of the Wall

Vallum Roman earthwork, consisting of a deep ditch running between two high mud or earth walls, that ran to the south of and parallel to the Wall

❏ Norse words

Squashed between the Saxons and the Scots, the area of the Borders and the Lake District has kept many Norse words that you'll find today in the local place names. Amongst them:

Norse	Meaning
fell	upper slope of hill
beck/burn	stream
haugh	flat land beside river
holm	island in river
hope	sheltered valley
moss	peat bog

❏ Haaf netting

If you're lucky, when visiting Bowness you may come across the strange sight of half a dozen men standing chest-deep in the waters of the Solway holding large nets secured to wooden frames. This practice, known as haaf netting, is the traditional means of fishing in the estuary. The practice is believed to have come from the Vikings in around the 10th century AD, and indeed the very word 'haaf' comes from the Norse word for channel. The haaf net itself is a wooden frame, or 'beam', 5.5m long which is said to be the length of an old Viking oar without the blade. The net is then suspended from this beam, and the fishermen, usually in groups of half a dozen or so, form a line across the channel to catch any fish, usually sea trout and Atlantic salmon, that pass their way.

APPENDIX B – GPS WAYPOINTS

Each GPS waypoint below was taken on the route at the reference number marked on the map as below. This list of GPS waypoints as well as instructions on how to interpret an OS grid reference can be found on the Trailblazer website: 💻 www.trailblazer-guides.com (click on GPS waypoints).

MAP	WAYPOINT	OS GRID REF	DESCRIPTION
1	001	N54 59.313 W1 31.846	Segedunum
1	002	N54 58.431 W1 32.376	Wincomblee Bridge
2	003	N54 57.722 W1 32.737	Top of steps
2	004	N54 58.017 W1 34.658	St Lawrence Rd
3	005	N54 58.280 W1 35.370	Ouseburn
3	006	N54 58.215 W1 35.993	Millennium Bridge
3	007	N54 57.965 W1 36.755	Copthorne Hotel
4	008	N54 57.731 W1 39.035	Car park
4	009	N54 57.831 W1 39.372	Riverside path joins road
4	010	N54 57.927 W1 39.866	Cross A695
5	011	N54 58.130 W1 41.204	Milepost
5	012	N54 58.364 W1 41.571	Path leaves road for Denton Dene
5	013	N54 58.611 W1 41.886	Bridge across A1
5	014	N54 58.459 W1 42.143	Join road (Ottringham Close)
6	015	N54 58.613 W1 42.902	Path goes under bridge
6	016	N54 58.807 W1 43.962	Over A6085 at Newburn
6	017	N54 58.900 W1 44.649	Boathouse
7	018	N54 58.884 W1 45.938	Gate at Ryton Island
7	019	N54 59.013 W1 45.985	Join the Wylam waggonway
7	020	N54 59.067 W1 47.485	Leave the Wylam waggonway
8	021	N54 59.273 W1 48.207	Bend in track
8	022	N54 59.463 W1 48.213	Track bends right (E)
8	023	N54 59.815 W1 47.322	Heddon Roman wall
8	024	N55 00.005 W1 48.629	Path leaves road and joins bridleway
9	025	N55 00.094 W1 49.482	Cross road by Rudchester
9	026	N55 00.217 W1 50.375	Join B6318 by Two Hoots
9	027	N55 00.284 W1 50.989	Cross B6318
10	028	N55 00.468 W1 52.160	Cross road to Albemarle Barracks
11	029	N55 00.590 W1 55.415	Robin Hood Inn
11	030	N55 00.680 W1 56.604	Walking in Roman ditch
11	031	N55 00.692 W1 56.977	Cross B6318
12	032	N55 00.745 W1 59.128	Over stile off road
13	033	N55 00.670 W1 59.764	Stile by B6318
13	034	N55 00.642 W2 00.355	Path to Corbridge
13	035	N55 00.767 W2 01.232	Port Gate
14	036	N55 01.091 W2 03.854	Off road onto path by Roman ditch
14	037	N55 01.161 W2 04.591	Track
15	038	N55 01.153 W2 05.742	St Oswald's Hill Head
15	039	N55 01.155 W2 06.050	Path to Acomb
15	040	N55 01.259 W2 06.669	Cross road by track to quarry
15	041	N55 01.335 W2 07.151	Join road at end of wood
16	042	N55 01.420 W2 07.605	Path to Brunton Turret
16	043	N55 01.564 W2 07.459	Join road to Chollerford

MAP	WAYPOINT	OS GRID REF	DESCRIPTION
16	044	N55 01.723 W2 08.297	Chesters entrance
16	045	N55 01.763 W2 09.203	Walwick junction
16	046	N55 01.946 W2 09.159	Leave road; enter farm

Corbridge–Hexham–Acomb alternative

MAP	WAYPOINT	OS GRID REF	DESCRIPTION
13a	*110*	*N55 00.122 W2 00.375*	*Junction of tracks*
13a	*111*	*N55 00.050 W2 00.647*	*Junction of roads*
13a	*112*	*N54 59.882 W2 00.870*	*Leazes Lane*
13a	*113*	*N54 59.023 W2 00.885*	*Under A69*
13b	*114*	*N54 58.276 W2 01.174*	*Join Tyneside path off road*
13b	*115*	*N54 58.141 W2 02.416*	*Bridge*
13b	*116*	*N54 58.001 W2 02.422*	*Cross river by A69*
13b	*117*	*N54 57.952 W2 02.657*	*Cross track*
13c	*118*	*N54 57.940 W2 03.090*	*Signpost to Duke's House*
13c	*119*	*N54 57.785 W2 03.897*	*Junction of paths*
13d	*120*	*N54 57.730 W2 04.803*	*Signpost to Hexham*
13d	*121*	*N54 57.911 W2 05.273*	*Signpost to Duke's House*
13e	*122*	*N54 59.103 W2 06.098*	*Junction of roads below Acomb*
13e	*123*	*N54 59.230 W2 06.327*	*Leave road*
13e	*124*	*N54 59.369 W2 06.350*	*Gate by mill*
13e	*125*	*N54 59.582 W2 06.452*	*Acomb*
13e	*126*	*N54 59.939 W2 06.515*	*Left across stile*

Main route

MAP	WAYPOINT	OS GRID REF	DESCRIPTION
17	047	N55 02.182 W2 11.043	Cross track to Green Carts Farm
17	048	N55 02.301 W2 11.558	Trig point
18	049	N55 02.183 W2 12.857	Stile to Brocolitia
18	050	N55 02.034 W2 13.366	Mithras Temple
18	051	N55 02.122 W2 13.624	Cross road
19	052	N55 01.861 W2 15.978	Milecastle 33
19	053	N55 01.685 W2 17.660	Grindon Turret 34a
20	054	N55 01.540 W2 18.395	Milecastle 35
20	055	N55 01.474 W2 18.844	Trig point
21	056	N55 00.880 W2 19.715	Knag Burn Gate
22	057	N55 00.731 W2 20.258	Milecastle 37
22	058	N55 00.229 W2 22.528	Castle Nick (Milecastle 39)
23	059	N55 00.092 W2 23.281	Gates at Peel Rigg leading down to Once Brewed
23	060	N55 00.120 W2 24.282	Green Slack (trig point)
23	061	N55 00.099 W2 24.433	Path to Winshields Farm
24	062	N54 59.809 W2 25.522	Bogle Hole
24	063	N54 59.629 W2 26.819	Hole Gap
25	064	N54 59.585 W2 27.117	Stile at Burnhead

Walking to and from Haltwhistle

MAP	WAYPOINT	OS GRID REF	DESCRIPTION
25	*130*	*N54 59.585 W2 27.117*	*Gate onto road by bridge over Haltwhistle Burn*
25	*131*	*N54 59.262 W2 26.959*	*Gate onto B6318*
25	*132*	*N54 59.232 W2 27.119*	*Gate off B6318*
25	*133*	*N54 58.645 W2 27.501*	*Bridge by Old Brickworks*
25	*134*	*N54 58.769 W2 27.746*	*Gate*
25	*135*	*N54 59.179 W2 27.516*	*B6318*

MAP	WAYPOINT	OS GRID REF	DESCRIPTION
Main route			
26	065	N54 59.598 W2 30.057	Stile by track to Walltown Farm
27	066	N54 59.205 W2 31.163	Walltown Refreshments
27	067	N54 59.268 W2 31.223	Path north by Roman ditch
27	068	N54 59.301 W2 32.050	Gate opposite Thirlwall Castle
27	069	N54 59.281 W2 32.353	Path leaves road; cross stile
28	070	N54 59.325 W2 33.365	Stile
28	071	N54 59.368 W2 34.156	Cross road leading to Samson Inn
28	072	N54 59.375 W2 34.720	Cross road near Turret 48A
29	073	N54 59.375 W2 36.245	Gate at Birdoswald
29	074	N54 59.007 W2 37.901	Farm road; gate
30	075	N54 58.845 W2 38.486	Track to Comb Crag
30	076	N54 58.604 W2 39.602	Stile off road at Pike Hill
30	077	N54 58.468 W2 40.171	Back onto road
31	078	N54 58.462 W2 40.952	Hare Hill Wall
31	079	N54 58.462 W2 40.813	Haytongate
32	080	N54 58.296 W2 44.435	Roman bridge abutment
32	081	N54 58.146 W2 45.362	Gate into woods
32	082	N54 58.118 W2 45.651	Gate heading into second field
33	083	N54 57.812 W2 46.431	Bridge over a stream
33	084	N54 57.219 W2 47.361	Gate leaving Newton
34	085	N54 56.805 W2 48.853	Gate by bus stop at Oldwall
35	086	N54 56.334 W2 51.308	Join bridleway known as Sandy Lane
35	087	N54 55.901 W2 51.053	Stile and gate off Sandy Lane
35	088	N54 55.755 W2 51.169	Onto road
36	089	N54 55.452 W2 52.510	Bridge over stream
36	090	N54 55.194 W2 52.922	Turn away from Eden River
37	091	N54 54.395 W2 54.431	Path off road by The Beeches
38	092	N54 54.273 W2 55.208	Bridge and kissing gate
38	093	N54 54.007 W2 56.091	Sands Sports Centre
39	094	N54 53.946 W2 57.775	Go under bridge over Eden
40	095	N54 54.752 W2 59.179	Grinsdale
40	096	N54 54.806 W2 59.883	Cross Sourmilk Footbridge
40	097	N54 55.517 W3 00.925	Gate into Beaumont
41	098	N54 55.287 W3 02.522	Join road
41	099	N54 55.301 W3 03.413	Greyhound Inn
42	100	N54 55.351 W3 05.013	Cattle grid at Dykesfield
43	101	N54 55.639 W3 08.904	Drumburgh
44	102	N54 55.346 W3 09.452	To Drumburgh Moss SSSI
44	103	N54 55.932 W3 10.198	Path onto road at Glasson
44	104	N54 56.052 W3 10.045	Junction by Highland Laddie Inn
44	105	N54 56.397 W3 10.708	Entry to Glendale Holiday Park
45	106	N54 56.983 W3 11.317	Port Carlisle
45	107	N54 57.240 W3 12.773	Start/end of path by gazebo at herb garden

APPENDIX C – TAKING A DOG

[See also p35] As noted on p35, the Hadrian's Wall Path is not that dog-friendly. Much of the land through which the path passes is grazed by livestock and dogs must be kept on a lead. However, if you're sure your dog can cope with (and will enjoy) walking 12 miles or more a day for several days in a row, you need to start preparing accordingly. Extra thought also needs to go into your itinerary. The best starting point is to study the village and town facilities table on pp32-3 (and the advice below), and plan where to stop and where to buy food.

Looking after your dog

To begin with, you need to make sure that your own dog is fully **inoculated** against the usual doggy illnesses, and also up to date with regard to **worm pills** (eg Drontal) and **flea preventatives** such as Frontline – they are, after all, following in the pawprints of many a dog before them, some of whom may well have left fleas or other parasites on the trail that now lie in wait for their next meal to arrive. **Pet insurance** is also a very good idea; if you've already got insurance, do check that it will cover a trip such as this.

On the subject of looking after your dog's health, perhaps the most important implement you can take with you is the **plastic tick remover**, available from vets for a couple of quid. These removers, while fiddly, help you to remove the tick safely (ie without leaving its head behind buried under the dog's skin).

Being in unfamiliar territory also makes it more likely that you and your dog could become separated. For this reason, make sure your dog has a **tag with your contact details on it** (a mobile phone number would be best if you are carrying one with you); you could also consider having it **microchipped** for further security.

When to keep your dog on a lead

● **Near the crags** It's a sad fact that more than one dog has perished after falling over the edge of the crags. It usually occurs when they are chasing rabbits (which know where the edge of the cliffs is and are able, unlike your poor pooch, to stop in time).

● **When crossing farmland**, particularly in the lambing season (around May) when your dog can scare the sheep, causing them to lose their young. Farmers are allowed by law to shoot at and kill any dogs that they consider are worrying their sheep. During lambing, most farmers would prefer it if you didn't bring your dog at all. It is also **compulsory to keep your dog on a lead through National Trust land**. The exception to the dogs on leads rule is if your dog is being attacked by cows. A couple of years ago there were three deaths in the UK caused by walkers being trampled as they tried to rescue their dogs from the attentions of cattle. The advice in this instance is to let go of the lead, head speedily to a position of safety (usually the other side of the field gate or stile) and call your dog to you.

● **Around ground-nesting birds** It's important to keep your dog under control when crossing an area where certain species of birds nest on the ground. Most dogs love foraging around in the woods but make sure you have permission to do so; some woods are used as 'nurseries' for game birds and dogs are only allowed through them if they are on a lead.

What to pack

You've probably already got a good idea of what to bring to keep your dog alive and happy, but the following is a checklist:

● **Food/water bowl** Foldable cloth bowls are popular with trekkers, being light and take up little room in the rucksack. You can also get a water-bottle-and-bowl combination, where the bottle folds into a 'trough' from which the dog can drink.

● **Lead and collar** An extendable one is probably preferable for this sort of trip. Make sure both lead and collar are in good condition – you don't want either to snap on the trail, or you may end up carrying your dog through sheep fields until a replacement can be found.
● **Medication** You'll know if you need to bring any lotions or potions.
● **Tick remover** See above
● **Bedding** A simple blanket may suffice, or you can opt for something more elaborate if you aren't carrying your own luggage.
● **Poo bags** Essential.
● **Hygiene wipes** For cleaning your dog after it's rolled in stuff.
● **A favourite toy** Helps prevent your dog from pining for the entire trek.
● **Food/water** Remember to bring treats as well as regular food to keep up mutt morale. That said, if your dog is anything like mine the chances are they'll spend most of the trek dining on rabbit droppings and sheep poo anyway.
● **Corkscrew stake** Available from camping or pet shops, this will help you to keep your dog secure in one place while you set up camp/doze.
● **Raingear** It can rain a lot!
● **Old towels** For drying your dog after the deluge.

When it comes to packing, I always leave an exterior pocket of my rucksack devoted to Daisy's kit. I have also seen several dogs sporting their own 'doggy rucksack', so they can carry their own food, water, poo etc – which certainly reduces the burden on their owner.

Cleaning up after your dog
It is extremely important that dog owners behave in a responsible way when walking the path. Dog excrement should be cleaned up to ensure it is not left to decorate the boots of others. In towns, villages and particularly in fields where animals graze or which will be cut for silage, hay etc, you must pick up and bag the excrement.

Staying with your dog
In this guide we have used the symbol 🐕 to denote where a hotel, pub or B&B welcomes dogs. However, this always needs to be arranged in advance and some places make an additional charge (usually per night but occasionally per stay) while others may require a deposit which is refundable if the dog doesn't make a mess. Hostels (both YHA and independent) do not permit them unless they are an assistance (guide) dog; smaller campsites tend to accept them, but some of the larger holiday parks do not. Before you turn up always double check whether there is space for them; many places have only one or two rooms suitable for people with dogs. In some cases dogs need to sleep in a separate building.

When it comes to eating, most landlords allow dogs in at least a section of their pubs, though few restaurants do. Make sure you always ask first and ensure your dog doesn't run around the pub but is secured to your table or a radiator.

INDEX

Page references in **bold** type refer to maps

Map key

♠ Where to stay	📖 Library/bookstore	● Other
○ Where to eat and drink	🔊 Internet	CP Car park
Λ Campsite	🎵 Museum/gallery	🕐 Bus station
⊠ Post Office	✝ Church/cathedral	🕐 Bus stop
© Bank/ATM	☎ Telephone	▬▬ Rail line & station
ⓘ Tourist Information	☑ Public toilet	Park
	□ Building	🔋082 GPS waypoint

⟋⟍ Walking Track	⟋╫ Gate	Stream
⟋⟍ Minor Track	⟋⟰ Bridge	River
⟋⟍ 4WD Track	Fence	Forest / Wood
⟋⟋ Road	Stone Wall	Boggy Ground
⟋‖‖ Steps	Hedge	Hadrian's Wall
⟋⟍ Slope	Water	Vallum
⟋⟍ Steep Slope	Sand	Ditch
⟋⟍ Stile	Stones	43 Map Continuation

TRAILBLAZER'S LONG-DISTANCE PATH (LDP) WALKING GUIDES

We've applied to destinations which are closer to home Trailblazer's proven formula for publishing definitive practical route guides for adventurous travellers. Britain's network of long-distance trails enables the walker to explore some of the finest landscapes in the country's best walking areas. These are guides that are user-friendly, practical, informative and environmentally sensitive.

● **Unique mapping features** In many walking guidebooks the reader has to read a route description then try to relate it to the map. Our guides are much easier to use because walking directions, tricky junctions, places to stay and eat, points of interest and walking times are all written onto the maps themselves in the places to which they apply. With their uncluttered clarity, these are not general-purpose maps but fully edited maps drawn by walkers for walkers.

● **Largest-scale walking maps** At a scale of just under 1:20,000 (8cm or 3 1/8 inches to one mile) the maps in these guides are bigger than even the most detailed British walking maps currently available in the shops.

● **Not just a trail guide – includes where to stay, where to eat and public transport** Our guidebooks cover the complete walking experience, not just the route. Accommodation options for all budgets are provided (pubs, hotels, B&Bs, campsites, bunkhouses, hostels) as well as places to eat. Detailed public transport information for all access points to each trail means that there are itineraries for all walkers, for hiking the entire route as well as for day or weekend walks.

Coast to Coast *Henry Stedman*, 6th edition, £11.99
ISBN 978-1-905864-57-7, 268pp, 110 maps, 40 colour photos

Cornwall Coast Path (SW Coast Path Pt 2) 4th edition, £11.99
ISBN 978-1-905864-44-7, 3526pp, 142 maps, 40 colour photos

Cotswold Way *Tricia & Bob Hayne* 2nd edition, £11.99
ISBN 978-1-905864-48-5, 204pp, 53 maps, 40 colour photos

Dorset & South Devon (SW Coast Path Pt 3) *Stedman & Newton*, £11.99
ISBN 978-1-905864-45-4, 336pp, 88 maps, 40 colour photos

Exmoor & North Devon (SW Coast Path Pt I) *Stedman & Newton*, £11.99
ISBN 978-1-905864-43-0, 192pp, 68 maps, 40 colour photos

Hadrian's Wall Path *Henry Stedman*, 4th edition, £11.99
ISBN 978-1-905864-58-4, 224pp, 60 maps, 40 colour photos

Offa's Dyke Path *Keith Carter*, 3rd edition, £11.99
ISBN 978-1-905864-35-5, 240pp, 98 maps, 40 colour photos

Peddars Way & Norfolk Coast Path *Alexander Stewart*, £11.99
ISBN 978-1-905864-28-7, 192pp, 54 maps, 40 colour photos

Pembrokeshire Coast Path *Jim Manthorpe*, 4th edition, £11.99
ISBN 978-1-905864-51-5, 224pp, 96 maps, 40 colour photos

Pennine Way *Stuart Greig*, 4th edition, £11.99
ISBN 978-1-905864-61-4, 272pp, 138 maps, 40 colour photos – due Aug 2014

The Ridgeway *Nick Hill*, 3rd edition, £11.99
ISBN 978-1-905864-40-9, 192pp, 53 maps, 40 colour photos

South Downs Way *Jim Manthorpe*, 4th edition, £11.99
ISBN 978-1-905864-42-3, 192pp, 60 maps, 40 colour photos

Thames Path *Joel Newton*, 1st edition, £11.99
ISBN 978-1-905864-64-5, 256pp, 120 maps, 40 colour photos – due mid 2015

West Highland Way *Charlie Loram*, 5th edition, £11.99
ISBN 978-1-905864-50-8, 208pp, 60 maps, 40 colour photos

'The same attention to detail that distinguishes its other guides has been brought to bear here'.

THE
SUNDAY TIMES

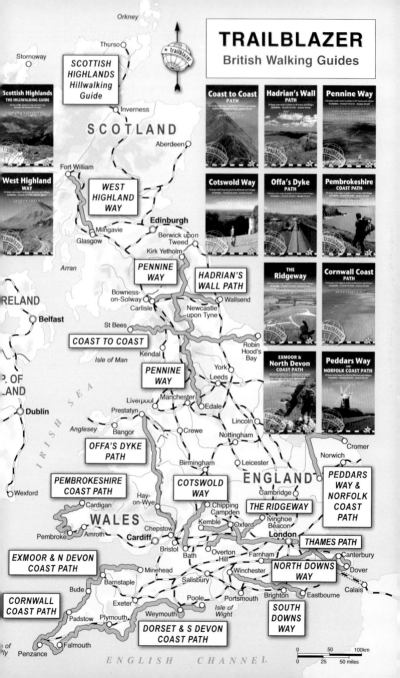

TRAILBLAZER TREKKING GUIDES

Africa
Kilimanjaro – Trekking Guide
Moroccan Atlas – Trekking Guide

Asia
Nepal Trekking & The Great
   Himalaya Trail
Sinai – the trekking guide
Trekking in the Everest Region

South America
Inca Trail, Cusco & Machu Picchu

Australasia
New Zealand – The Great Walks

Europe
Corsica Trekking – GR20
Dolomites Trekking – AV1 & AV2
Scottish Highlands – The
   Hillwalking Guide
Tour du Mont Blanc
Walker's Haute Route:
   Mt Blanc to the Matterhorn

Kilimanjaro – the trekking guide to Africa's highest mountain
Henry Stedman, 4th edn, £13.99
ISBN 978-1-905864-54-6, 368pp, 40 maps, 50 photos
At 19,340ft the world's tallest freestanding mountain, Kilimanjaro is one of the most popular destinations for hikers visiting Africa. It's possible to walk up to the summit: no technical skills are necessary. Includes town guides to Nairobi and Dar-Es-Salaam, and a colour guide to flora and fauna. Includes Mount Meru.

Sinai – the trekking guide   *Ben Hoffler,* 1st edn, £14.99
ISBN 978-1-905864-41-6, 288pp, 74 maps, 30 colour photos
Trek with the Bedouin and their camels and discover one of the most exciting new trekking destinations. The best routes in the High Mountain Region (St. Katherine), Wadi Feiran and the Muzeina deserts. Once you finish on trail there are the nearby coastal resorts of Sharm el Sheikh, Dahab and Nuweiba to enjoy.

Inca Trail, Cusco & Machu Picchu
Alexander Stewart, 5th edn, £13.99
ISBN 978-1-905864-55-3, 320pp, 65 maps, 35 photos
The Inca Trail from Cusco to Machu Picchu is South America's most popular trek. Practical guide with detailed trail maps, plans of Inca sites, guides to Lima, Cusco and Machu Picchu. Includes the Santa Teresa Trek, the Choquequirao Trail and the Vilcabamba Trail and a challenging trek linking all three. With a history of the Incas by Hugh Thomson.

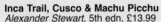

Moroccan Atlas – the trekking guide
Alan Palmer, 2nd edn, £13.99   **new edition due Oct 2014**
ISBN 978-1-905864-59-1, 272pp, 54 maps, 40 colour photos
The High Atlas in central Morocco is the most dramatic and beautiful section of the entire Atlas range. Towering peaks, deep gorges and huddled Berber villages enchant all who visit. With 44 detailed trekking maps, 10 town and village guides including Marrakech.

Tour du Mont Blanc
Jim Manthorpe 1st edn, £11.99
ISBN 978-1-905864-12-6, 208pp, 60 maps, 30 colour photos
At 4810m (15,781ft), Mont Blanc is the highest mountain in western Europe, and one of the most famous mountains in the world. The trail (105 miles, 168km) that circumnavigates it, passing through France, Italy and Switzerland, is the most popular long distance walk in Europe. Includes Chamonix and Courmayeur guides.

TRAILBLAZER TITLE LIST

Adventure Cycle-Touring Handbook
Adventure Motorcycling Handbook
Australia by Rail
Australia's Great Ocean Road
Azerbaijan
Coast to Coast (British Walking Guide)
Cornwall Coast Path (British Walking Guide)
Corsica Trekking – GR20

Cotswold Way (British Walking Guide)
Dolomites Trekking – AV1 & AV2
Dorset & Sth Devon Coast Path (British Walking Gde)
Exmoor & Nth Devon Coast Path (British Walking Gde)
Hadrian's Wall Path (British Walking Guide)
Himalaya by Bike – a route and planning guide
Inca Trail, Cusco & Machu Picchu
Japan by Rail
Kilimanjaro – the trekking guide (includes Mt Meru)

Morocco Overland (4WD/motorcycle/mountainbike)
Moroccan Atlas – The Trekking Guide
Nepal Trekking & The Great Himalaya Trail
New Zealand – The Great Walks
North Downs Way (British Walking Guide)
Norway's Arctic Highway
Offa's Dyke Path (British Walking Guide)
Overlanders' Handbook – worldwide driving guide
Peddars Way & Norfolk Coast Path (British Walking Gde)

Pembrokeshire Coast Path (British Walking Guide)
Pennine Way (British Walking Guide)
The Railway Anthology
The Ridgeway (British Walking Guide)
Siberian BAM Guide – rail, rivers & road
The Silk Roads – a route and planning guide
Sahara Overland – a route and planning guide
Scottish Highlands – The Hillwalking Guide
Sinai – the trekking guide

South Downs Way (British Walking Guide)
Tour du Mont Blanc
Trans-Canada Rail Guide
Trans-Siberian Handbook
Trekking in the Everest Region
The Walker's Anthology
The Walker's Haute Route – Mont Blanc to Matterhorn
West Highland Way (British Walking Guide)

For more information about Trailblazer and our
expanding range of guides, for guidebook updates or
for credit card mail order sales visit our website:

www.trailblazer-guides.com

MAP 45

Bowness-
on-Solway

Port
Carlisle

MAP 44

Glasson

MAP 43

Drumburgh

Easton

Boustead
Hill

Dykesfi

Longburg

MA

Fingland

Angerton

B5307

Kirkbride

Thurstor

Kirkbampton

B5307

Little
Bampton

Newton
Arlosh

0   1   2   3km

0   ½   1   1½   2 miles

Bowness-
on-Solway

Port
Carlisle

Glasson

Drumburgh

Turn for
Boustead Hill

14   13   12   11   10   9   8

Maps 38-45
Carlisle to Bowness-on-Solway

14 miles/22.5km — 4¾-5hrs

NOTE: Add 20-30% to these times to allow for stops

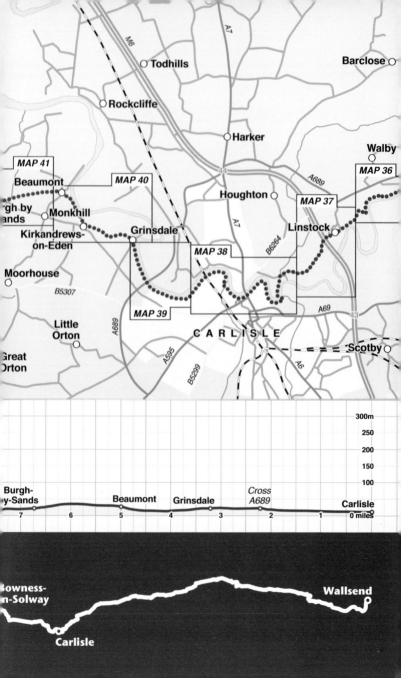

MAP 41

Beaumont

gh by
ands

Monkhill

Kirkandrews-
on-Eden

Moorhouse

B5307

Little
Orton

Great
Orton

MAP 40

Grinsdale

A689

A595

B5299

Todhills

Rockcliffe

Harker

Houghton

A7

B6264

MAP 38

C A R L I S L E

A689

A69

43

A6

Barclose

Walby

MAP 36

MAP 37

Linstock

MAP 39

Scotby

300m
250
200
150
100

Burgh-
y-Sands

Beaumont

Grinsdale

*Cross
A689*

Carlisle

7   6   5   4   3   2   1   0 miles

Bowness-
n-Solway

Carlisle

Wallsend

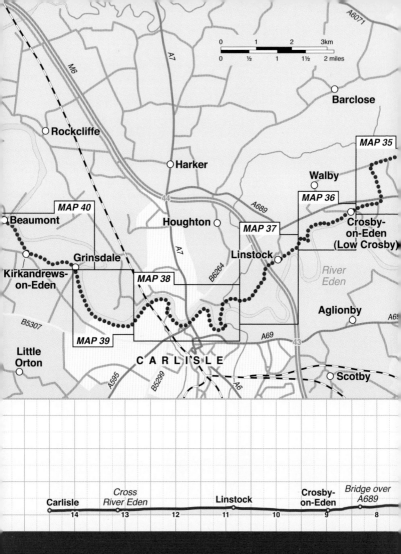

MAP 35

MAP 36

MAP 40

MAP 37

MAP 38

MAP 39

Barclose

Rockcliffe

Harker

Walby

Beaumont

Houghton

Crosby-
on-Eden
(Low Crosby)

Grinsdale

Linstock

Kirkandrews-
on-Eden

*River
Eden*

Aglionby

Little
Orton

C A R L I S L E

Scotby

Carlisle

*Cross
River Eden*

Linstock

Crosby-
on-Eden

*Bridge over
A689*

14   13   12   11   10   9   8

Maps 30-38
Banks to Carlisle
14½ miles/23.3km – 6-6¼hrs
NOTE: Add 20-30% to these times to allow for stops

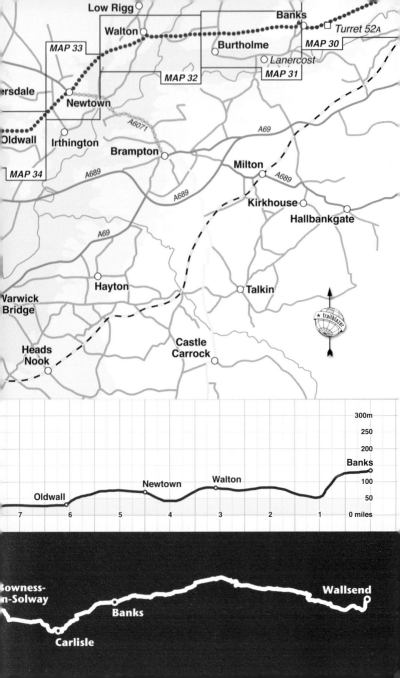

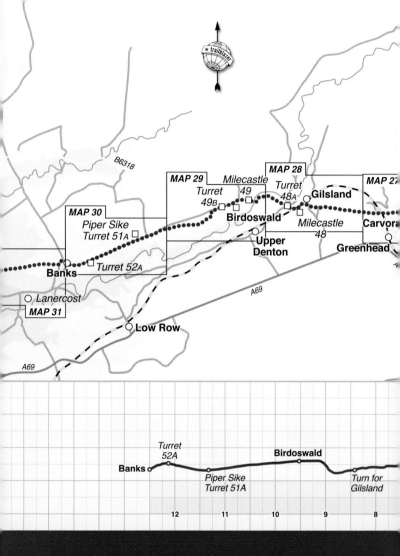

Maps 23-30
Steel Rigg to Banks

12½ miles/20km – 6-6¼hrs

NOTE: Add 20-30% to these times to allow for stops

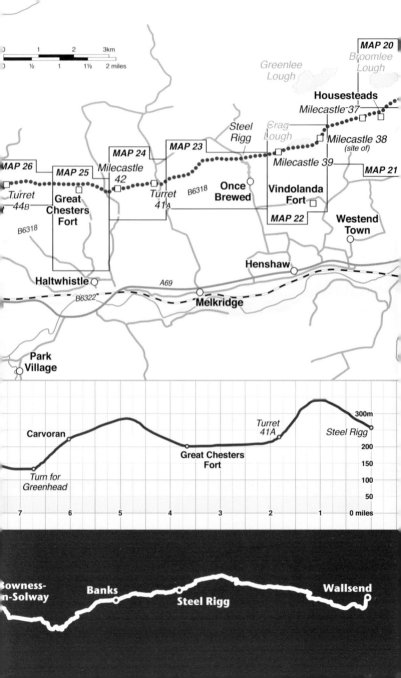

MAP 20
Greenlee
Lough
Broomlee
Lough

Housesteads

Milecastle 37

MAP 23

Steel
Rigg

Crag
Lough

Milecastle 38
(site of)

Milecastle 39

MAP 21

MAP 24

Milecastle
42

Once
Brewed

Vindolanda
Fort

MAP 25

Turret
41A

B6318

MAP 22

MAP 26

Great
Chesters
Fort

Westend
Town

Turret
44B

B6318

Henshaw

Haltwhistle

A69

Melkridge

B6322

Park
Village

Carvoran

Turret
41A

Steel Rigg

300m

Great Chesters
Fort

250

Turn for
Greenhead

200

150

100

50

7   6   5   4   3   2   1   0 miles

Bowness-
on-Solway

Banks

Steel Rigg

Wallsend

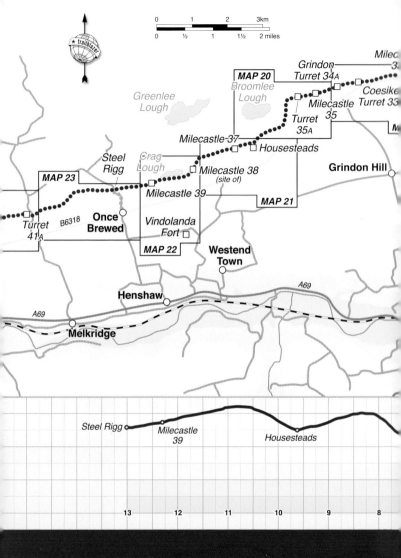

Maps 16-23
Chollerford to Steel Rigg

13 miles/21km – 5¼-6½hrs

NOTE: Add 20-30% to these times to allow for stops

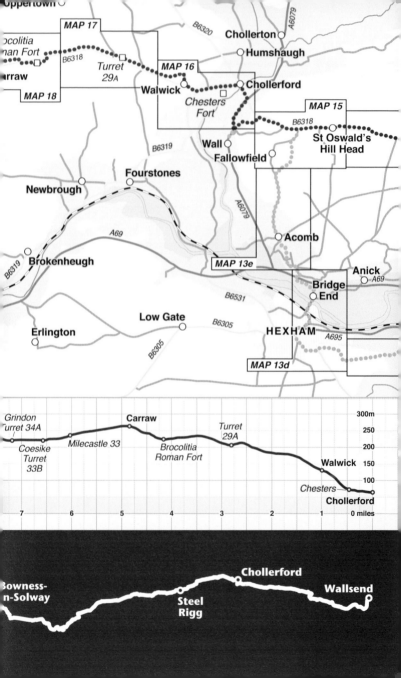

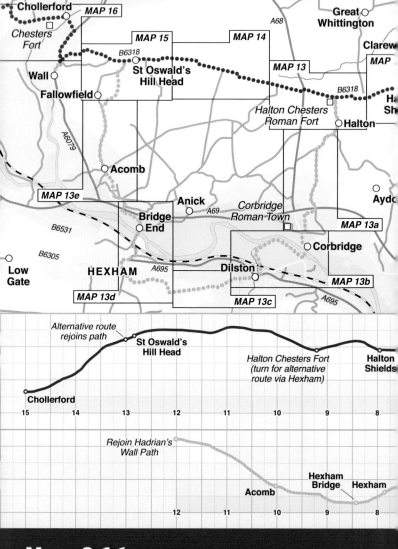

Maps 8-16
Heddon-on-the-Wall to Chollerford

15 miles/24km – 6¾-7hrs

Alternative route: Halton Chesters Fort to St Oswald's Hill Head – 12 miles/19.5km – 4½-4¾hrs

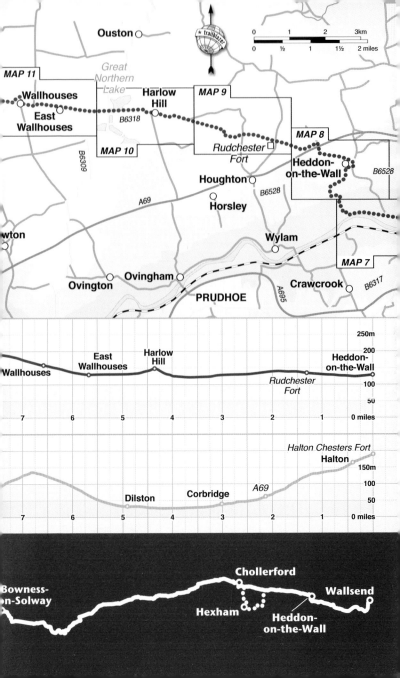

MAP 11

Great Northern Lake

Ouston

Wallhouses

East Wallhouses

MAP 10

B6318

Harlow Hill

MAP 9

Rudchester Fort

MAP 8

Heddon-on-the-Wall

B6528

B6309

Houghton

Horsley

B6528

A69

Wylam

MAP 7

B6528

...wton

Ovingham

Crawcrook

B6317

Ovington

PRUDHOE

A695

Elevation profile 1

250m
200
Heddon-on-the-Wall

East Wallhouses

Harlow Hill

Wallhouses

Rudchester Fort

100

50

7   6   5   4   3   2   1   0 miles

Elevation profile 2

Halton Chesters Fort
Halton

150m

Corbridge

A69

100

Dilston

50

7   6   5   4   3   2   1   0 miles

Route map

Chollerford

Bowness-on-Solway

Wallsend

Hexham

Heddon-on-the-Wall

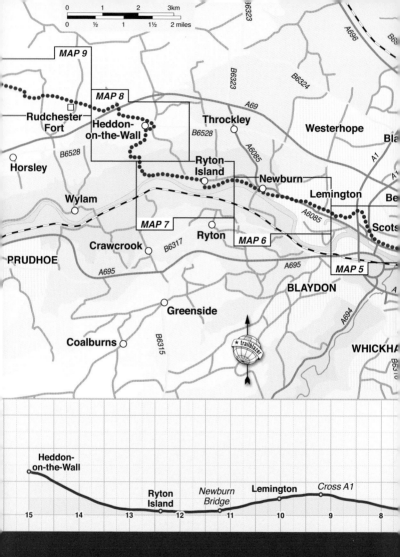

0 **1** **2** **3km**
0 ½ **1** 1½ **2 miles**

MAP 9

MAP 8

Rudchester
Fort

Heddon-
on-the-Wall

Horsley

B6528

Wylam

MAP 7

Crawcrook

PRUDHOE

A695

Greenside

Coalburns

B6315

B6323

B6323

B6324

A69

A696

Throckley

Westerhope

Bla

B6528

Ryton
Island

Newburn

Lemington

Be

A6085

A6085

Ryton

MAP 6

Scots

B6317

MAP 5

A695

BLAYDON

A694

WHICKHA

B63

★ trailblazer

Heddon-
on-the-Wall

Ryton
Island

*Newburn
Bridge*

Lemington

Cross A1

15   14   13   12   11   10   9   8

Maps 1-8
Wallsend to Heddon-on-the-Wall
15 miles/24km – 4¾-5hrs
NOTE: Add 20-30% to these times to allow for stops

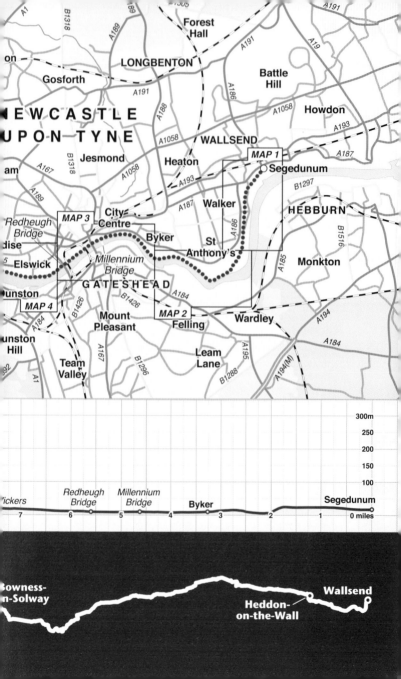

Distance chart (miles above, kilometres in italics below):

	Wallsend (Newcastle)	Newburn	Heddon	East Wallhouses	Port Gate	Wall	Chollerford	Housesteads	Steel Rigg	Carvoran	Gilsland
Newburn	11 / *17.6*										
Heddon-on-the-Wall	15 / *24*	4 / *6.4*									
E Wallhouses	21 / *33.6*	10 / *16*	6 / *9.5*								
Port Gate	25 / *39.9*	14 / *22.4*	10 / *16*	4 / *6.4*							
Wall	29 / *46.3*	18 / *28.8*	14 / *22.4*	8 / *12.8*	4 / *6.4*						
Chollerford	30 / *47.9*	19 / *30.4*	15 / *24*	9 / *14.4*	5 / *8*	1 / *1.6*					
Housesteads	39 / *62.4*	28 / *44.8*	24 / *38.4*	18 / *28.8*	14 / *22.4*	10 / *16*	9 / *14.4*				
Steel Rigg	43 / *68.8*	32 / *51.2*	28 / *44.8*	22 / *35.2*	18 / *28.8*	14 / *22.4*	13 / *20.8*	4 / *6.4*			
Carvoran	48.5 / *77.6*	37.5 / *60*	33.5 / *53.6*	27.5 / *44*	23.5 / *37.6*	19.5 / *31.2*	18.5 / *29.6*	9.5 / *15.2*	5.5 / *8.8*		
Gilsland	51 / *81.6*	40 / *64*	36 / *57.6*	30 / *48*	26 / *41.6*	22 / *35.2*	21 / *33.6*	12 / *19.2*	8 / *12.8*	2.5 / *4*	
Birdoswald	53 / *84.8*	42 / *67.2*	38 / *60.8*	32 / *51.2*	28 / *44.8*	24 / *38.4*	23 / *36.8*	14 / *22.4*	10 / *16*	4.5 / *7.2*	2 / *3.2*
Banks	55.5 / *88.8*	44.5 / *71.2*	40.5 / *64.8*	34.5 / *55.2*	30 / *48*	26.5 / *42.2*	25.5 / *40.8*	16.5 / *26.4*	12.5 / *20*	7 / *11.2*	4.5 / *7.2*
Walton	58 / *92.8*	47 / *75.2*	43 / *68.8*	37 / *59.2*	33 / *52.8*	29 / *46.4*	28 / *44.8*	19 / *30.4*	15 / *24*	9.5 / *15.2*	7 / *11.2*
Newtown	60 / *96*	49 / *78.4*	45 / *72*	39 / *62.4*	35 / *56*	31 / *49.6*	30 / *48*	21 / *33.6*	17 / *27.2*	11.5 / *18.4*	9 / *14.4*
Crosby-on-Eden	65 / *104*	54 / *86.4*	50 / *80*	44 / *70.4*	40 / *64*	36 / *57.6*	35 / *56*	26 / *41.6*	22 / *35.2*	16.5 / *26.4*	14 / *22.4*
Carlisle	70 / *112*	59 / *94.4*	55 / *88*	49 / *78.4*	45 / *72*	41 / *65.6*	40 / *64*	31 / *49.6*	27 / *43.2*	21.5 / *34.4*	19 / *30.4*
Grinsdale	73.5 / *117.6*	62.5 / *100*	58.5 / *93.6*	52.5 / *84*	48.5 / *77.6*	44.5 / *71.2*	43.5 / *69.6*	34.5 / *55.2*	30.5 / *48.8*	25 / *40*	22.5 / *36*
Burgh-by-Sands	77 / *123.2*	66 / *105.6*	62 / *99.2*	56 / *89.6*	52 / *83.2*	48 / *76.8*	47 / *75.2*	38 / *60.8*	34 / *54.4*	28.5 / *45.6*	26 / *41.6*
Drumburgh	79.5 / *127.2*	68.5 / *109.6*	64.5 / *103.2*	58.5 / *93.6*	54.5 / *87.2*	50.5 / *80.8*	49.5 / *79.2*	40.5 / *64.8*	36.5 / *58.4*	31 / *49.6*	28.5 / *45.6*
Glasson	80.5 / *128.8*	69.5 / *111.2*	65.5 / *104.8*	59.5 / *95.2*	55.5 / *88.8*	51.5 / *82.4*	50.5 / *80.8*	41.5 / *66.4*	37.5 / *60*	32 / *51.2*	29.5 / *47.2*
Port Carlisle	83 / *132.8*	72 / *115.2*	68 / *108.8*	62 / *99.2*	58 / *92.8*	54 / *86.4*	53 / *84.8*	44 / *70.4*	40 / *64*	34.5 / *55.2*	32 / *51.2*
Bowness-on-Solway	84 / *134.4*	73 / *116.8*	69 / *110.4*	63 / *100.8*	59 / *94.4*	55 / *88*	54 / *86.4*	45 / *72*	41 / *65.6*	35.5 / *56.8*	33 / *52.8*

Hadrian's Wall Path

DISTANCE CHART

miles/*kilometres*
(approx)

	Birdoswald	Banks	Walton	Newtown	Crosby-on-Eden	Carlisle	Grinsdale	Burgh-by-Sands	Drumburgh	Glasson	Port Carlisle
Banks	2.5										
	4										
Walton	5	2.5									
	8	*4*									
Newtown	7	4.5	2								
	11.2	*7.2*	*3.2*								
Crosby-on-Eden	12	9.5	8	5							
	19.2	*15.2*	*12.8*	*8*							
Carlisle	17	14.5	12	10	5						
	27.2	*23.2*	*19.2*	*16*	*8*						
Grinsdale	20.5	18	15.5	13.5	8.5	3.5					
	32.8	*28.8*	*24.8*	*21.6*	*13.6*	*5.6*					
Burgh-by-Sands	24	21.5	19	17	12	7	3.5				
	38.4	*34.4*	*30.4*	*27.2*	*19.2*	*11.2*	*5.6*				
Drumburgh	26.5	24	21.5	19.5	14.5	9.5	6	2.5			
	42.4	*38.4*	*34.4*	*31.2*	*23.2*	*15.2*	*9.5*	*4*			
Glasson	27.5	25	22.5	20.5	15.5	10.5	7	3.5	1		
	44	*40*	*36*	*32.8*	*24.8*	*16.8*	*11.2*	*5.6*	*1.6*		
Port Carlisle	30	27.5	25	23	18	13	9.5	6	3.5	2.5	
	48	*44*	*40*	*36.8*	*28.8*	*20.8*	*15.2*	*9.6*	*5.6*	*4*	
Bowness-on-Solway	31	28.5	26	24	19	14	10.5	7	4.5	3.5	1
	49.6	*45.6*	*41.6*	*38.4*	*30.4*	*22.4*	*16.8*	*11.2*	*7.2*	*5.6*	*1.6*

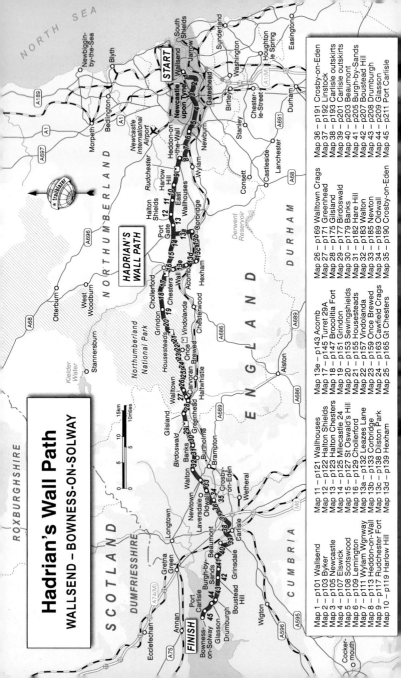

Hadrian's Wall Path
WALLSEND – BOWNESS-ON-SOLWAY